Penguin Education SH 5

Britain in the Modern World:
the Twentieth Century

E. N. Nash & A. M. Newth

Miss E. N. Nash (Mrs E. N. Jull) is a graduate of Oxford and of
Durham Universities, with wide experience of teaching in
grammar schools, a secondary modern school, a college of education, and Birmingham University Education Department. She
has taught for two years in South Africa and spent some time in
Nigeria after her marriage to a Nigerian civil servant.

Mrs A. M. Newth was educated at Haberdashers' Aske's School,
Acton, and spent a year in Germany including a term at the
University of Munich, before reading for the History Tripos at
Newnham College, Cambridge. She taught for several years in a
girls' high school and later in a boys' grammar school, where
she was Head of the History Department.

A History of Britain

Britain in the Modern World: the Twentieth Century

E. N. Nash & A. M. Newth

Penguin Books

Design: Arthur Lockwood

Illustration research: Rosemary Barnicoat

Penguin Books Ltd, Harmondsworth, Middlesex, England
Penguin Books Inc., 3300 Clipper Mill Road, Baltimore, Md 21211, U.S.A.
Penguin Books Australia Ltd, Ringwood, Victoria, Australia

First published 1967, Reprinted with corrections 1968
Copyright © E. N. Nash and A. M. Newth, 1967

Printed in Great Britain, web offset, by Hazells Offset Ltd, Leigh Road, Slough, Bucks.
Set in Lumitype Plantin

Contents

Chapter 1
England 1901–14

The end of Victorian England

Queen Victoria's funeral was a solemn and splendid occasion. The famous cream-coloured horses, wearing nodding black plumes on their bridles, pulled the hearse very slowly through the streets to the sound of muffled drums. Behind it there walked almost all the kings of Europe, and almost all of them were closely related to the dead queen. The procession passed between silent crowds in dark clothes; one woman who appeared in Bond Street dressed in a bright suit was mobbed and had to take refuge in a shop. The newspapers came out with black borders, and door-knockers all over England were tied with black ribbon. The nation was united not only by a common loss, but also by the feeling that something important which Victoria represented had come to an end.

They were right. Great changes were on the point of happening.

The dizzy speed of change in the twentieth century

When you read about the earliest years of history, you may have noticed how slowly things changed in the far past. For the greater part of a *million* years man learned only to control fire and to make tools of flint and bone. Then some unknown genius discovered bronze, and only a few *thousand* years later, iron was discovered. In the last *hundred* years, man has learnt to use electricity and atomic energy as sources of power, and now, every *week* we hear of new discoveries and inventions.

The people who watched Queen Victoria's funeral procession thought that they could count upon their grandchildren living in a world which would be very like the one they lived in themselves, a world in which kings would reign over most countries, in which England would remain the richest and most powerful country, in which Africans and Asians would remain inferior in position, in which the labouring classes would remain poor and humble, and servants would be cheap and plentiful.

In this they were wrong, and this book will describe the changes which have taken place in Great Britain, and in her place in the world, during this century.

Edwardian England

The years between the death of Victoria and the outbreak of World War I in 1914 are called the 'Edwardian' period, because Edward VII, Victoria's eldest son, reigned until 1910.

Above: The Queen is dead. February, 1901.

Below: Queen Victoria's funeral service at Windsor Castle. The two men on the left are her grandson, Kaiser Wilhelm of Germany (far left) and her eldest son, King Edward VII of England.

The court and the world of the rich changed immediately after the accession of the new monarch; it became much livelier, and much less respectable, than it had been in the days of Victoria. The king loved pleasure more than he loved work, which is not surprising when one remembers how he had been brought up, and the Edwardian age was frivolous and gay. Edward VII carried his duties lightly, and was more often at the races or the theatre than in his study. But he was a magnificently dignified figure and did the public part of a king's job well. He never learned much from books, but he could pick things up from people, and was clever enough to talk as if he knew much more than he really did. He could exert charm and make friends, which was useful in an age when kings still had a great deal of influence, and in which most of them were related to him by blood. He is likely to be the last of our royal family to have much space in the history books, because he was the last one who influenced politics at all seriously. Our friendship with France was important if we were to resist Germany (see page 32) and Edward went on a state visit to France at a time when the French people were hostile to us, and was so tactful that he softened French hostility and made it easier to get agreement between their government and our own. He had courage, and on this visit terrified the French police who were responsible for his safety by walking amongst crowds, and he delighted the French public by going on to the stage after a performance and kissing the chief actress when he congratulated her. This was the kind of duty he did not find unpleasant.

Aristocrats and commoners enjoy the races.

A daring bathing costume for the fashionable, 1901.

The court gave a lead to a glittering social life. The stalls of London theatres were occupied by people in full evening dress. Ascot was as elegant as it has ever been, and the enclosures were more select than they are now. Lavish house-parties were held in country mansions; this is the kind of breakfast which might face the guests, less than twelve hours after they had finished a proportionately enormous dinner:

The porridge was disposed of negligently, people walking about and watching the rain descend on the Italian garden. Then would come whiting and omelette, and devilled kidneys and little fishy messes in shells. Then tongue and ham and a slice of ptarmigan. And then scones and honey and marmalade. Then a little melon and a nectarine or two, and just one or two of those delicious raspberries.

In those days the aristocracy did not need to show the public over their houses at half a crown a head.

The first motor-cars had appeared on the roads. They were uncomfortable and unreliable, and it was very difficult to look elegant in them, but even so they had advantages over horses, which could only average twenty miles a day, and which needed stabling at the end of a journey. Progressive people discarded their carriage and pair for a Daimler and a chauffeur.

Where the money came from

This gay social life was based upon our enormous wealth. We saw how, in the nineteenth century, the manufacturers supplied goods such as cotton and woollen materials and steel to all the world, and made huge profits, which they could spend on pleasure and display in their own homes.

What do people do after they have as much as they can possibly spend, and still have money come pouring in?

Such people invest their money. If, for instance, in Edwardian times a railway was to be built in China or the Argentine, the money for it might be borrowed in the city of London. People told their stockbrokers to buy for them shares in Chinese or Argentinian railways. They got interest on this money for an indefinite time, perhaps after they had received several times more than the sum they had originally lent. The people of China or the Argentine would have to pay this money by charging higher fares and freights. It is true that the underdeveloped countries needed the help of our capital but nevertheless they suffered and we profited from the continuous drain of their money to ourselves.

In 1902 we had about £2,000,000,000 invested abroad. By 1914 we had £4,000,000,000, and our export trade also doubled. No wonder life for the rich was gay and optimistic!

It was particularly profitable to invest in tropical countries where the workers could live on a bowl of rice or maize a day, and needed only huts for shelter. Wages in such countries were very low and

profits were therefore very high. This is one of the reasons why our Empire added to our wealth. The Empire also had the advantage that it provided managerial and Civil Service jobs for a number of middle-class boys. The sober virtues of our middle class came in useful here, for we created an overseas Civil Service famous for its incorruptibility, staffed by men most of whom were devoted to the colonies in which they served.

Look at a map of the British Empire before 1914 to see the vast extent of our resources.

Danger signals for our economy

For those who had their eyes and ears open, there were plenty of signs that the comfortable world of Edwardian England was not going to last long.

There was a new, dangerous tendency in our exports. Before 1900 we had exported chiefly finished consumer goods, such as our textiles.

After 1900 we exported more and more machine tools, factory equipment which was setting up our future rivals.

Another alarming tendency was that real wages, which had been rising during the nineteenth century, dropped four and a half per cent during the Edwardian period. 'Real' wages are wages reckoned by how much they will buy, so real wages drop if prices go up, even if workers get the same money. If you look at the Smith family budget on page 20 you will understand that even a small drop in real wages, four and a half per cent, would cause suffering and was bound to cause strife. You will read later in this chapter of the struggle over wages between employers and trade unions which lay ahead.

The third change in our position was caused by the growth of powerful rivals who were soon to have greater wealth and resources than ourselves. Germany and America were already advancing to overtake us, and, although this was not yet understood in Great Britain, we had to learn to play a different part in world affairs from the masterful, independent part we had played in the past.

The politics of Edwardian England

During the first years of this period we had a Conservative government under Arthur Balfour. The most important reform which it made was the Education Act of 1902, which began our present system of secondary education. Local Education Authorities were from now on to be responsible for running secondary schools, as well as the elementary ones which School Boards had run since 1870. At first they charged fees for secondary schools, but soon they gave some free places to children from elementary schools. For the first time, there was a ladder by which a child from a poor home could reach a University and qualify for professional work. But it was a very narrow ladder, and only a very clever, lucky and determined child could climb it.

1906 Election   The great Liberal triumph

The country had been governed by the Conservatives for a long time. Why did they lose control in the general election of 1906?

One reason was that great changes were taking place in our society, and the country was ready for new men and new policies. Another reason was that working men now had the vote, and they either voted for candidates of the new Labour Party, or they voted for Liberals who had promised that if they were elected they would give the trade unions a stronger position.

But perhaps the chief reason why the Conservatives lost was because the public thought they might put a tax on corn. Joseph Chamberlain, one of the leading Conservatives, believed that we ought to bind the Empire together by letting its goods into the United Kingdom on more favourable terms than those offered to foreign countries. He proposed that we should let Empire goods in free, and put a small tax on foreign goods, including corn.

This may have been a good idea, but it was not a popular one. People in this country remembered that we had grown rich under a policy of free trade, and you may remember reading (*A History of Britain* SH4, Chapter 4) how people thought that John Bright and the work of the Anti-Corn Law League had saved them and their children from hunger by ensuring that corn should come into the country free from tax.

Your Food Will Cost you More,
if you Vote Conservative,

said the Liberal election propaganda, and posters such as the one above did the trick. At a time when the working people's food was still very simple and bread was indeed the staff of life, they voted for the Big Loaf.

The result was that the new parliament contained thirty Labour members, a group big enough to have influence, and the Liberals had a majority of 243 over the Conservatives.

A government of reform   1906–11

The new and energetic government which was set up by the Liberals was different from any we had had before in that it was led by middle class men, instead of by the aristocracy and the rich upper middle class. Mr Asquith, who became Prime Minister in 1908, was a Yorkshire lawyer who got to Oxford by means of a scholarship, and David Lloyd George, the most brilliant member of his government, was also a lawyer, and came from a very humble Welsh background; he had been brought up by an uncle who was a shoemaker.

War on poverty

The new men had the new idea that poverty was *not* a crime. It had

A Liberal Party procession from a poster of the 1906 election campaign. The Conservative Party was under attack for its failure to keep down the price of bread, and its support for the exploitation of Chinese workmen in cruel conditions in South African goldmines. This last is shown by children in tropical clothes, bullying Chinese.

Election Result   1906

Liberals	400
Conservatives	157
Labour	30

been thought that the poor were poor because they were idle, drunken, vicious or incompetent, and since the Poor Law Act of 1834 the policy was to 'deter' them from becoming destitute by making the workhouses so unpleasant to live in that nothing but starvation would drive people to them.

At the beginning of the century the first scientific investigations into the earning and spending of working people were made, and the results were horrifying. Thoughtful people learnt for the first time the extent of poverty in prosperous England, and they learnt that its causes were such things as wages being too small to keep a family, the ill-health of the wage-earner, and so on. There had always been complaints against the old, cruel Poor Law of 1834, which had set up workhouses which were feared and hated as much as prison, and now the government appointed a committee to report on the working of the Poor Law.

A room in a Victorian workhouse, opened in 1851: wooden bed-boards, which could be swung up to make living-space in the daytime; roof windows; meagre gas-lighting for the evening; cold brick floors. Such workhouses were still in use at the beginning of this century.

The 'Minority Report' on the Poor Law   1909

The main report of this committee was a rather timid affair which proposed no big changes, and nobody took much notice of it. But a few of its members, including George Lansbury, disagreed with this report and wrote a 'Minority Report' of their own. This Report has become famous because it described the evils of the old Poor Law so vividly, and because its suggestions pointed the direction for future changes. It said of the workhouses:

We have seen feeble-minded boys growing up in the workhouse year after year untaught and untrained, alternately neglected and tormented by the other inmates, because it had not occurred to the Board of Guardians to send them to . . . suitable institutions. We have ourselves seen . . . idiots who are physically offensive or mischievous, or so noisy as to create a disturbance by day and by night with their howls, living in ordinary wards . . . We have seen imbeciles annoying the sane, and the sane tormenting the imbeciles. We have seen half-witted women nursing the sick, feeble-minded women in charge of babies, and imbecile old men put to look after the boys out of school hours.

The 'Minority Report' said that there should be different kinds of treatment in different kinds of institutions for people who needed different kinds of help, and that certainly the sick, feeble-minded, children, widows, old, unemployed, should not be herded together in a kind of barracks.

Poverty and ill-health

If you look at the diagram below, taken from a survey published in 1902, you can work out that the people who suffered most from poverty were the growing children, because it was children who made the families too big for the wage packet to buy enough food: this was a serious matter, for if children are not well fed during their growing

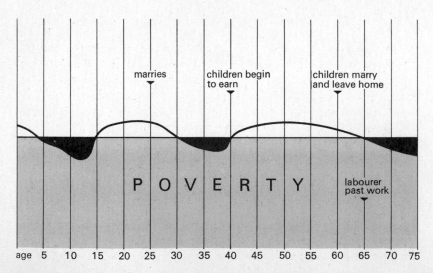

This diagram, based on a survey made in 1902, shows the years in the life of an average working-class labourer who started work at the age of fifteen. The shaded part, below the line, represents periods of extreme poverty, when he could not afford to buy enough to eat.

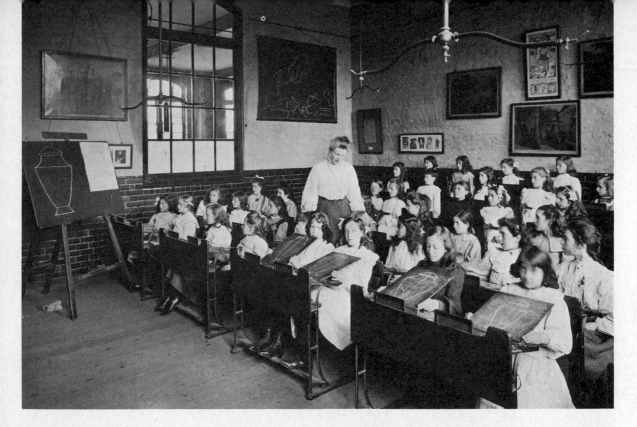

A drawing lesson in 1907.
Learning to copy a dull picture.

years, their constitution is damaged, and they may carry through life such things as deformities caused by rickets.

There was also anxiety because army doctors who examined recruits for the Boer War had found that many had to be rejected for physical defects and rotten teeth. After the war there was an investigation into the nation's health, and as a result of what was found out it was decided that something must be done.

The School Meals Act   1906

One of the first reforms of the Liberal government was a law making it possible for schools to provide meals for ill-fed children. Headmasters asked questions if children were pale and thin, found out if they had come to school without breakfast and were going home to nothing better than a slice of bread and jam, and put them down for a free dinner. A little later a school medical service was started.

These were very important measures. They mark the beginning of recognition that it is no use trying to educate sickly and hungry children, and perhaps we can say that these laws mark the beginning of the welfare state.

The triumph of the 'Welsh Wizard'

David Lloyd George was born in a cottage and brought up in a strict, Nonconformist society. But he became the most vivid personality in

15

'I'll make 'em pity the aged poor!' Lloyd George caricatured as a highwayman who compels the rich to pay up, August 1908.

politics. It was said that his speeches 'could charm the black off a kettle', and he had the energy of a dynamo. He might be up in the House of Commons until three in the morning, and then, at 9.15, come bouncing down to one of the little breakfast parties for which he was famous, and delight his guests with funny stories. He was not really popular with people who knew him personally, for they believed that he was as artful as a cartload of monkeys and in this they were right. He had no close personal friends. The House of Commons is like a very good club, where members are friendly and use Christian names, but Mr Lloyd George was scarcely ever called 'David' by anyone. However he had great public virtues; although he enjoyed moving in the world of rich and powerful people, unlike some other successful politicians, he never forgot the interests of the ordinary people who had voted for him.

A seat by the fireside for the old

Lloyd George was Chancellor of the Exchequer under Asquith, who was Prime Minister, and he was responsible for the Old Age Pensions Act of 1908, which gave five shillings a week to people over seventy. Nobody thought that this sum would enable them to support themselves in their own houses, but it would enable them to pay for their keep in the home of one of their children, and enable them to live there without feeling that they were taking the bread out of their grandchildren's mouths.

Five shillings was not a large sum, even for those days, but the idea of payments of this kind was new, and there was some indignation at this extravagance. Lord Rosebery, the racehorse owner and former Liberal Prime Minister and statesman, said, 'A scheme so prodigal of expenditure might be dealing a blow at the Empire from which it would never recover'.

'Ninepence for Fourpence' National Insurance Act of 1911

Lloyd George studied the social insurance scheme which Bismarck had set going in Germany, and decided to do something similar for the sick and unemployed in this country. By the National Insurance Act, each worker was to pay fourpence a week into the fund, the employer threepence and the State twopence. After so many weeks of payment the worker (but not his wife and children) would be entitled to free doctoring. There was also an unemployment insurance by which the worker, the employer and the State each paid twopence halfpenny a week, and then the worker could claim seven shillings a week if he was unemployed.

The benefits were small, but the Act was a beginning. Thirty years after the Act was passed men who were drawing their sickness or unemployment pay would still speak of 'being on Lloyd George'. This is perhaps a better tribute to him than all the books about him which stand on library shelves.

The workers demand a share of the national wealth

The workers were demanding a larger slice of the rich national cake, and the most effective way, perhaps the only way, in which they could do this was through their trade unions.

You may have read in the last volume how the unions received a disastrous blow by the Taff Vale decision which said that they had to pay their employer for any loss he suffered through a strike. They now organized to get this altered; their members promised to vote for Parliamentary candidates who were pledged to reverse the Taff Vale decision. When the new Liberal Parliament of 1906 met, it fulfilled the promises its members had made to their working-class supporters by passing a law which said that the trade unions were not to be held responsible for financial losses which the employers incurred through strikes. So now the unions were again able to use the threat to strike

Propaganda like this made out that the workers did not want Lloyd George's insurance scheme, and resented the idea of having to pay fourpence a week for sickness benefit. From *Punch*, 1911.

in their negotiations over wages and hours. But a little later another blow befell them, the Osborne Judgement.

The Osborne Judgement   Trade union funds for politics?

At this time M.P.s did not receive a salary, and the socialist M.P.s depended on funds provided by the trade unions to keep them whilst they were in Parliament. The unions put aside a proportion of their members' contributions into a 'Political Fund' for this purpose.

In 1909 a trade unionist named Osborne objected to part of his subscription being used in this way, claimed that it was illegal, and took the matter to court. The House of Lords decided in his favour. What were the Labour M.P.s to do? They asked the Liberal government to pass a law legalizing the political use of trade union funds. They did not get their way over this until 1913, when the 'Second Trade Union Act' was passed.

The Osborne Case was one of the things which made the working-classes decide that a Liberal government could not be relied upon to serve their interests and that a Labour government was necessary. But in 1911 the government did grant a salary of £400 to M.P.s. This was very important for democracy; it would not do if only people who had private means, or who had rich backers, could represent the nation in Parliament.

The battle for the wage rates

At this time the workers were finding out that it was only through trade union action that they could bargain for better wages, and the employers had not yet come to accept, as they do now, that wage agreements must be negotiated with the unions. There were bitter battles because workers and employers were struggling to establish their position with regard to one another. These struggles reached a climax in 1911 when a strike of transport workers brought London to the verge of a food famine. As a result of this strike the unions won their wage demands.

Ben Tillett, one of the trade unionists who had led the great strike for 'the Docker's Tanner' in 1889, described what it was like:

Everywhere the docks were at a standstill and the transport ceased to move. Pickets were unnecessary because there were no workers to be found willing to blackleg on their fellows. The great markets of the City were idle; the rush and turmoil of the City's traffic congesting the principal ways, dwindling to a little trickle as motor-buses, motor-cars and private vehicles of all kinds felt the pressure of shortage of petrol, and all the immense volume of trading traffic through the city streets from the docks to the warehouses and the great railway terminals ceased to move . . . no trade was handled except by permission of the Strike Committee.

Naturally these measures taken by the Strike Committee gave great offence to the fire-eating, bloodthirsty gentlemen sitting in their clubs and offices, apoplectic with indignation against the dockers and their leaders.

Our modest demands – we were asking for the dockers a minimum rate of eightpence an hour and a shilling an hour overtime, a working day from 7 a.m. to 5 p.m. . . . were resisted with a bitterness, a fury, a stubbornness which I still find inexplicable.

A journalist described what he saw when he went to Liverpool during the strike:

A number of men denounced as 'scabs' or 'blacklegs' by the strikers were found to run the trams, but were stoned on their journeys. On a Sunday morning I saw many trams brought to a standstill and then set on fire.

In one tramcar were passengers, including women and children, who became panic-stricken as stones came hurtling through the glass . . . The car was travelling at a furious speed. The driver had lost his nerve, as well he might under that fusillade of stones . . . There had been no scavenging for weeks. Dead rats lay about with rotting cabbage stalks and other ill-smelling refuse. The stench came through the windows, and someone suggested we should form a scavenging party and clean up the square . . . and a party of us, armed with brooms from the hotel, went out on the job, clapped by maidservants who watched from the windows . . . a crowd gathered and booed us and shouted out 'scabs . . . scabs'. They were very hostile, regarding us as strike-breakers, but they did not attack, and we did some pretty good work with the dead rats and the garbage.

On occasion troops were brought out to maintain order, and in 1912 the following leaflet was printed by the workers and circulated amongst the soldiers:

Don't Shoot.
You are Working Men's Sons.
When we go on strike to better Our lot which is the lot also of Your Fathers, Mothers, Brothers and Sisters, *You* are called upon by your officers to *Murder Us*.
Don't do it . . .
Don't you know that when you are out of the colours and become a Civvy again, that You, like Us, may be on strike, and You, like Us, be liable to be Murdered by other soldiers.
Boys, Don't Do It;
'Thou shalt not Kill,' says the Book.
Don't forget that.
It does not say, 'unless you have a uniform on'.
No. *Murder is Murder* . . .
Think things out and refuse any longer to Murder Your Kindred. Help us to win back Britain for the British and the World for the Workers.

The people who were responsible for this leaflet were sent to prison, but nevertheless Great Britain was very liberal compared with most countries in allowing people to express their views, and such punishments were rare. So long as people are free to express their opinions without fear of punishment, there is hope for peaceful, legal reform.

The Smith family budget

This is the weekly budget of a steady worker with a careful, capable wife. He had three children. It is the budget of a real, not an imaginary family.

Budget of the Smith family   1900

Wages: 20s. a week

Expenditure:

Food for five people	11	0
Rent	3	2
Coal and Light	2	0
Soap, etc.		5
Sick Club		6
Life Insurance		4
Clothing Club		3
Personal expenditure for father	2	0
	19	8

Mr Smith's 2s.

Beer (1d. each day)	7
Tobacco	3
Children's savings box	3
	1 1

Mr Smith clothed himself with the rest.

You can see how prices and wages were changing if you compare the Smith family budget with the following budget of a family living in a town just before the war in 1914. It is a family of father, mother, and three children. Wages then averaged 32s. 6d. a week.

Meat 9 lb.	5	7½
Bread and flour 32½ lb.	3	11½
Tea 13 oz.	1	3
Sugar 6 lb.	1	1
Milk 9½ pints	1	5
Butter and margarine 2¼ lb.	2	10
Cheese 13 oz.		6½
Eggs 10	1	0½
Potatoes 17 lb.	1	0
Total for Food	18	9
Other expenses		
Rent	5	0
Clothing	3	9
Fuel and light	2	6
Sundries	1	3
£1	11	3

Most working-class people in cities lived in grim and crowded conditions. An alley like this probably had one lavatory which everyone shared.

Votes for women

We were a free society in that we were freer than other nations to express our opinions, and most men had the vote, but one half of our people, the women, could do nothing directly to influence the government.

Looking back on history we see that women have nearly always had a raw deal. They have been really the slaves of their husbands, and though they might be very happy if he were kind, they were absolutely at the mercy of an unkind one. A hundred years ago a husband had the right to every penny his wife possessed, even if she earned it herself; he could wait at the factory gate on pay-day and take his wife's earnings from her as she came out. Once, when a woman was making a speech demanding the right of married women to their own property, a man in the audience said, 'Dost mean to say, that if your bill was passed, and my wife came into a bit of money, I should have to *ask* her for it?' The House of Commons was more generous than this man, for in 1882 it passed the Married Women's Property Act which gave a married woman control of her property, but this did nothing to give women rights in public life, and during the reign of Edward VII women organized to demand the vote.

Emmeline Pankhurst and her two gifted daughters were the centre of the women's suffrage movement. The two girls, Christabel and Sylvia, grew up to be both clever and good-looking, and Christabel had besides a beautiful speaking voice and a quick wit. In 1903 the Pankhursts and their friends formed the Women's Social and Political Union to demand votes for women. All through the years of which we are writing in this chapter, the activities of women who were demanding the vote filled the newspapers and harassed the government.

Mrs Pankhurst and her daughter Christabel in prison clothes, in December 1908.

Suffragists and suffragettes

The Pankhursts soon found themselves the leaders of a great movement, whose members ranged from rich and elegant women to working girls who wore clogs and shawls.

At one time or another most of the leaders of the demand for votes for women went to prison. This is because many of them thought that the only way to compel people to listen to them was to create public disturbances. In the early days of the movement they contented themselves with heckling at meetings and refusing to leave when ordered to do so. Even for this they were arrested and often treated roughly by the police. When they marched through London some of their processions were violently broken up by the mounted police.

After a time the movement divided between those called suffragists, who thought that only peaceful means of persuasion should be used, and the militant members, called suffragettes, who were prepared to defy the police and break the law. Of course we hear more of the suffragettes because their story is more exciting; so did the people of their own time, and no wonder.

Suffragettes about to set off on a tour of London from the headquarters of the Women's Social and Political Union in 1913.

Some of the suffragettes, when they went to Downing Street or the House of Commons with petitions or banners, padlocked themselves to the railings, and their friends ran away with the keys, so that it took the police a long time to remove them. Some of them set fire to mail by dropping lighted, paraffin-soaked rags into pillar boxes. At one time they slashed pictures in the National Gallery. Some refused to pay their taxes, and bailiffs removing their furniture was a common sight for their neighbours. One of them followed Winston Churchill round to his meetings with a muffin bell to drown what he said, because he opposed votes for women. On one occasion, when the Prime Minister, Mr Asquith, was speaking in Birmingham two women got on the roof and made such a noise that they had to be dislodged with fire-hoses. Once they went up in a balloon and showered leaflets down on London. When they were in prison they broke the windows of their cells, and many of them went on hunger-strike.

The government was afraid of having the hunger-strikers die on its hands, so it had them forcibly fed. This is a disgusting and unpleasant process and there was indignation at the women being subjected to it. Despite this feeding, some of the women became weak and ill, so the government put through the 'Cat and Mouse Act' by which women were let out when they became dangerously weak, and re-arrested when they had recovered.

The most famous demonstration of the militants was when Emily

Wilding Davidson threw herself in front of the King's horse at the Derby and was killed. Her sympathizers organized a funeral procession which would, they hoped, make her death serve the cause in which she believed. Thousands of women walked behind the hearse, women in purple carrying irises, and women in white carrying laurels. And hundreds of thousands who did not follow the coffin were moved to sympathy. But of course many did not sympathize, thought that she was foolish, and pointed out that the jockey might have got hurt.

What came of it all?

Votes for women did not come immediately. The Liberal Party was afraid of giving them the vote because it thought that women were more conservative than men and would vote against them. Votes for women did not come until after the war, in 1918, and some people think that they got it because of their war-work and that the earlier agitation had nothing to do with it. We shall never be certain about this. But the suffragists and suffragettes achieved much. For years everybody, from cabinet ministers to the idlest newspaper reader, thought and talked about votes for women. Perhaps if it had not been for this no-one would have thought of giving them the vote after the war.

Some people said that the 'antics' of the militants only proved that women were unfit to vote. Others argued that no-one would have

Mrs Pankhurst arrested after the suffragettes made an attack on Buckingham Palace in May 1914.

noticed the suffrage movement but for the suffragettes. It is rather like the Campaign for Nuclear Disarmament of 1958, of which you will read in Chapter 7; which also had a militant branch, the Committee of 100. Did the Committee of 100 discredit CND by having sit-downs in Trafalgar Square? Or would CND have been forgotten if it were not for this sort of thing? But even the wildest actions of the Committee of 100 were tame compared with the exploits of the suffragettes.

You can see from this extract from the *Daily Mail* of 2 March 1906, what it was like when the suffragettes got going:

From every part of the crowded and brilliantly lighted streets came the crash of splintered glass. People started as windows shattered at their side; suddenly there was another crash in front of them; on the other side of the street; behind; everywhere. Scared shop assistants came running out on the pavements; traffic stopped; policemen jumped this way and that; five minutes later the street was a procession of excited groups, each surrounding a woman wrecker being led in custody to the nearest police station.

Jane Bull: 'High time for a good spring clean!' From a suffragettes' magazine, in which women appeal for the reform of the system which excludes them from public life.

Attack on the House of Lords

Lord Rosebery's remark about Old Age Pensions shows that there was strong disapproval at this time of any 'redistribution of income', which means taxing those who can afford to pay and providing with the money services for those who need them. Lloyd George was determined to do some redistribution of income, and was afraid that the House of Lords would veto his legislation; it had in fact already vetoed some of his bills. In any case he disapproved on democratic grounds of the House of Lords. So he plotted to clip its wings.

The People's Budget   1909

First he drew up a budget which he said was a 'War-time budget', made to fight the war against poverty. It contained proposals which horrified property owners. For instance, income tax was raised from one shilling to one shilling and twopence, and a new tax, a super-tax of sixpence in the pound, was put on incomes over £3,000. Spirits were taxed so that the price of a bottle of whisky went up to four shillings. He included a land-tax which infuriated the land-owning peers, but pleased Liberal Party members, who used to sing,

The Land. The Land. T'was God who made the land.
The Land. The Land. The ground on which we stand.
Why should we be beggars with the ballot in our hands?
God gave the Land to the People.

The outcry against this budget was tremendous, as Lloyd George had hoped, and, as he hoped, the House of Lords refused to pass it. Now he had got what he wanted, a head-on collision with the House of Lords in which the Lords were in the wrong. They were in the wrong because by tradition the Lords never reject a Bill which concerns money. The theory is that it is the 'tax-payers' money, and only the elected representatives of the tax-payers should decide how it is spent.

There had to be another General Election, because a government cannot carry on if the Budget is not passed. The speeches in this election were amongst the most violent in our history.

Lloyd George said:

A fully equipped duke costs as much to keep as two Dreadnoughts, and dukes are just as much a terror and last much longer.

He said of the Lords:

They have no qualifications – at least they *need* have none. No testimonials are required. There are no credentials. They do not even need a medical certificate. They need not be sound either in body or in mind. They only need a certificate of birth – just to prove that they are first of the litter. You would not choose a spaniel on these principles . . .

The other side was not quite so good at calling names as Lloyd George, but they did their best, and he was described, amongst other things, as 'a snivelling little Welsh attorney'. The Duke of Bedford said 'I should like to see Winston Churchill and Lloyd George in the middle

The Tory cry is – 'HANDS OFF THE LAND!' The Liberal Policy is – '. . . the best use of the land in the interests of the community.' From a Liberal Party publication, December 1909.

Mr Asquith to Mr Lloyd George: '500 coronets dirt cheap!' This cartoon shows Asquith and Lloyd George doing well out of cheap peerages. Although peerages would not actually have been sold, men who had contributed generously to Liberal Party funds would doubtless have been offered them.
From *Punch*, December 1910.

of twenty couples of dog-hounds'. Winston Churchill was then a member of the Liberal Party.

The Lords defeated   The Parliament Act   1911

The Liberals and their allies won the two elections which were held over the refusal of the Lords to pass the budget, and this showed that the country was prepared for the Lords to have their power reduced. But the battle was not over, because the Lords themselves had to agree to any law limiting their power. There were many 'Ditchers' in the House of Lords who said that they would die in the last ditch rather than surrender any of their privileges. However, they changed their minds when they learned that if they did not give way the government would, as was its right, ask the king to create enough new Liberal peers to pass the Bill. A great many new peers would have 'cheapened' titles, and the Lords usually yield when they are threatened with this. You may remember that they yielded because of this in 1832, over the Great Reform Bill.

So the Parliament Act was passed. By it a bill becomes law even if it is vetoed by the Lords, if it is passed three times by the Commons. After this Act the Lords had the power to make the government pause and think again, but they could not absolutely prevent any legislation. In 1949 the powers of the House of Lords to delay legislation were further reduced.

White supremacy established in South Africa

The great mistake of the Liberal Government

In 1910 the Union of South Africa was set up. This meant that the two white peoples, the Boers and the English, were united and given self-government. People said at the time how wonderful it was that the struggles of the Boer War were forgotten, and how generous we were to trust the Dutch with a share in the government. Only a very few people realized that we had forgotten to safeguard the interests of three-quarters of the population of South Africa who were neither Dutch nor English, but African. A member of the House of Lords, supported by a bishop, did propose that Africans should have the right to stand for Parliament in South Africa, but the idea was pushed aside, and the Africans were left without protection in the hands of their white employers. So South Africa started off in the direction which led to Apartheid: a system of government about which you will read in Chapter 9.

At this time Africans were usually forgotten; they had not won any power and could not make their voice heard.

Other Liberal reforms

This Liberal government was one of the most important reforming governments in our history. Many other Acts besides the ones we have described were passed by it. For instance, a Shops Act was passed, which gave shop-assistants a weekly half-holiday. Another act set up children's courts and forbade sending children to prison, and this government also began the probation system, by which first offenders are not sent to prison but are given supervision to help them to go straight. These acts were very valuable, because if children and first offenders are sent to prison they may learn there all the habits and ideas of the old lags, and 'serve an apprenticeship to a life of crime'.

The government was occupied with the task of giving Home Rule to Ireland when the First World War broke out, putting a stop to all reform for four years.

Dates to remember

1909　Blériot flew the Channel
1912　Captain Scott reached the South Pole
1912　The *Titanic* sank in the Atlantic

Things to do

1　Find out what your own town or village was like at the beginning of this century. There may be pictures at the local library showing the streets and buildings at that time. If so, notice how the streets were lit, what sort of traffic was on the roads, and how people were dressed. If you recognize the spot, go there yourself and describe how the scene has changed.

2　Find out if there was a local newspaper at this time. If so, look at copies of it at the local library and see what you can find of interest.

3　Calculate how much a week the dockers would have earned after winning their strike, and decide whether you think that their claims were reasonable. Use the family budgets to decide what wages would have been suitable.

4　Find out how much trade unionists pay into a political fund today, and what the money is used for now.

5　Make a list of all the things which your family bought last week which would come under the heading of 'sundries' in the family budgets. Discuss the difficulties of living in those times compared with the present.

Make a list of the foods which your family bought last week which do not appear on the budgets.

Things to discuss

1　Which of the activities of the suffragettes were wise or justifiable?
2　What are the advantages and disadvantages of having a House of Lords?

From 14s. 6d. to 28s.

From 12s. 3d. to 16s.

28

3 Should people be allowed to print such leaflets as 'Don't Shoot'?
4 In what ways should juvenile crime be treated differently from adult crime?

Books to read

M. Cathcart-Borer, *Women Who Made History*, Warne
Charlie Chaplin, *My Autobiography* (part about his childhood in London), Penguin
W. Churchill, *My Early Life*, Odhams
W. Holwood, *Captain Scott*, Muller
R. Fulford, *Votes for Women*, Faber
C. L. Mowat, *Lloyd George*, Oxford University Press
H. G. Wells, *History of Mr Polly*, Collins

Advertisements for boys' and girls' clothing (*left*) and a lady's cycling costume, at the turn of the century.

Chapter 2
The First World War 1914-18

Behind the scenes

There was plenty of excitement in British politics at home during the ten years before the war broke out. The papers were full of the doings of the suffragettes, Lloyd George's speeches and the troubles in Ireland. Only a few people saw cause for alarm in what was happening abroad.

Look at the map of Europe and notice the position of the great powers on the Continent. The strongest of them was Germany, a comparative newcomer, because it was only since 1871 that she had been a united country. Under Bismarck, a clever German statesman, Germany had become a great industrial power.

The figures opposite show how successful she had been:

If you went into the shops you might have seen pots and pans and knives marked 'made in Germany', and the manufacturers would tell a sorry tale of how their old customers in South America were now buying their goods from Germany. In fact Germany had become a dangerous trade rival to Britain.

1914 Steel Production

Britain	7·7 million tons
France	5·0 million tons
Germany	17·3 million tons

Germany's ambitions

German industrialists looked with envy at the British and French Empires. Germany had few overseas possessions, and in these had no valuable raw materials, so that her colonies were more of an expense than an advantage. The steel barons of the Ruhr, where the coal and iron fields were, wrote in the German newspapers about the necessity of Germany having 'a place in the sun', and 'room to live'. They argued that Germany had nowhere to send her surplus population. They wanted to get cheap raw materials and to find new markets. The two European countries which had acquired large empires were Britain and France, and if Germany was to expand overseas it must obviously be by claiming parts of the world already conquered by these two imperial powers.

As part of her efforts to force her way to new supplies and new markets, Germany planned a Berlin–Baghdad railway which would connect her with the warm waters and oil lands of the Mediterranean and the Middle East, and she made treaties with Italy, Austria and Turkey.

France fears Germany

France had special reason to fear the rapid German advance. Whilst the German population was going up, that of France was declining; there were already 20,000,000 more Germans than Frenchmen.

Australian troops in the front trenches. The German trenches were near by. After the German advance had been checked at the Battle of the Marne, both sides dug a system of trenches reaching from the North Sea to Switzerland. For three and a half years all along this line, neither side advanced more than a few miles.

France, therefore, formed an alliance with Russia, hoping that the prospect of having to fight on two fronts at once would deter Germany from attacking.

Great Britain had not made alliances with other countries because she thought that, since she was an island, so long as she controlled the sea she had no need of military help. But when Germany began to build a large navy, the situation changed. In 1897 Germany started making submarines, and, later, battleships. What was the point of this? She had no empire to defend. The answer seemed to be that she was anxious to build an empire, and it would most likely be at our expense. Great Britain replied by adopting what was called the 'two power standard'. This meant that we should have a navy strong enough to defeat any two powers combined against us. When Germany built four Dreadnoughts we built eight. This was one of the reasons why Lloyd George brought out such stiff budgets; the naval building was very expensive, and people grumbled at the high taxes.

'Entente Cordiale' with France   1904

You have read in *A History of Britain* SH 4, Chapter 7, how France and Great Britain entered into an agreement after the dispute at Fashoda. We left the French free to operate in Morocco; in return France recognized our influence in Egypt. So in 1904 we signed an agreement with her which was called the 'Entente Cordiale'. It was a friendly understanding, not an alliance which compelled us to support her in war, but it made quite clear which side we were on.

This was rather bewildering for the British people who had for so long regarded France as an enemy. Children had played a war game with flags called 'French and English'. Now they had to make friends.

We also made friends with another old enemy, Russia. We had fought her in the Crimean War and had criticized the autocratic government of the Tsars, but now our newspapers had articles which pointed out that the Russians were not so bad after all, and in 1907 we made an agreement with her. Both we and the French sent experts to train her army.

If you look at the map you can see how Europe was divided into two groups, Germany/Austria/Italy and Britain/France/Russia.

Crises and alarms

There were several occasions when the international situation became tense, because Germany seemed to be probing to find the weaknesses of her opponents.

For instance, in 1911 a German battleship sailed into Agadir, a small town on the coast of Morocco. The Germans gave the explanation that they were protecting their trade, but as the land was a sandy waste and there was no trading station there, the British government thought that the Germans wanted to set up a naval base, and ordered the battleship to withdraw.

1914 Population

Britain	40,000,000
France	40,000,000
Germany	60,000,000

'The Glutton', Wilhelm II, German Emperor and King of Prussia. In this Italian cartoon, he greedily tries to bite off a hunk of the world for his empire. Britain and France had already claimed most of it.

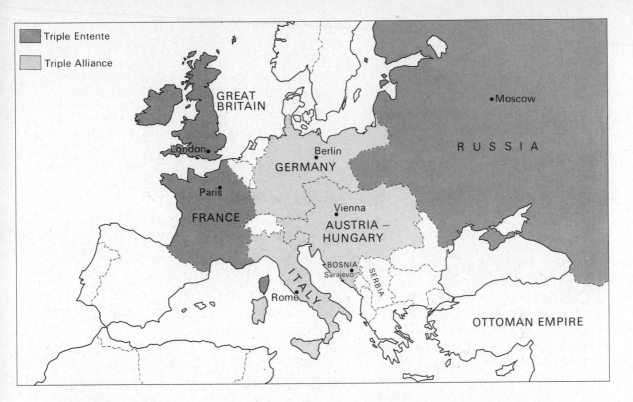

Triple Entente
Triple Alliance

Europe in 1914 was divided into two power blocs. Italy deserted her German ally in 1914 and in 1915 she joined in the war on the side of Britain and France.

The fact that this order was obeyed seemed to point to our superiority; the Germans did not seem prepared to pit their navy against ours.

But since Agadir did not belong to us, you may think that we, too, were behaving in a high-handed way.

The First World War breaks out

Between 1900 and 1914 the major powers in Europe spent vast sums in arming themselves, but few people believed that these expensive weapons would ever be used. A learned German professor said to the author: 'Germany will never start a war. Every family would have to lose their sons and this fear will always prevent us from making war.' In England an economist argued that a modern war would be too expensive; no country, he declared, would be able to fight for more than a few months. The socialist parties in Europe said that the working classes would not attack each other. The general opinion was that wars belonged to past ages, and not to civilized men of the twentieth century.

The summer of 1914 began peacefully. Then on 28 June the heir to the Austrian throne, the Archduke Ferdinand, was assassinated, together with his wife, in the town of Sarajevo in Bosnia. The man who fired the shots was a Serbian student called Gavrilo Princip. It was headline news in the papers, and there were pictures of the dead Archduke, and later of his funeral. The whole affair, however, had little interest for the English. Bosnia was a faraway country and the politics of that part of the world seemed of small importance.

A fortnight later, when the matter had been forgotten in England, there were rumours of disagreement between Austria and Serbia. The Austrian Government had demanded an apology from Serbia, though there was no proof that the Serbian Government had had any hand in the murders. The apology sent did not seem sufficient to Austria; she dictated humiliating terms to Serbia. Russia encouraged Serbia to refuse them and ordered a general mobilization. Germany entered the fray, demanding that the Russian mobilization should stop. Russia refused this demand.

On 1 August Germany declared war on Russia, and two days later on France. In a space of four days the fate of millions of people had been disastrously decided.

Britain enters the war

The English people went away as usual for the August Bank holiday, not thinking that the war in Europe affected them. But the Cabinet knew better and met all through the weekend. From 1 August to 4 August our Foreign Office worked at full pressure and lights shone from its windows all night. Telegrams of warning were sent to our consuls in every part of the world.

Should we declare war in support of France or not? Some members of the Cabinet were against our doing so; on the other hand, if France were defeated, would not the Germans then attack our Channel ports? During this time of hesitation the editor of *The Times* called upon the French Ambassador, Monsieur Cambon, at the French Embassy, and found him pacing up and down his study with clenched fists. 'What are you doing, Monsieur Cambon?' he asked. The ambassador turned on him passionately and said 'I'm waiting to see if the word "Honour" is to be expunged from the English language.'

It would have been particularly bitter for the French if we had not come in, because at our suggestion they had sent their fleet to the Mediterranean, and depended on us to defend the Channel.

Finally, when the news came that Germany was advancing on France through Belgium, a country whose neutrality both we and the Germans had guaranteed, the government decided that we should fight, and at midnight on Monday, 4 August, an excited crowd outside Buckingham Palace heard that we were at war with Germany. Violent indignation was felt at the contemptuous way the German Chancellor referred to the treaty with Belgium as 'a scrap of paper'.

Within a few days the British Expeditionary Force had landed in France, and we began to recruit for further armies amongst our civilian population.

The first weeks of the war were a hopeful time. People said 'It will be over by Christmas', and the slogan 'Christmas in Berlin' was chalked on the troop trains which steamed out of Victoria Station.

Farewell to a humdrum life.

Off to defend their country.

34

These stirring words printed in bold letters with the picture of Field-Marshal Kitchener stared from every hoarding. The response to it was overwhelming. Look at the picture on the previous page showing the crowds lining up at a recruiting office. The same scene could be seen in every town. Thousands of young clerks, who had been used to working every day from nine till six o'clock with only one fortnight's holiday a year, joyfully left their offices to serve their country in a more romantic way. Students at the universities threw away their books on Anglo-Saxon, Latin or Chemistry. Schoolboys were terrified that the war might

BRITONS

"WANTS" YOU

JOIN YOUR COUNTRY'S ARMY!
GOD SAVE THE KING

Reproduced by permission of LONDON OPINION

Lord Kitchener, War Minister, started a campaign in which over 3,000,000 men volunteered to serve in the armed forces.

NATIONAL SERVICE
WOMEN'S
LAND ARMY

'GOD SPEED THE PLOUGH
AND THE WOMAN WHO DRIVES IT'

'Every woman in a man's job
releases a man for the
firing line.'

be over before they were old enough to enlist. Clergymen preached that it was a holy war, a crusade against evil, and the origins of the war in the remote town of Sarajevo were forgotten. All that people understood was that the big bully, Germany, was invading gallant little Belgium.

Women flung themselves as eagerly as the men into the war effort. They were needed to replace the men who left their jobs to join up. They worked on the land, made munitions, became conductresses on the buses. More nurses were needed and young women enrolled in the V.A.D. (Voluntary Aid Detachment). The W.A.A.C. (Women's Auxiliary Army Corps) was founded. In fact women did everything except the actual fighting. In the past many parents had refused to allow their daughters to leave home and earn their living. Now it suddenly became their duty to leave home and they tasted freedom for the first time.

Support from the Empire

Not only in Great Britain did men rush to enlist. They came from Canada, Australia and New Zealand, and in South Africa, generals who had fought against us in the Boer War, were now prepared to fight on our side. On the streets could be seen the lines of marching recruits singing lustily:

It's a long way to Tipperary,
    It's a long way to go,
It's a long way to Tipperary,
    To the sweetest girl I know;
Goodbye Piccadilly,
    Farewell Leicester Square;
It's a long, long way to Tipperary,
    But my heart's right there.

The enthusiasm often turned to hysteria. The hatred of all things German made some people say that no more German music should be played, though by no manner of reasoning could Bach or Beethoven be accused of having started the war. Numbers of German Jews who had come to this country learned to their cost what it meant to have a German name, when their shops were wrecked and looted. There was a spy mania. Anyone who was eccentric or who seemed mysterious was labelled a spy, rather in the way that women were accused of being witches in the Middle Ages. There were atrocity stories about the Germans, who were labelled 'Huns' after a barbarian tribe of the fifth century which had a reputation for great cruelty. Nothing was too bad to be believed about the Germans. How these stories grew in the telling of them is shown by these quotations from newspapers:

When the fall of Antwerp became known, the church bells were rung. *Kölnische Zeitung.*

According to the *Kölnische Zeitung* the clergy of Antwerp were compelled to ring the church bells when the fortress was taken. *Le Matin.*

According to what *The Times* has heard from Cologne, via Paris, the unfortunate Belgian priests who refused to ring the church bells when Antwerp was taken have been sentenced to hard labour.

According to the information which had reached the *Corriere della Sera* from Cologne via London, it is confirmed that the barbaric conquerors of Antwerp punished the unfortunate Belgian priests for their heroic refusal to ring the church bells by hanging them as living clappers to the bells, with their heads down. *Le Matin*.

Stories such as these fanned the flames of hatred and the war became a holy war against a wicked nation. Rupert Brooke, the young Cambridge poet wrote 'Now God be thanked who has matched us with His Hour'.

The War in France

The German High Command planned to knock out France in one tremendous, rapid campaign, and then to transfer their armies to Russia, which they knew would be slow to mobilize. By the 'Schlieffen Plan' German troops were to sweep round north of Paris, surround and capture the city. They were to go through Belgium, in defiance of the treaty of neutrality about her, because, as a neutral country, she had unfortified frontiers.

Fortunately for us the Schlieffen Plan was never properly carried out. For one thing, the Belgians delayed the German advance by resisting;

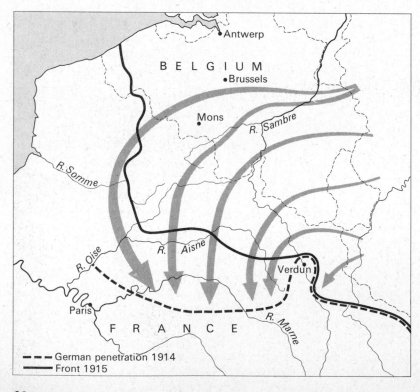

- - - German penetration 1914
——— Front 1915

The German attack on France.

the railway workers tore up the railway lines, and the Belgian army put up a gallant fight. For another thing, the distances to be marched proved too much for the German troops, who were sleeping on their feet by the time they got within range of Paris. The time of mechanized transport for armies had not yet arrived. And lastly, there was the splendid resistance of the French army and the small, but highly trained, British Expeditionary Force. When the citizens of Paris heard the booming of the German guns, many of them thought that their city was doomed and prepared to flee.

But at the Battle of the Marne, east of Paris, the Germans were halted and pushed back to the River Aisne. Both armies dug themselves into trenches, and held lines which stretched from the North Sea to Switzerland. For more than three years these lines changed very little, and in some places they were so close together that when the guns were silent each side could hear the other talking.

It was a new kind of war. In the past wars had meant movement. This was a deadlock because the weapons of defence were much stronger than the weapons of attack. The people at home were expecting to hear of the Germans being driven back by great advances; no such news came. Instead, after fierce attacks and heavy casualties in some sector, we might capture a few yards of enemy trench, but this did not mean that the enemy was dislodged, for behind the first line of trenches there was a second and a third line.

The mud of the battlefield. War without romance.

The generals of both sides were unable to adapt themselves to the new situation. They were further handicapped by the fact that new inventions, such as tanks, came into production far more slowly than had been hoped. The generals had mostly been trained as cavalrymen, and imagined charging forward to victory. They seldom went to the front line, and some of them owed their appointments to family connexions rather than to intelligence. In World War II generals who failed were immediately replaced. In World War I we hesitated to do this, although Sir Douglas Haig did replace Sir John French. Yet hundreds of thousands of lives were in the hands of these generals.

If you look at the picture on page 31, you will see what the trenches looked like. The men who manned them had to contend with mud, rats, lice, as well as constant shelling. When an attack was planned, there would first be a bombardment, then the men 'went over the top' in a rush to capture a German trench. In the territory between the front lines of trenches, the part called 'No-man's-land', there was barbed wire, on which a man might be caught and linger in agony until he died. Men were kept ten days in the trenches, and then were given a week behind the lines to rest.

In 1915 the Germans first used chlorine gas. This filled the lungs, so that the men choked and gasped. The British followed this practice. Here is an account by Robert Graves, one of our greatest modern poets, of what happened the first time it was used by us.

A tank in 1917. Tanks, invented in England in 1915, were designed to travel over very rough country and to cut through the barbed wire of German trenches. They took the Germans by surprise in the Battle of the Somme, 1916. The early tanks often broke down, and the one shown here is an improved model.

After a gas attack. The men are blinded, their lungs choked with gas.

The spanners for unscrewing the cocks of the cylinders proved, with two or three exceptions, to be misfits. The gasmen rushed about shouting for the loan of an adjustable spanner. They managed to discharge one or two cylinders; the gas went whistling out, formed a thick cloud a few yards off in no-man's-land, and then gradually spread back into our trenches . . . Then their batteries opened on our lines. The confusion in the front trench must have been horrible; direct hits broke several of the cylinders, the trench filled with gas. The gas company stampeded.

After this gas was used by neither side. It was too uncertain a weapon, for if the wind changed, the gas would be blown back in the opposite direction.

The Battle of the Somme 1916

There was a demand for more munitions, more shells, and, because of his tremendous drive, Lloyd George was appointed Minister of Munitions. Soon, all over England could be seen small wooden huts where the shells were filled; separate huts, because of the danger of explosion. In 1916 Lloyd George became Prime Minister instead of Asquith, and his energy in speeding up the making of munitions did much to ensure our final victory.

The French and British commanders decided in 1916 on a combined attack which by its sheer weight could end the war. They chose the

Somme as the best place for launching this. It is difficult to understand this decision. The land sloped upwards to the German lines so that the Germans were entrenched on high ground. The land there was chalky, and easy to dig and the German front trenches were very deep – in fact they had an almost impregnable position. Also there had been numerous small attacks by the British in this sector, attacks which had encouraged the Germans to strengthen their defences in the area.

The battle of the Somme began with a five days' bombardment. Then the attacking force went in. They were ordered to go forward in a straight line. They fell and stumbled in the craters formed by the previous British bombardment. Then the Germans opened fire, and on that first day there were 20,000 casualties. Still the attack went on, and day after day the British were thrown against the enemy. In the end the total British casualties were 420,000. The battle was fought by the volunteer army, the brave, who had enlisted at their own free will. Conscription had been introduced in the spring of 1916, but the conscripts were not yet trained.

We gained a small advance on part of the line by great effort, but victory was as far away as ever.

After this battle the mood of the soldiers changed. They still fought on stubbornly, but their faith in their leaders had gone. Siegfried Sassoon wrote:

'Good morning, good morning,' the General said,
   When we met him last week on our way to the line.
Now the soldiers he smiled at are most of 'em dead,
   And we're cursing his staff for incompetent swine.
'He's a cheery old card,' grunted Harry to Jack
   As they slogged up to Arras with rifle and pack.
But he did for them both with his plan of attack.

There was only one more big attempt at a breakthrough by British troops, that was at Passchendaele, sometimes called the Battle of the Mud. The men had to wade waist high through mud, and some drowned when they stumbled into bomb craters. Like the other attempts, it was a failure. After it was over Haig's Chief of Staff visited the front for the first time. When he saw the mud, he burst into tears and said: 'Good God, did we really send the men to fight in that?'

Wilfred Owen, the poet, wrote 'An Anthem for doomed Youth'.

What passing-bells for these who die as cattle?
   Only the monstrous anger of the guns.
   Only the stuttering rifles' rapid rattle,
Can patter out their hasty orisons.
No mockeries now for them; no prayers nor bells,
Nor any voice of mourning save the choirs,
The shrill, demented choirs of wailing shells;
And bugles calling for them from sad shires.

The British 'Tommy' and his equipment.

The Dardanelles

Lloyd George from the beginning had had doubts about the wisdom of concentrating on the western front. Churchill suggested a way out from the deadlock in France by attacking Turkey (which was allied with Germany), so that the British forces could link up with the Russians and attack Germany from the south. You can see from the map that this was a promising idea. If we succeeded we should cut Turkey off from Germany, and we would be able to supply Russia with munitions by her Black Sea ports. But the best of plans fail if they are not carried out properly, and many of the commanders thought this a wildcat scheme and gave it only half-hearted support.

In order to succeed, the attack needed to be a surprise, but the Turks had got wind of it. When our troops, most of them the tall Australians and New Zealanders, landed, they were met by machine-gun fire from prepared positions. Many men were killed. Those who survived could not go out from such cover as they had found to bury the dead, and they lay under a burning sun, attacked by dysentery and overwhelmed by the increasing stench from the decaying bodies. They could neither retreat nor advance.

Finally, one night we took off all the survivors. The Turks never knew that we were withdrawing, and we got every man down the cliff paths and into boats without a single casualty. It was a brilliant end to a tragic failure.

Lawrence of Arabia.

War in Arabia

Turkey, however, was defeated in another part of the world. Her empire then stretched right across the Middle East, and the allies took advantage of the fact that the Arabs were in revolt against their Turkish masters. Indian troops were sent into Mesopotamia, and other troops were sent into Syria to help the Arabs. This desert war produced one remarkable leader, T. E. Lawrence. He was an Oxford scholar who had worked for several years in the Middle East on archaeological sites. In 1916 he went to Arabia to lead the tribesmen of King Feisal in a series of dashing raids against the Turks. He wore Arab dress and spoke Arabic; King Feisal said he loved him as his son. To the Arabs there was something miraculous about this little Englishman with the blue eyes. He became a legend in Arabia in his lifetime, and indeed he was a brilliant leader.

General Allenby, commander of our forces in Syria, entered Jerusalem in December 1917. He was the first Christian master of the city since the time of the Crusades.

We had destroyed the Turkish empire in Asia.

The Russian steamroller

While this grim struggle went on in the west, the allies had little comfort from the eastern front. The Russian army, though its size was impressive, was not a powerful fighting machine. The individual

Russian soldier was as brave as any other, but he was sent to fight without proper equipment; sometimes six men had to share a rifle. The railway system was inadequate, so that food and supplies could not be transported to the troops.

The German general Hindenburg won a decisive victory over the Russians at the Battle of Tannenberg, and eventually they were pushed back 300 miles.

How did it happen that a country of 120,000,000 people could not produce a more efficient army? Russia was in all technical ways very backward, and the system of Government was old-fashioned and corrupt. The Tsar of all the Russias was an absolute monarch. He alone decided policy and made all the appointments. The last of the tsars, Nicholas II was an amiable, weak-minded man, who would have been really happy if he could have lived a quiet life with his family. The one idea to which he held firmly was that he must hang on to his power and hand over the country one day to his son in the same state in which he had inherited it, as an absolute monarchy. This son, the youngest of a family of five, was delicate. He was a haemophiliac, which meant that his blood had not the quality which causes a wound to heal, so that his hold on life was precarious. The Tsarina was a superstitious woman, and when someone brought to the palace a so-called 'Holy Man', who said he had the power of healing, she believed in him. His name was Rasputin, and he was in fact a shameless scoundrel who made a fortune for himself. It so happened that on three occasions when the little Tsarevitch was ill, he recovered after Rasputin visited him.

From that time onwards Rasputin controlled the palace and also the affairs of state. If a manufacturer wanted a government contract he only had to bribe Rasputin to get it. Coveted posts were given away to those whom Rasputin recommended. No wonder that the soldiers shivered and starved at the front. Patriotic Russians, who saw the war as a defence of their country were indignant at the sight of the dirty, disreputable Rasputin controlling affairs.

A group of young Russians, headed by Prince Yussupov, determined to get rid of him. They invited him to supper with them and gave him poisoned cakes. They knew he was greedy and saw with satisfaction that he ate eighteen of them, enough to poison a dozen people. Strange to say nothing happened to him, and they almost began to believe that he really had supernatural powers. Die he must, they thought, so they stabbed him and then threw his body into the River Neva. But the death of Rasputin did not change things very much. The corruption had gone too far. In March 1917 the Tsar was forced to abdicate and a provisional government set up. The leaders tried to rally the army to a renewed fight, but with little success. Later in the year, after the second revolution, Russia made peace with Germany.

The War at sea

The great Dreadnought battleships which we had built at such cost

The Government employed artists to record scenes of the war. Their paintings can be seen today in the Imperial War Museum. (See also the painting on page 101.)

Above: 'Over the Top', by John Nash.
Below: 'We are making a new world', by Paul Nash.

A Dreadnought.

fought only one major battle, for the German Grand Fleet only once came into the North Sea to meet them. This occasion was the Battle of Jutland, 1916. Both sides claimed the victory. We lost more ships, but the German fleet steamed back to port and did not emerge again.

Submarines were a much greater menace to us than the unwieldy battleships, for we had to keep the sea lines open for merchant shipping if we were to maintain our food and military supplies. The Germans launched a submarine campaign against us; first sinking ships which they suspected of carrying armaments to Britain. When in 1915 they sank the *Lusitania* a hundred Americans were amongst the passengers who were drowned. This drew a protest from President Wilson, and the Germans offered to call off the submarine campaign if we would call off our blockade of German ports. We refused to do this because we realized that the battle for supplies might prove to be the decisive battle of the war.

Submarines were a deadly menace to our merchant shipping, and were difficult to destroy because they could escape by submerging.

In times past merchant ships had sometimes disguised themselves as

A German submarine in 1914.

men-of-war in order to deceive pirates. In World War I we reversed this trick, and harmless-looking old tramp steamers and trawlers were fitted up with anti-submarine guns hidden behind hinged panels. These were called 'Q-ships'.

Manning these ships was dangerous and skilled work, for they had to court attack by torpedoes, and the deception had to be perfect. For instance, a boat pretending to be a trawler had to carry decaying fish to attract the cloud of gulls which always accompanies a fishing vessel. Since merchantmen nearly always have a pet, a stuffed parrot in a cage was part of the equipment. The only men ever to be seen on deck either at sea or in port were a handful of merchant seamen in a mixture of old working clothes, and 'Mr Mate' in baggy trousers.

When they were at sea they rehearsed their parts for when they met a submarine. A 'panic party' acted the part of the merchant crew. They ran about shaking their fists at the submarine and cursing. They lowered the boats with such speed that one of them upset. The parrot's cage was handed overboard, and then, as they rowed away with frantic haste, a black-faced fireman rushed up from below and yelled for them to come back for him. All the time the gun-crews were lying silent behind their guns, waiting until the submarine surfaced in order to collect the ship's papers. Then, when the submarine lay helpless on the surface of the water, the naval White Ensign was run up the mast, the secret panels were flung open, and the guns fired.

Several submarines were destroyed by Q-ships. In time their work became more dangerous, for the submarines became more cautious and would not surface until their victim was on the point of sinking. The crews faced hours of waiting in a leaking, disabled ship, or in open boats for rescue to arrive.

The submarine danger grew so great that neutral ships refused to sail to Britain. So we started a convoy system, by which fifty ships would sail together, protected by half a dozen destroyers.

In February 1917 Germany declared unrestricted submarine warfare; any ship in the eastern Atlantic would be sunk. This made the Americans very angry.

A Q-ship. The hatch is a dummy, concealing an anti-submarine gun.

America enters the war 1917

The majority of Americans sympathized with the Allies, but they did not want to be involved in a European war, and in the presidential election of 1916 Wilson was re-elected on the promise that he would keep America out.

But by 1917 it was by no means certain that the Allies would win. American businessmen had given a great deal of credit to Britain and France for buying war material, and if the Allies lost they would never be paid. Many of them urged that the United States should declare war on Germany. The German declaration of unrestricted submarine warfare was the final affront to America, and in April 1917 she broke off relations with Germany.

The American navy immediately helped us to tighten the stranglehold of our blockade of Germany, but it was three months before soldiers from the United States appeared to help the exhausted allied armies in France. Perhaps they came just in time; the French were so short of manpower that they were putting boys of sixteen in the army.

The Americans arrive, fresh and vigorous, to replace men who were war-worn, exhausted, or dead.

The defeat of Germany

The Germans prepared through the winter of 1917–18 for one final assault. In March 1918 they mounted the greatest offensive of the war and reached as near to Paris as they had been in 1914. They could not keep it up because they had no reserves to fall back on and when the Allies mounted their last great offensive in August 1918, the Germans were finally driven from France. They were unable to continue the war. The people in Germany were starving and there was unrest everywhere. Later, as you will notice, the Nazis made a great point of the fact that their army had held together, and that Germany had been defeated not by a superior army, but by the blockade.

President Wilson had issued what he called his 'Fourteen Points' explaining what sort of peace he would want. The peace was to be just, the losers were not to be punished, and the peoples to be free to choose their own governments. The German cabinet realized that their hope for a merciful peace lay with President Wilson, and that the Kaiser was a stumbling block. If they could get him out of the way and form a more democratic government, which was pleasing to the Americans, then they would get better terms.

On 9 November 1918, from the town of Spa, the military German headquarters, a train slid out of the station carrying one passenger who knew the Germans could not win the war. It was the Kaiser, the 'All Highest' as he had been called. When the train got to the Dutch frontier, there was a car waiting for him and he ended his journey in Holland. He never returned to Germany.

Two days later on 11 November the armistice was signed. All over England and France sirens announced the good tidings. There was relief and in some cases wild rejoicing. Whatever else might be in store for people, at least the awful slaughter was over.

Settling the affairs of our enemies

'I will make Germany pay', declared Lloyd George to an applauding audience, and then added under his breath, 'as much as she can'. He had also promised to hang the Kaiser, in order to please the people who had been taught by propaganda to think that the Kaiser was chiefly responsible for the war. When Lloyd George went off to the

An armistice scene in London. The Kaiser's better hole was a pleasant country house in Holland.

The new nations. Europe, 1920.

Peace Conference in Paris he knew that he had to satisfy the electors at home, and that this would be difficult because Germany could not pay, and to talk of hanging the Kaiser was nonsense.

The important people at the conference besides Lloyd George were President Wilson, Clemenceau of France, and Orlando of Italy. President Wilson represented the nation to whom all the others owed money, so they were debtors facing their creditor. Wilson, therefore, was in the strongest position.

Wilson believed that all nations should be free from domination by other nations, and was determined to allow the countries which had been under the Austrian Empire to set up separate governments of their own. You can see from the map the new nations which resulted from this policy.

The final treaty has been bitterly criticized, but some good and lasting arrangements were made. Poland became independent, after having been ruled by Prussia, Austria and Russia for a hundred years. Czechoslovakia and Yugoslavia were created as free nations out of the Austro-Hungarian Empire. It would have been impossible to draw the borders between all these new countries in a way which would have been satisfactory to everyone; the races were too much intermingled. However, on the whole, national feeling was taken into account. Compare this to the way in which the victors settled Europe at the Congress of Vienna in 1815. (See *A History of Britain* SH 4.)

France wanted back her provinces of Alsace and Lorraine, and was granted these. She also wanted payment for the rebuilding of her ruined cities, and this raised the question of how much Germany could be made to pay. In the end an impossible sum was agreed upon, which caused prolonged wrangles between the nations.

Lloyd George returned home in triumph, and after the signing of the Peace Treaty in June 1919 there were celebrations in every town and village. Heavy though the cost of their victory had been, people thought that they had won the war to end war.

The League of Nations set up

Wilson was anxious to create an organization of states which could settle disputes and maintain peace between the nations.

This was set up as the League of Nations. All nations of the world had the right to join it. It was the first time in the history of the world that the people – as apart from kings – had an opportunity to join together to outlaw war as uncivilized and barbarous. Unfortunately the American Congress, despite Wilson's advocacy, refused to join the League, and as Germany was not at first allowed to join, it was not strong enough to settle disputes between the larger nations. Nor was it able to save us from another war in twenty years' time. But it did much good work in settling smaller disputes, and was a pointer towards the future.

The question of who should have the German colonies was settled by the League, which took responsibility for them, and handed them to members of the victorious alliance to govern. In this way, Britain obtained control of Tanganyika and South-West Africa.

The cost of the War in human lives:

Great Britain	750,000
France	1,500,000
Germany	1,500.000
America	88,000

Dates to remember

1914   Outbreak of the First World War
1917   America entered the war
1918   The Armistice was signed
1919   The Treaty of Versailles

Things to do

1   Go to your local library and look at the old newspapers and any other documents and find out how many men from your town went to the war and how many of them were killed.
2   Make a list of the authors and poets who wrote about the war.
3   Find out what was the origin and the purpose of 'Poppy Day'.

Books to read

A. F. Alington, *The Lights Go Out*, Faber
J. Cadell, *Young Lawrence of Arabia*, Max Parrish
R. Graves, *Goodbye To All That*, Penguin
A. J. P. Taylor, *The First World War*, Penguin
Erich Maria Remarque, *All Quiet on the Western Front*, Putnam

Chapter 3
Politics in Britain   1918–29

Back to normal?

When England came to count up the cost of the war she realized that she had lost the pick of a generation, and there were a million 'surplus' women who would not marry because the men had been killed. Fifteen years later a writer visited a village where everything looked at first sight much the same as in 1914; but when he talked to the old men he found that there was a difference:

'There's no one between them (the very young) and chaps like us.'
'All the rest were killed you mean?'
'Most of them, sir. Forty-two were killed in this village, and they'd be men of thirty-five and forty by now.'
'Ah. That war didn't do any of us any good,' said Mr Stillway.
'Nothing's been the same since.'

England set about the vast undertaking of demobilizing her armies, getting the wheels of industry turning again, and returning to democratic elections. But things were not the same in political fields either. When we come to politics we find that the great Liberal Party was reduced to a small minority, and the Labour Party was rising to take its place.

This was probably because Lloyd George in 1916 took over from Asquith as leader of the Liberals and Prime Minister of a coalition war-time government. The Liberal Party split because most Liberals remained loyal to Asquith, and Lloyd George thought that if he led the Liberal Party in an election in 1918 he would be beaten. He wanted to stay Prime Minister, so he proposed to the Conservatives that they should continue their war-time alliance with him and fight the election together as a coalition.

The Coupon Election   1918

The Conservatives wanted Lloyd George's help to deal with the problem of the peace. Winston Churchill said, 'He was the greatest master of the art of getting things done and putting things through that I ever knew,' and the Conservative leader, Mr Bonar-Law said, 'We must never let the little man go.' So an agreement was made between Lloyd George and the Conservatives; in every constituency one candidate had a letter signed by both Bonar Law and Lloyd George saying that he was the coalition candidate. Asquith contemptuously called this letter a 'Coupon', and the election was called after it.

November 1917. Petrograd. Lenin proclaiming the end of seven months of parliamentary government and the establishment of a communist state. The Russian Revolution greatly influenced British politics of this period.
(See page 54.)

The Coupon Election is considered rather shoddy now. The supporters of Lloyd George won votes by promising that Germany should be 'squeezed until the pips squeaked', although he knew quite well that every one would have to share in paying for four years of destruction.

Nevertheless the coalition won by a huge majority. People voted for Lloyd George as 'the man who won the war', and he remained Prime Minister. The Liberal Party, made up of supporters of Asquith, had only half as many members in Parliament as the Labour Party. We have arrived at the time when Labour became the rival of the Conservatives for the government of the country. This had not happened merely because Lloyd George had shouldered aside his old colleagues and split the Liberals; it was largely because the workers were now better educated and more independent; they were no longer prepared to let parties based on middle-class ideas and interests govern them; they wanted a party controlled by themselves. Also, their self-confidence was very much increased by what had happened in Russia.

Election Result   1918

Coalition of Conservatives and Lloyd George

Liberals	478
Labour	63
Asquith Liberals	28

The workers take over in Russia   1917

The Tsarist Russian government imprisoned, or exiled in Siberia, those who dared to oppose it, so that the leaders of popular movements worked in secret and lived much of their lives in exile. Most of these died without ever knowing that their cause was to succeed. But one of them, Vladimir Ilyich Ulyanov, whom we know as 'Lenin', a name he used in his secret work, became the greatest figure in Russian history.

When Lenin was seventeen his elder brother, who was a student, was executed for having taken part in a plot to assassinate the Tsar. Lenin loved and admired his brother, and was deeply moved by his death, but when he heard of the plot he said, 'No. That is not the way we must do it.' He meant that assassination was useless; the way was to be by organization and political education.

He devoted his life to the organization of opposition to the Tsarist government. Like other Russian socialists and liberals, he spent long periods in prison, where he continued his political work by writing pamphlets. He wrote them with milk and made 'inkwells' out of bread, which could be swallowed in an emergency. His future wife used to spend hours standing at a particular spot on the pavement outside the prison in the hope that he would be comforted by a glimpse of her when he was going to exercise.

During the 1914 war he lived in exile in Switzerland. You have read in Chapter 2 how in 1917 the Russian armies, ill-fed, ill-armed, ill-led, began to collapse. The Germans realized that if there were a Bolshevik government in Russia, it would make peace because the Bolsheviks did not believe in fighting for the Russian Empire.* This would release the German Eastern army for use on their western front. They believed, rightly, that Lenin was the most able and dangerous Bolshevik leader. Therefore, they arranged to take him and thirty other

*The word 'Bolshevik' means 'majority'. It was the name given to the communists who believed that socialism could only be achieved by a well-organized party of men, dedicated to the overthrow of the ruling classes. They had got this name because they had been the majority at one of the conferences of Russian socialists.

Russian revolutionaries in secret in a sealed train through Germany, across the Baltic to Finland, and so to Russia.

When Lenin stepped out of the Finland Station in St Petersburg (the city which was after his death to be called Leningrad), he found Russia in a ferment of suffering and hope; he found that everyone in the streets, in the factories, in the blocks of flats, was talking about the future. Was it to be peace or war? Liberalism or Socialism? Parliaments or Soviets?†

Lenin began to make the speeches which promised them bread, land and peace, and a society in which power would belong to the workers instead of the wealthy and aristocratic classes. He won his way, and in the seven years which were left before he died the Bolsheviks had won the civil war against the supporters of the old, Tsarist parties (who were called the 'Whites') and had set up the new state of the U.S.S.R., the Union of Socialist Soviet Republics.

The Russian Revolution was perhaps the most important event of this century, because it set up the first communist state. Communism is a kind of socialism based on the idea that private profit is wrong. Communists say that no man should make profit out of the work of another, as they maintain that employers do when they sell the things made by their workers for more than they pay them in wages. Therefore the communists believe that the means of production (the factories and the land) should belong to the state, or to public bodies, so that the profits go back to the people.

You may have read about Karl Marx, the German exile who lived in London from 1849 to 1883 and wrote about these ideas in his famous book *Capital*.

Lenin led the Russian people in setting up a state which carried out the ideas of Karl Marx. The land and factories in Russia were taken from the landlords and industrialists. Power was exercised by the Communist Party and Workers' Committees.

At first the capitalist countries thought that communism would not work, and that the Soviet government would collapse. But in fact, after the first desperate years of famine and civil war, the standard of living went up in Russia, and showed that communism could make a backward, hungry society into a powerful and prosperous one in a short time. In 1949 the example of Russia was followed by China, and now more than one-fifth of the world's population lives under governments inspired by the ideas of Marx and Lenin.

The wars of intervention

The Russian Revolution was regarded with horror by our middle and upper classes. Not only were the Tsar and Tsarina (who was a granddaughter of Queen Victoria) executed, but also foreign investment and property, including the Lena goldfields, where much British money was invested, were confiscated. They realized that socialism of this kind put an end to the business world they knew and which had made

† The Soviets were committees of ordinary people, who, when the Tsarist government of Russia broke down, met to decide what should be done.

The Communist Manifesto

A spectre is haunting Europe, the spectre of communism. All the powers of old Europe have entered into a holy alliance to exorcize this spectre; Pope and Tsar, French liberals and German police spies...

Communists demand –
Abolition of all property in land.
Abolition of all inheritance.
Ownership of all factories by the state.
Everyone to be obliged to work.
All education to be free.

The communists scorn to hide their ideas and aims. They openly declare that their ends can only be reached by the forcible overthrow of existing governments. Let the ruling classes tremble at a communist revolution. The workers have nothing to lose but their chains. They have a world to win. Workers of the world, unite.

Britain wealthy and powerful. No investment was safe if communist governments were to be set up. Our newspapers were full of stories of Bolshevik atrocities, and the British, French, American and Japanese governments actually sent armed forces to Russia to help the Tsarist 'Whites' against the communist 'Reds'.

The Jolly George

The workers on the whole differed from the wealthier classes in their attitude towards Russia. There were 350,000 ex-soldiers unemployed, and they had learnt that the Russian system of planning and organizing industry provided plenty of work at all times. They felt sympathy with their Russian comrades who were fighting a civil war, struggling to set up a new kind of society, and who were also faced by hostile armies from abroad.

In London docks there was the cargo ship the *Jolly George*, waiting to be loaded with military supplies to be used against the Red Russians. The dockers refused to load the *Jolly George* and the Labour Party supported the dockers. This was a danger signal to the government. It learnt that, partly from war weariness, and partly from political feeling, it would be useless to ask the people of this country to fight a war to put an end to communism in Russia. Intervention in Russia was called off.

Lloyd George as Prime Minister in peacetime   1918–22

Lloyd George showed his energy and originality in peace as he had done in war.

Housing Act 1919   'Homes Fit for Heroes'

He made an effort to carry out his promise to build homes. By Addison's Act the local authorities were given the job of building houses. The government ordered them to do this, and helped them by giving them subsidies of about £260 for every working-class house that they built. Although this first housing act was not entirely successful, it pointed to the way in which the vast housing estates of today have been built, and is another way in which the government of Lloyd George has left its mark on our national life.

The Forestry Commission   1919

He left his mark on the countryside as well as the cities. He cared about the waste of the poor, unprofitable lands of marsh and hillside, and he recognized our need for timber. Therefore he founded the State Forestry Commission. We can see the results in the forests in many of the lonelier parts of the British Isles.

Wages and prices gone mad

He was very clever in foiling the strikes which were threatened as a result of changes in wages and prices.

October 1921. 'I don't say these hot-water bottles will absolutely cure you, but they should relieve the trouble.' Lloyd George's help for the unemployed.

There was a wild boom in England after the war. Everybody wanted goods, new firms were set up to make these and profits were enormous. Prices rocketed up, partly because there was more money than things to buy with it; the government had set the money, paper money, in circulation during the war, but it could not provide the goods to buy. Imagine a desert island with ten shipwrecked sailors on it, and ten tins of corned beef as the only food available; if each sailor had five pounds in his trouser pocket, the price of a tin of corned beef might be five pounds. It was rather like that in England in 1919. A family's food which had cost 12s. 10½d. in 1914 would cost, for the same items, in 1919 £2 3s. 5d., an increase of 236 per cent. Wages had gone up too, but not so much. Therefore there were threats of strikes.

Lloyd George set up committees to discuss wage rates for industries in which there was trouble. The committees could decide nothing, only examine the problem and give an opinion, but whilst they were spending months preparing their reports, the workers did not strike, because they hoped that some agreement would be made in their favour. Lloyd George thought that by the time the committees had finished talking things would have settled down. At any rate, serious strife was put off until a later date.

You will read on page 62 what happened later in the battle for wages.

The Geddes Axe and the slump   1922

The Government thought in 1922 that it was time to make a great effort to bring down both prices and wages, and return so far as possible to price levels of 1914. It did this by sudden, drastic economies, planned by one of the cabinet ministers, Sir Eric Geddes.

The army and navy were docked of millions of pounds, which was perhaps not unreasonable since the war was over, and no one was prepared to fight another immediately. Other government departments were also cut. In education, for instance, nearly all the 'Day Continuation Schools' for children over fourteen were closed. The state gave less money for health and child welfare services. Every organization paid for by the government got less money.

This did in one way save money, but it also caused more unemployment because it meant that people could not afford to buy so much. Think how many people you employ, each of them for a fraction of a second, every time you buy a quarter of sweets or a box of matches, and you will see how this policy would make unemployment. Prices did, indeed, come down, but the factories slowed down too, and men were turned off.

By March 1921 there were 1,355,000 unemployed. Unemployment had become our most serious national problem, and it remained so until 1939 when war broke out again. Since the 1939–45 war we have had booms instead of slumps almost all the time, and people now can hardly remember the suffering of the years between the two wars.

The troubles between the wars

Lloyd George had plenty of trouble on his hands. Besides the unemployment and labour unrest at home, there was trouble overseas. There was a revolt against us in Egypt, and India was enraged by the 'Amritsar Massacre', of which you will read in Chapter 8.

But perhaps the worst trouble for the government was caused by the old question of Ireland. When you read about Ireland in Chapter 9 you will understand how the scandals and bloodshed there would damage the reputation of the British Prime Minister who was responsible.

The discarding of Lloyd George   1922

It was not only that the scandals in India and Ireland damaged Lloyd George's reputation; but the Conservatives were also angry with him because he had quarrelled with Turkey. In any case, they would naturally rather have had a Conservative than a Liberal Prime Minister, and by 1922 they thought that the magic of 'the man who won the war' had faded and that they could win an election without his help.

Therefore, there was the famous 'Carlton Club meeting' of the senior members of the Conservative Party, and the most important speech at it was made by Stanley Baldwin. He was a quiet man of whom the public had at that time heard little. He spoke against the leadership of Lloyd George; he said that Lloyd George had smashed the Liberal Party, and that if they went on with the coalition he would smash the Conservatives too, and they should get rid of this dangerous ally, leave the coalition, and fight the next election on their own. They agreed to do this, and withdrew their support from Lloyd George, who was therefore forced to resign. When he did so the king said, 'He will be Prime Minister again'. But he never was. Brilliance is no use to a politician who has not got a strong party behind him.

The Conservatives won the election of 1922, and in 1923 Stanley Baldwin became the Conservative Prime Minister. The Labour Party was still advancing; it had nearly three times as many members elected as it had had in 1918. The Liberals, divided between Asquith and Lloyd George, were sinking.

MacDonald becomes Prime Minister   1924

Baldwin held another General Election only a year after he had won the last one, and asked the country to vote for protection. You remember that the country had said 'No' to protection in 1906; it did the same in 1923. Baldwin resigned after his defeat and the king sent for Ramsay MacDonald, leader of the Labour Party, and asked him to form a government.

The first Labour government

Should he accept? He could only govern if the Liberals supported him, because it needed the combined votes of Labour and Liberal members

Every box of matches needs the work of these people:

Foresters
Lumberers
Paper and Cardboard makers
Gum makers
Paintmakers
Phosphorus workers
Sailors who bring the matches or materials here
Men who make the ships, and those who mine the metals of which the ships are made
Harbour workers
Those who design the covers of the boxes
Those who make up the jokes on the boxes
Those who put the matches in the boxes
Shopkeepers who sell them

Can you think of anyone else who takes part in the process?

Election Result   1922

Conservatives	345
Labour	142
Liberals	116

Election Result   1923

Conservatives	258
Labour	191
Liberals	159

Ramsay MacDonald, Prime Minister, addressing a Labour Party conference in January 1924.

in the House of Commons to beat the Conservatives. This would be a 'Minority' government. Labour would only be able to do things with which the Liberals agreed, and would be bound to disappoint many Labour supporters. In the end MacDonald decided to accept. 'At any rate, we have the handsomest of all Prime Ministers,' said one of the Conservatives. But good looks, a golden voice, ambition and social gifts were not enough for the tremendously difficult tasks he faced, and we shall see that before the end of his career Labour Party members regarded him as the chief cause of their most disastrous defeat.

One of his difficulties was that his followers were inexperienced in big jobs. Some of the Labour men could hardly believe the sudden change in their lives. J. R. Clynes, who became Lord Privy Seal, wrote:

. . . as we stood waiting for His Majesty amid the gold and crimson of the palace, I could not help marvelling at the strange turn of Fortune's wheel, which had brought MacDonald, the starveling clerk, Thomas, the engine-driver, Henderson, the foundry labourer, and Clynes, the mill-hand, to this pinnacle.

As well as more serious worries, they bothered about what clothes they should wear on formal occasions, and in the end three sets of court uniform were bought and worn by ministers in turn when necessary. MacDonald was also harassed by his poverty; he could not afford the cost of entertaining in the usual way at Downing Street, but when he accepted the gift of a motor-car from a friend to whom he gave a knighthood, there was an outcry and he was accused of corruption. Yet it did not seem right that the Prime Minister of Great Britain should have to waste his time and energy travelling by tube and bus.

More money for housing, education and old age pensions

The Labour government could not do much, but it did end the Geddes cuts on education; unemployment benefits were raised and old age pensioners were given a little more. Perhaps most important, it put good teeth into Lloyd George's housing schemes by Wheatley's Housing Act of 1924. This Act gave much larger subsidies for council houses, and arranged for the training of building workers so that many more houses could be built.

The League of Nations and world peace

MacDonald was more successful abroad than at home. He believed in the League of Nations, and arranged an agreement by which League member states were bound to apply 'sanctions' against a state which attacked another. Sanctions are a form of pressure, or punishment; for instance, League of Nations members might try to stop a war by preventing the supply of petrol to a country which had attacked its neighbour.

MacDonald enjoyed international conferences at which he was a distinguished personality, and he did good work in making better relations between France and Germany. He also recognized the Russian government and made a trade treaty with Russia. This friendship with Russia led to bitter attacks on the government by both Liberals and Conservatives.

MacDonald was exasperated by the weakness of his position, his dependence on the Liberals, and attacks from all sides. He was perhaps relieved to be able to resign after a defeat in Parliament when he had been in office only nine months.

The fall of the Labour government caused a General Election in 1924.

General Election   1924   The Zinoviev letter

The voting was to take place on Wednesday, 29 October. On Saturday, 25 October, the Conservative *Daily Mail* came out with this headline:

CIVIL WAR PLOT BY SOCIALIST MASTERS

What was it all about?

Zinoviev was a high official in the Russian government, and *The Times* had got from the Foreign Office a letter which he was supposed to have written to communists in this country urging them to work in and through the Labour Party to make a revolution in Britain. This letter, which was circulated among the other major newspapers said that the Labour Party should plan for 'armed

CIVIL WAR PLOT BY

MOSCOW ORDERS TO OUR REDS.

GREAT PLOT DISCLOSED YESTERDAY.

"PARALYSE THE ARMY AND NAVY."

AND MR. MACDONALD WOULD LEND RUSSIA OUR MONEY!

DOCUMENT ISSUED BY FOREIGN OFFICE

AFTER "DAILY MAIL" HAD SPREAD THE NEWS.

A "very secret" letter of instruction from Moscow, which we publish below, discloses a great Bolshevik plot to paralyse the British Army and Navy and to plunge the country into civil war.

The letter is addressed by the Bolsheviks of Moscow to the Soviet Government's servants in Great Britain, the Communist Party, who in turn are the masters of Mr. Ramsay MacDonald's Government, which has signed a treaty with Moscow whereby the Soviet is to be guaranteed a "loan" of millions of British money.

The letter is signed by Zinoviev, the Dictator of Petrograd, President of the Third (Moscow) International, and is addressed

paign of disclosure of the foreign policy of MacDonald.

ARMED INSURRECTION.

The IKKI [Executive Committee, third (Communist) International] will willingly place at your disposal the wide material in its possession regarding the activities of British imperialism in the Middle and Far East. In the meanwhile, however, strain every nerve in the struggle for the ratification of the Treaty, in favour of a continuation of negotiations regarding the regulation of relations between the S.S.S.R. and England. A settlement of relations between the two countries will assist in the revolutionising of the international and British proletariat not less than a successful rising in any of the working districts of England, as the establishment of close contact between the British and Russian proletariat, the exchange of delegations and workers, etc., will make it possible for us to extend and develop the propaganda of ideas of Leninism in England and the Colonies. Armed warfare must be preceded by a struggle against the inclinations to compromise which are embedded among the majority of British workmen, against the ideas of evolution and peaceful extermination of capitalism. Only then will it be possible to count upon complete success of an armed

Zinoviev, whose real name is Apfelbaum.

Daily Mail, 25 October 1924.

insurrection'. They should do propaganda 'in all units of the troops, particularly amongst those quartered in large cities, and also in factories working on munitions and at military storage depots . . .'

What could this mean except that the Russians were not only encouraging the British workers to make a revolution, but also were prepared to help them to defeat 'capitalists and bourgeoisie' by armed intervention? It did not seem impossible to the British that the Russians should make such plans. After all, we had been prepared to intervene to overthrow the Russian Revolution; why should they not intervene to help a revolution here?

There was widespread alarm and excitement; many who had voted Liberal in 1923 because they opposed protection now swung to the Conservative Party which defeated Labour by a large majority.

Later it was believed that the letter was a forgery, and in any case, even if it had been real, it would not have influenced the Labour Party.

Election Result   1924

Conservatives	415
Liberals	152
Labour	42

But in the meantime it had done its work, and there were people who said that the Foreign Office had given it to the Press just at the right moment to swing the election.

Baldwin Prime Minister 1924-9

Baldwin again became Prime Minister after this election, and Winston Churchill, who had by now become a Conservative, was his Chancellor of the Exchequer. Churchill was chiefly responsible for a valuable Act this government passed, which saved many people from misery. It was the Widows and Old Age Pensions Act, 1925. It was based on the same idea as health and unemployment insurance; the worker paid a bit each week, and in return widows and people over sixty-five received 10s. a week, and orphan children 7s. 6d.

But everything else which happened during this time was overshadowed by the General Strike of 1926.

The General Strike 1926

'The most dramatic event of the mid-twenties'

Unrest 1918-26

During the war the people had seen everybody, rich and poor, united in the struggle, agreeing to rationing and mobilization, and they thought that we would use the same kind of effort and justice to improve life in peacetime. They were soon sadly disillusioned. Lloyd George had talked of providing 'Homes fit for heroes to live in', but many soldiers found that they could not get a home at all, let alone one fit for a hero, and had to take up married life in a back bedroom of their in-laws' house.

It was the same with wages. During the war wages had rocketed up, and girls were drawn into the factories so that many families had several incomes coming in. You can see from the *Punch* joke opposite how funny it seemed then that working families should have savings-bank accounts.

After the war these good times ceased. The soldiers were demobilized, and even though the girls were soon turned out of the factories, there was not enough work for the men. Prices had gone up during the war, but 'real' wages had not kept up with them. When men have been fighting for their country for four years, and living on good army rations all this time, they are prepared to fight for their standard of living when they get home.

Trouble in the mines

The miners were the most important section of men in industry. Transport and all other industry depended on their work. It was hard work, it was particularly dangerous, and the miners, living

Charwoman: 'I ain't coming to work for you no more after this week. My man is earning so much now that we are forced to put money in the savings-bank.'

62

together in mining villages where every man worked in the pits, were strongly united and organized in trade unions. Some of them were well paid, those who worked in pits where the coal seams were easy to work and the coal was easy and cheap to get out. Others, in less profitable pits, were very badly paid.

After the war, when workers were again plentiful and our exports of coal were dropping, the employers tried to bring down wages and it was the miners who resisted most strongly.

The battle for wages began in 1920, when the mine-owners put up notices at the colliery gates giving new wage rates which were much lower than the old ones. The miners went on strike against these rates. They had formed the 'Triple Alliance' with two other powerful unions, the National Union of Railwaymen and the Transport and General Workers' Union, and it was understood that these would strike too in support of the miners. But on Friday, 15 April 1921, these two unions decided not to strike. The miners called the date 'Black Friday', a disaster for themselves and other trade unionists. They carried on their strike alone until they were defeated and forced to go back to work for lower wages. Soon afterwards workers in the shipyards and docks, in the building trade, cotton spinning, printing, and on the railways were also forced to accept lower wages. By this they learnt the lesson of 'Black Friday', that a defeat for one trade union meant a defeat for all, and in future they intended to stand together.

Red Friday, 31 July 1925

So when, four years later, the colliery owners gave notice that they were again going to reduce wages, the General Council of the Trades Union Congress promised to support the Miners' Federation. They told their members that they must not touch coal. Coal was 'black'. This statement of unity was greeted with delight by the miners, who called the day on which it was made 'Red Friday'. They felt that the shameful mistake of 'Black Friday' was now wiped out.

The refusal of all workers to handle coal would have brought industry to a stop, so the employers gave way, and the government gave £10,000,000 to the collieries to keep them going whilst new wage agreements were made. This appeared to be a great victory for the unions. But was it really a triumph? It was more like a truce; both sides had as long as the £10,000,000 lasted in which to get ready for the struggle.

The government did not waste its time. It set up the 'Organization for the Maintenance of Supplies'. Food and fuel depots were quietly established, and lists of people who would be prepared to help were drawn up, people who would lend cars, drive trains, enrol as special constables. Everything was made ready for industrial war.

On the other hand the trade unions did waste their time. They made

Nottinghamshire pits
17s. 6d. a shift

Bristol pits
6s. 4d. a shift

no plans for the tremendous strike which they expected, and did not even arrange to publish and distribute a news-sheet giving their point of view, although they knew that no ordinary newspapers would be printed. The miners actually weakened their position by getting a record output of coal from the pits, which made it easier for the government to build up reserve stocks of fuel.

'Not a penny off the pay, not a minute on the day'

In six months, when one side at least was ready, the coal owners brought out their new terms. These demanded a separate agreement for each district instead of a national wage and much lower wages. In South Wales, for instance, a coal hewer would get 55s. 10d. instead of 78s. for a five shift week. And the owners also proposed longer hours. When he was faced with these terms the miners' leader, Mr A. J. Cook, said 'Not a penny off the pay, not a minute on the day'. He was prepared to fight, and if it came to a strike, 'Red Friday' meant that it would be a strike not only of the miners, but also of any unions the T.U.C. chose to call out.

On 4 May 1926, the General Strike began.

Nine days of battle

In a sense the General Strike was, from the unions' point of view, a success, for the men who were called upon to down tools did so almost to a man, and seemed prepared to stay out as long as their leaders asked them to do so. The furnace fires died out, and in industrial towns of perpetual cloud the people experienced clear, country light for the first time.

There was at the beginning rather a holiday air of good humour and excitement. In some places idle workers played football, and policemen who were off duty joined in the game. The T.U.C. organized a system of dispatch riders who roared from place to place on motor-bikes with the cheering news that fellow-workers in other towns were also loyal to their unions. And for the young men of the upper classes it was great fun because they volunteered to drive trains and trams in order to break the strike and many Oxford and Cambridge students took a week's holiday to go to work at the docks.

The amateur tram-drivers were encased in wire mesh to protect them from stones, and they had put mottoes like these on their vehicles:

A stone in the hand is worth two in the bus

I have no pane dear mother now

The driver of this bus is a student of Guys Hospital. The conductor is a student of Guys. Anyone who interferes with either is liable to be a patient at Guys.

But many of the volunteer strike-breakers were very serious about their work for they thought that a general strike was the road to

Convoy of food lorries leaving London docks during the General Strike. On some of the lorries you can see a few soldiers, wearing 'tin hats' to protect them from stones.

The army is called in, in force. Hyde Park Corner at 6 a.m. on 10 May, the seventh day of the General Strike: armoured cars and troops prepare to escort the food convoy.

64

GREAT SILENT CITY OF DOCKLAND

Peep at East London: Strikers' Fine Discipline

EASY TIME FOR POLICE

(By Our Special Commissioner.)

The whole East End of London is a great silent city, even quieter and more peaceful than on a Sunday.

Not a workshop, factory, or commercial concern of any kind is doing business.

At all the district strike headquarters that I have visited, the instructions that are prominently displayed are being rigidly observed.

KEEP CALM. KEEP COOL.
DON'T CONGREGATE.

On vacant plots of land I saw many games of football, and a few by the pickets and told that they would be strike-breaking, they left quietly, and not one case of black-legging is reported throughout the whole of the area.

The police are having a very easy time—no traffic whatever to attend to, no crowds to move on. I saw many of them chatting with the strikers, the best of friends, and with the best of good humour.

SUPPLIES FOR THE SICK

The hospitals and infirmaries are receiving their supplies, and the escorts are not police, or O.M.S., but trade unionists carrying out

---

Every man who does his duty by the country and remains at work or returns to work during the present crisis will be protected by the State from loss of trade union benefits, superannuation allowances, or pension. His Majesty's Government will take whatever steps are necessary in Parliament or otherwise for this purpose.

STANLEY BALDWIN.

The General Council does not challenge the Constitution.
It is not seeking to substitute unconstitutional government.
Nor is it desirous of undermining our Parliamentary institutions.
The sole aim of the Council is to secure for the miners a decent standard of life.
The Council is engaged in an Industrial dispute.
There is no Constitutional crisis.

HOLD-UP OF THE NATION

Government and the Challenge

NO FLINCHING

The Constitution or a Soviet

When King and People understand each
*   other past a doubt,*
It takes a foe and more than a foe to
*   knock that country out.*
                                    Kipling.
" *Be strong and quit yourselves like*
men."

The general strike is in operation, expressing in no uncertain terms a direct challenge to ordered government. It would be futile to attempt to minimise

---

The *British Worker (left)* claimed that the strikers were well disciplined and only wanted an industrial settlement *within* the Constitution. The *British Gazette (right)* saw the strike as a crisis, an attempt by the strikers to overthrow the government by force.

anarchy and ruin. They and the government thought that any means to break it were justified; for instance some members of the government brought out a special news-sheet called the *British Gazette*, which was prepared to print any news, true or false, which would get the men back to work. The unions replied by getting out a news-sheet of their own, the *British Worker*.

The radio greatly helped the government. The B.B.C. started the practice of giving daily news bulletins, which has continued ever since, and when the strike stopped the supply of ordinary papers everybody listened to these bulletins. Naturally, members of the government made statements to the public over the radio, and appeals were broadcast for cars and volunteers to help break the strike. But Ramsay MacDonald, the Labour leader, was not allowed to speak.

Not all the students were on the government side. Hugh Gaitskell, who was then at Oxford, and later became leader of the Labour Party wrote this:

The vast majority of undergraduates went off to unload ships or drive trams or lorries. For me this was out of the question. All my sympathies were instinctively on the side of the miners, the unions, and the Labour Party and the left generally. It was their cause I wanted to help.

My main job was to act as driver to the liaison officer between the Oxford Strike Committee and the T.U.C. in London, and to bring back copies of the

A bus provided with boarding and wire netting to protect the volunteer driver.

British Worker. I was given a union card (Printers and Paper-makers), fully paid up, to get me through the pickets and crowds in Fleet Street.

He remembered trying vainly to climb into his college one night when they got back after twelve, and being in consequence fined £1. He added:

After the collapse of the strike, there followed the long-drawn-out agony of the miners' lock-out. We collected money for them, and argued hotly with the more conventional about the merits of striking and the whole system . . .

Underneath the humour and cheerfulness it was very serious, and became graver as the days went on. The government quietly moved troops into the cities, and many of the trade union leaders themselves feared that if the strike went on it would lead to serious fighting between troops and workers; they were frightened of the responsibilities which would fall on their shoulders if the unions won and the government was overthrown. They were determined to call the strike off, even if it meant the defeat of the miners, and after nine days they called on Baldwin and said that they were prepared to advise their men to go back to work. The General Strike was over.

The miners were very bitter about this; they said that the workers had shown no signs of wanting to go back, and that the strike was not broken. They were angry because the T.U.C. had called it off unconditionally; they had not even asked for an undertaking that men who had taken part in the strike should not be victimized, and as a result of this omission many had to go back to work for lower wages.

The miners struggled on alone. By July, poverty in the grey, silent mining villages was driving the men back to work, but it was not until November that their strike officially ended, and they were forced to go back for lower wages.

Trades Disputes Act   1927

The next year Parliament passed this law, which said that strikes in aid of other unions were illegal; each union has the right to strike over its own concerns, but not over the interests of other unions. So a general strike could now happen only in direct defiance of the law of the land.

The Trades Disputes Act was the last important event before the 'Great Slump' hit America, Europe and Great Britain with such force that all politics and governments were altered by it.

Dates to remember

1926   General Strike
1927   Trades Disputes Act

Things to do

1 Are there any municipal houses in your district which were built before 1930? If there are, photograph them, or draw them. Compare them with houses built since 1945. Pay attention not only to the houses themselves, but also to the layout of the estate.

2 Make a list of any forestry plantations you have seen.

Things to discuss

Should sympathetic strikes be allowed?

Books to read

A. B. Allen, *Twentieth Century Britain*, Barrie & Rockliffe
D. G. Fry, *Russia, Lenin and Stalin*, Hamilton
J. Hitchman, *King of the Barbareens*, Penguin
E. Huxley, *The Flame Trees of Thika*, Penguin
J. Montgomery, *The Twenties*, Allen and Unwin
B. Mullen, *Life is My Adventure*, Faber
S. Pickering, *Twentieth-Century Russia*, Oxford University Press
W. Pickles, *Between You and Me*, Werner Laurie
J. B. Priestley, *The Good Companions*, Heinemann

Chapter 4
Approach of war   1929–39

The Great Crash of 1929

You have already read of slumps and unemployment in the 1920s, but what happened then was nothing to what happened in 1929, when American wealth and employment crashed, and all the capitalist world went down with it.

Why did it happen?

First the boom

When business is good, and people are buying food, clothes, houses, motor-cars, and all the other necessities and luxuries of civilized life, then investment is profitable and shares in industry are worth a lot. If you have £100 to invest, and you think that there is going to be a tremendous sale of motor-bicycles next year, you may buy shares in a company which makes motor-bikes. You may buy twenty £5 shares, and this makes you a part-owner of the company, and you have a right to a share of the profits. If the company does well, you may get, say, £8 each year for the £100 you have lent. If the company prospers, people may be so anxious to buy your shares that they are willing to pay more than £5 for them, and you might be able to sell them for as much as £10 each. If, on the other hand, young men cease to buy motor-bicycles, and your firm gives little or no interest, the value of your shares goes down. If you suspect that motor-bicycles may not do so well in future, you will try to sell your shares before other people know that the firm is in difficulties, and you can still get a good price for them.

In America between 1919 and 1929 business did well. Americans bought a tremendous amount themselves, and lent money abroad. For instance, they lent a great deal to German concerns, because the Germans were skilled industrial workers and money was needed to start their industries after the war. The Americans thought that investment in Germany would be particularly profitable, but they also helped found businesses in other countries, and firms had such faith in continuing prosperity and success that they offered high rates of interest to persuade people to lend.

Then the slump

It all depends on the ability of the public to buy. In 1929 there began to appear signs that the public would not be able to buy all

The Jarrow March, October 1936. Unemployed men from Jarrow, where the shipbuilding yards had closed, are setting out on a 270-mile march to London, to ask the government to provide work for their dying city. The march became a symbol of the discontent of the 1930s, when skilled men went unemployed.

that was being produced; one reason for this was that most of the working class had little or limited spending money; therefore they could not buy enough to keep things going at the same speed. Looking ahead, directors of businesses decided that less of their products would sell next year, and so they decided to make less, and ordered less raw material. Therefore the first danger signal was that raw material producers, such as timber workers in Finland and Canada, miners of various metals all over the world, found that less of their product was wanted, and some of them became unemployed. When people are unemployed they buy less, and so unemployment becomes worse everywhere. (You remember the importance of the box of matches, page 58.)

Investors realized that prices of many kinds of share would drop, and became anxious to sell their shares while they still had good value. This selling was a danger signal to all other investors, who all tried to sell their shares before they crashed in value, or the businesses in which they had invested became bankrupt. There was what is called 'panic selling' on the stock exchanges of the world, and especially in Wall Street, the American business centre. This had often happened before in the history of business, but never before to the extent of October 1929.

On the night of 23 October 1929, an English journalist was dining at the house of very wealthy people in New York. It was the kind of house which ran like well-oiled machinery, the servants skilled and respectful, and the food superb. The large staff of servants had, of course, a radio in their sitting-room, and like many humble Americans, because there was no social insurance in the USA, they had invested their savings in various kinds of stocks and shares.

In the middle of dinner an extraordinary thing happened for an orderly house of this kind. The door of the dining-room opened, the butler appeared, and behind him the guests could see the white faces of the other servants. The master, he said, must come at once and advise them. They had been listening to stocks and shares prices, and it seemed that they were ruined. The dinner was abandoned. The guests were forgotten and made their way home. The master, after speaking to his domestic staff, went to his office to see what he could do about his own fortune.

The next day, 24 October, 12,894,650 shares changed hands, many of them at prices which meant poverty for those who had owned them, and all the following week shares fluctuated between disastrous falls and slight recoveries. Many elderly people faced a destitute old age. The nerves of Americans were stretched to breaking point; in Chicago a boy exploded a cracker, and, like wildfire, the rumour spread that a lot of gangsters whose savings had gone were shooting up the street, and several squads of police arrived to make them take their losses peacefully. In New York the body of a stockbroker was found in the Hudson River; he had only $9.40 in his pockets.

"NEW POOR" IN AMERICA.

FROM WALL-STREET TO PAWNSHOPS.
NEW YORK.
Wednesday. Oct. 30.

MILLIONAIRES and small investors have been mourning together throughout America today over their losses as the stock market completed its week of upheaval.

A new list of America's millionaires is being made, and many familiar names will be found to have vanished.

The seven Fisher brothers, of Detroit, who are famous for making Fisher bodies on General Motors cars, are among those who are understood to be among the heaviest losers. Their combined resources were recently estimated to be about £200,000,000. Their paper losses since last Thursday are believed in Wall-street to have been "several hundred million dollars."

Daily Express, 31 October 1929

New York, 1930. Hungry,
penniless people queue in the
rain for a dole of bread
and soup.

The effects of the crash and the slump which followed it were felt
throughout the world. In Germany, for instance, much American
investment was on 'short term' agreements, which meant that the
investors had the right to get back their money at short notice, and
much was withdrawn when hard times hit America. Distress therefore
spread to Germany, where the unemployment figure rocketed. This
was how the slump affected ordinary people who were not investors;
it meant unemployment.

This book is about Great Britain, but since our concerns are inter-
locked with those of the rest of the world, we must consider what effect
the slump had, not only on our own finances and politics, but also on
those of the two great countries whose affairs most influenced our
future. These were America and Germany.

What America did about the slump

Roosevelt and the 'New Deal'

The crash and the slump which followed it made 13,000,000 people
unemployed in the U.S.A. by 1933, and some people starved to death.
The American President, Hoover, thought that 'things would right
themselves' and was not in favour of any government measures. The
American people were not content with this helpless attitude, and in
the presidential election of 1932 they elected Franklin Roosevelt, a

confident, courageous man who had plans for dealing with unemployment, and who had an infectious faith that something could be done. He was destined to be one of the greatest American Presidents. He started the threefold plan, known as the 'New Deal'. The first part of it planned *Relief* of the distressed; the second part the *Recovery* of the economy, and the third part the *Reform* of industry and commerce.

'F.D.R.' founded camps for the unemployed, where they could do useful work such as forestry, road making and school building: they were paid for this work, and their families also received some money. He set up temporary schemes (the Americans objected to permanent 'welfare' measures) to give unemployment pay and old age pensions. His government supported trade unions, so that workers were better able to bargain with employers. He started the huge Tennessee Valley scheme, by which a power-dam and lake were made to provide water, electricity and work in a poverty-stricken country area.

Slowly, the tide turned, unemployment figures fell, and Americans began to believe that there was hope, that something could be done. America had chosen the positive, progressive way out. We shall see that Germany chose a very different solution.

The German answer to slump and unemployment

Germany was hit very hard by the slump. At one time one-third of her workers were unemployed. If you think of your street with every third house occupied by a destitute family whose breadwinner was unemployed, you can imagine what it was like. But countries which fall into poverty do not all of them go fascist; you will see that the fascists failed in Great Britain, for instance. It is possible that Germany went fascist because she had not got a tradition of democracy such as we had. Before World War I she had been governed by the Kaiser and a military group of aristocrats. After World War I she was given a democratic government with a parliament and elections to decide who should exercise power, but this government had to deal with the problems which followed defeat, and many Germans looked back with regret to the days of the kaisers and generals when they had been powerful and prosperous. They were used to being commanded, and in a crisis they easily surrendered their democratic rights and responsibilities.

Hitler comes to power   1933

During World War I one of the corporals in the German army was a small man from Vienna named Adolf Hitler. He had a poor physique and not much education, and no one could have foreseen the dramatic future which was in store for him. He was happier in the army than he had been in his rather unsuccessful civilian life; he loved armies, and felt passionately that Germany must again become a great military power.

After the war he left his trade of house painting for politics, and

This statue of the American President, Franklin D. Roosevelt (idealized since Roosevelt spent most of his presidency in a wheelchair) was set up in Grosvenor Square, London, after the Second World War.

made speeches telling the Germans that they were the 'master race', and had been defeated in the 1914–18 war only because 'Socialist-Jewish traitors' in factories engineered strikes and so halted supplies to the troops.

His party was called the 'National-Socialist' party, known generally as the 'Nazi' party.

During the hard years, 1929–33, Adolf Hitler was finding bigger and bigger audiences for his speeches, and he was receiving more and more money for his party funds from rich industrialists who believed that he would 'save Germany from socialism'. He promised the Germans jobs, power, conquest, grandeur. He built up the private army of the 'Brownshirts', unemployed members of the middle classes most of whom were glad of a uniform, a little money, and the chance to swagger through the streets beating up both their private enemies and Jews.

The government could not keep order and in the end the President decided he must ask Hitler to take over power. Hitler, with the aid of his Brownshirts, and the secret police system he had set up, could keep order, and once in power he set to work to establish a complete dictatorship.

His secret agents appeared in factories, buses, streets, blocks of flats, and even schools. Whispering campaigns of terror frightened his opponents into silence, for they knew that those who spoke against Hitler were liable to hear the knock on the door at midnight, be arrested, taken away, and not heard of again. Leading Jews, socialists and liberals disappeared in this way. Others were murdered openly in the streets. Trade union funds were confiscated, all political parties except the Nazi Party were forbidden, all newspapers were taken over by the Nazis, and 'gauleiters' were appointed to organize everything for the Nazi Party; there were big 'gauleiters' in charge of provinces, little 'gauleiters' in charge of streets, whose job it was to know the comings and goings, who spoke to whom, and about what.

The 'Night of the Long Knives'   1934

After a year Hitler felt strong enough to get rid of rivals amongst his followers. He organized the murder of about 200 members of the Brownshirts, including their leader Captain Röhm. One of them, when he was stood against a wall to be shot, cried 'Heil Hitler' defiantly to his executioners. He did not know that Hitler had ordered his death and thought that he was the victim of a rising against the Nazis. No one in Germany dared to protest. The most fantastic, destructive dictatorship the world has known was firmly established.

What is Fascism?

The German Nazi Party was a particularly brutal kind of fascist party. All fascist governments are alike in some ways, and if we think of these, we can see what fascism is, and why some countries choose it.

In *My Struggle*, the book in which he explained his ideas, Hitler wrote:

The German state must gather all Germans to itself . . . It will be the duty of German foreign policy to provide large spaces for the nourishment and settlement of the growing population of Germany . . .

Education and training must be directed towards giving them a conviction that they are superior to others . . . this education should be completed by service in the army . . .

Most of the people have very little intelligence, therefore propaganda must consist of a few points put into a few simple words, and repeated again and again until even the most stupid know them.

1 *It is government by a popular leader* who promises to solve the people's problems for them. All they have to do is to obey, and follow him devotedly. In order to get this public affection and absolute obedience, a tremendous barrage of propaganda is turned on. Stirring military parades are arranged, followed by mass meetings at which the 'Leader' makes emotional speeches. The young in particular are given a strong dose of propaganda treatment, and in Germany every boy at the age of ten took the following oath – 'I consecrate my life to Hitler. I am ready to die for Hitler, the Saviour, the Leader.' It was said that every girl in Germany imagined herself as the bride of Hitler, who remained conveniently a bachelor until a few hours before his death.

2 *Fascist governments believe in war.* Hitler said that war was the test of a nation's manhood, and German boys were taught to look forward to army life. They believe in war because, first they deal with unemployment by putting men in the forces and in armament factories. Then, having given the nation's energy to the army, they hope, if they are strong enough, to use it to win land and wealth from their neighbours. Hitler spoke frequently of the Germans needing more 'living space', and of his plans to colonize the lands of his 'inferior' neighbours, Poland and Russia.

3 *Fascists believe in 'race',* by which they mean that they believe in the inferiority of every other race to their own. In particular, most fascist governments are anti-Semitic, and persecute Jews. Hitler confiscated Jewish property and dismissed Jews from their jobs; he set going every kind of slander about them, and finally, as the last wickedness and madness, he planned to exterminate them. Intelligent fascists at the top did not really think that the Jews were inferior, but they went in for anti-Semitism because it was useful to them. Confiscating Jewish property brought in money, and dismissing them from their jobs enabled the 'Leader' to reward his followers with these jobs. But, most important, blaming everything on the Jews prevented people from blaming themselves or their government for their misfortunes.

4 *Fascism is against trade unions and socialism.* Although fascist parties sometimes call themselves 'national socialist' they are really anti-socialist. One of the first things fascist governments do is to dissolve the trade unions so that there are no strong workers' organizations to oppose their policies. Fascist parties have been given large sums by rich employers because they do this. Hitler paid for his propaganda and his 'Brownshirt' organization with the contributions of rich German manufacturers, especially the arms manufacturers.

5 *Fascism is against rights for women.* Hitler said that the place of women is in the kitchen, and that the only job they should do besides

Adolf Hitler in 1935. He called himself 'der Führer', 'the leader' of the German people.

Jewish men and women rounded up by Hitler's Storm Troopers and sent to concentration camps where a total of 6,000,000 were put to death. This photo was taken in France, in 1943, but Hitler had begun to persecute German Jews during the 1930s.

cooking was looking after babies. He took the jobs away from women; even the headships of girls' schools were given to men.

Does Fascism work?

It did not work for its two most important, powerful and successful leaders. Both Hitler and Mussolini of Italy took to the sword, and perished by the sword within a few years, and ruined the people who had supported them in the process. As for the other fascist countries in Europe, Spain and Portugal, they keep many brave men and women who oppose the government in prison; there is a strict censorship of news, so that their citizens are ignorant of much that is happening, and their prosperity has not increased as much as that of the free countries in Europe.

Britain 1929–39

In Great Britain we watched with concern whilst Germany under Hitler left the League of Nations (1933), arranged for the murder of the ruler of Austria (1934), and introduced military conscription in defiance of the Versailles Treaty (1935). But we felt unable to act, and we had plenty of problems at home to occupy us.

In May 1929, just before the international financial crisis broke, a General Election was held. Labour got 288 seats, the Conservatives 260 and the Liberals 59. So once again MacDonald became Prime

Election Result   1929

Labour	288
Conservatives	260
Liberals	59

Minister in a Labour government which was dependent upon Liberal consent for everything it did. This government was soon to be overwhelmed by the international crisis of which you read at the beginning of this chapter.

MacDonald and Snowden, the Chancellor of the Exchequer, had the old, accepted ideas of economic policy; they believed that a country, like an individual, must have a 'balanced budget' which means that it must spend no more than it gets in taxation. It is agreed now that a government need not necessarily do this; in hard times it may need to spend more to keep enough money in circulation, people in work, and so on. If the Labour government had had more modern ideas, our history in the 1930s might have been very different.

The crisis hits Britain

The test came in August 1931. The number of our unemployed was very high and was increasing. Funds were running low, and the government desperately needed an American loan to keep going. America would not give us a loan unless we made a number of economies, including a 10 per cent cut in unemployment pay. What were MacDonald and Snowden to do? It was the votes of the working class, the people to whom unemployment pay was vitally important, which had put their government in power. They could either stick to the old, conventional ideas of finance, put the burden on the working class, and get the American loan, or else adopt new, bold policies, tax business and the rich more highly perhaps, and do without the American loan.

A National Government to save the country?

The cabinet split over the question, and there was intense political struggle. There were:

. . . Headlines, crowds, police, hectic movement, day and night meetings, the door of Downing Street loosened on its hinges by the constant passage of leading figures of all three parties as they hurried by the ever-present battery of photographers.

MacDonald could not persuade his cabinet to agree to cuts in unemployment pay, and did not think that the government could carry on without the American loan. Therefore, on a hot August evening, tired and despairing, he went to the palace to hand in his resignation to the King.

The King, who had discussed the matter earlier in the day with the Conservative and Liberal leaders, offered MacDonald the position of Prime Minister of a National Government of members of all parties formed in order to deal with the crisis. MacDonald accepted. He never even consulted his Labour ministers. He simply announced, to their astonishment, that he had accepted the request of the King that he

Average wage, 1930, 33s. 6d. a week

Unemployment pay:

Man	16s. a week
Wife	9s. a week
First child	3s. a week
Other children	2s. a week

Money needed at 1931 prices to keep man, wife, and three children, 35s. a week

The newspaper clipping:

No. 510   Press Telegrams: "Daily Worker, London."   TUESDAY, AUGUST 25, 1931   Telegraphic Address Workadai, Finsqure   One Penny

Down With The "National" Government!

The Government Of Dictatorship And Starvation

THE second Labour Government has fallen and the political leaders of capitalism are engaged in setting up a new "National" Government, under the leadership of Ramsay MacDonald.

In this Parliamentary intrigue centring around that hot-bed of reaction, Buckingham Palace, the working class has no voice. A handful of politicians, capitalists and bankers are deciding the future lives of millions of men, women, and children and conspiring to form a new Government of Dictatorship and starvation. Even a General Election is ruled out until their plans become law. Parliament will not be called together until the Starvation Plan is all cut and dried.

The working class is faced with the greatest crisis since the war. Never before have the capitalists and their Labour agents moved so swiftly and dramatically against the workers. They are prepared to resort to any measures, no matter how dictatorial and unconstitutional, in order to compel the masses to submit to cuts in unemployment benefit, reduced social services, and lower wages.

never have been possible to have formed a Government of this character. The Cabinet, including the eight dissentient Ministers, has pursued a Coalition policy from its first days of office; it carried on propaganda for sinking Party differences and treating Parliament as a Council of State; it consulted Baldwin and Lloyd George before deciding any important political question; it appointed the Royal Commission on Unemployment with its capitalist majority.

The Labour Cabinet appointed the Economy Committee, whose report led up to the present crisis. The Cabinet put a Liberal and Tory majority on the Committee, and deliberately excluded consideration of the War Debt and the £360,000,000 yearly interest from its terms of reference. Moreover, the chief discussions on how to apply the report were carried on last week, not in the Cabinet, but in the Committee of six, consisting of MacDonald, Snowden, Samuel, Maclean, Hoare and Chamberlain.

The "National" Government was born last week not this, and the Labour Cabinet was the mid-wife.

A majority of the Cabinet was prepared

BUT A SINGLE THOUGHT

MacDONALD and BALDWIN, who are expected to be members of the "National" Government, which is to push through the Economy Report.

T.U.C. GENERAL COUNCIL'S BLUFF

Actions Which Expose Words Of T.U. Leaders

RAMSAY MACDONALD HEADS NEW COALITION CABINET

With £120 Million Economy Programme Against Workers

UNITE AGAINST STARVERS!

THE Labour Government resigned yesterday, and Ramsay MacDonald has been charged by the King to form a new "National" Government with the inclusion of Liberal and Conservative leaders.

The Cabinet resigned because of disagreements on the carrying out of the Economy Report. Eight Ministers were opposed to the plan of the majority for cutting unemployment benefit by 10 per cent.

The Labour Party's two-year co-operation with the Liberals and Tories has now resulted in the formation of an open Coalition Government with only one point in its programme: the carrying out of the plan of starvation, proposed by the Labour Government's Economy Committee.

The apportionment of the principal offices in the new Government among the three Parties is likely to be as follows:—

LABOUR	 10	CONSERVATIVES	 6
		LIBERALS	 4

The Conservative representatives in the Cabinet are likely to include Baldwin, Neville Chamberlain, Sir Samuel Hoare, and Lord Hailsham. The Liberals will include Sir Herbert Samuel and Lord Reading. Sir Donald

---

An angry headline from the *Daily Worker*, the newspaper of the Communist Party. Most Labour supporters felt betrayed by the coalition government.

should be Prime Minister of a National Government, with the Liberal leader and Mr Baldwin as his supporters. Many people believed that he had planned to remain Prime Minister in this way.

MacDonald enjoyed his new position, and was relieved to be working with men whose ideas and social tastes were more like his own. 'Every duchess in London will want to kiss me,' he joked cheerfully. But he had smashed the party which had brought him to such a high position that he could hob-nob with duchesses.

The new government immediately reduced unemployment pay by 10 per cent. It also introduced household Means Tests, by which a man had his unemployment pay reduced by the amount any other member of his family brought home. This Means Test was hated bitterly; it led to snooping, with official investigators coming round to see whether any grown-up children of the family were bringing in wages. In many cases it drove children to leave home so that their father could claim full benefit. Also, the unemployed thought of their benefit as an insurance right for which they had paid contributions, not as a charity which they could get only on Poor Law conditions.

Not only the working-classes and the unemployed were called upon to make sacrifices; according to the usual policy of spending less in times of slump, all salaries controlled by the government were reduced. Teachers and civil servants for instance, had their salaries reduced by 15 per cent.

The General Election 1931 'A Doctor's Mandate'

The Conservatives pressed for a General Election directly after the National Government had been set up. The Conservatives argued that it was right to get public support and agreement for the policies of the new government; the Labour Party argued that the Conservatives wanted the election because the Labour Party was broken as a fighting force by having its leaders desert to the other side, and therefore there would be a large Conservative majority in the House of Commons which would make the government national in name only, and in actual fact, Conservative.

MacDonald asked the country for 'a Doctor's Mandate' to cure the nation's ills. He was given his mandate. The Conservatives got 473 seats, and the Labour followers of MacDonald 13. The Labour Party only got 52 seats. Because there was so little Labour support for MacDonald, the 'National' government did indeed become to all intents and purposes a Conservative one, and we had Conservative governments until the Second World War, when we had a National Government again, a really national one then.

Amongst the cures proposed in the scheme for a 'Doctor's Mandate' was a tariff on foreign goods, and one of the first steps taken by the National Government was to impose this. The British people had agreed to protection at last. Probably, because of our changed position in the world, it was by this time a wise decision.

The dark thirties

Until 1933 unemployment in Great Britain continued to get worse. The poorer streets of the cities contained peeling, unpainted houses,

Election Result	1931	
Conservatives	⎫	
MacDonald Labour	⎬	554
Liberals	⎭	
Labour		52
Independent Liberals		4

Looking for work.

The unemployed demanded work or 'maintenance', by which they meant enough unemployment pay to keep their families.

and boarded-up shops. The men hung about the street corners with nothing to do, too dispirited to talk. This is a description of a Durham miner:

He was standing there as motionless as a statue, cap pulled over his eyes, gaze fixed on the pavement, hands in pockets, shoulders hunched, the bitter wind blowing his thin trousers tightly against his legs. Waste paper and dust blew about him in spirals, the papers making harsh sounds as they slid on the pavement.

Hard times lead to extreme politics

Many people thought that a different political system was needed to improve things, and two parties, the Communist and the Fascist, made recruits.

The Communist Party grows

Many people joined the Communist Party, because the Soviet Union was not affected by the slump. In that country the setting up of industries and providing employment did not depend upon whether it was profitable to investors, but upon whether the government thought that the goods and services which the industry would produce were needed; things were run rather as our Post Office is run. There was no unemployment in Russia, and therefore many of the working class, and also members of the middle class who had read Karl Marx and descriptions of the new society in Russia thought that their system might be better than ours. You may remember reading in Chapter 3 about the ideas of the communists.

Fascism for Britain?

Others adopted political ideas like those of Hitler in Germany. Oswald Mosley set out to be dictator of Great Britain, with the same policy as the Nazis for attacking the Jews and abolishing the trade unions. His blackshirted followers held aggressive marches, especially through streets where many Jewish people lived; they would shout out insults to the Jews and try to create disorder, for they hoped to break down orderly government so that a fascist dictator could take over. They also held meetings in halls, where Mosley, trimly dressed in a black shirt and lit by spotlights, would make speeches full of anti-Jewish, anti-socialist, and anti-democratic remarks.

This is a description of an Olympia Hall, London, meeting:

London's Fascist Defence Force turned out in full strength, well briefed and trained to the task of the evening. Its members were swelled to thousands by contingents from as far north as Liverpool. Many of these wore kid gloves, containing knuckle-dusters or heavy rings; in many a trouser-pocket, 'black-jacks' lay ready to hand . . . They were to take up positions in groups of half a dozen or so at all points in the Olympia amphitheatre – round the arena

and the tiered gallery which rose from it . . . On the slightest interruption from any part of the hall a signal would be flashed. Immediately Mosley, **standing in dramatic isolation on the vast stage, would cut off his harangue.** The battery of twenty-four loudspeakers, capable of drowning a great chorus of hecklers, would fall silent. Powerful searchlights stationed near the stage would focus their full glare instantly on the interrupter. The nearer squads would move into action while the rest of the Blackshirts round the hall would set up a roar of 'We Want Mosley – Mosley'.

As you can imagine, the Blackshirts did not handle the interrupters gently, and even women were badly knocked about.

But the British showed a healthy dislike for fascism on the whole, and they defeated Mosley. On one occasion he had planned a march down Mile End Road in London, where many Jewish people lived. Anti-fascists determined to stop it. For two hours they blocked the road at the beginning of the march, despite police baton charges to clear the way. When there was a rumour that the Blackshirts were going to dodge the obstruction by going down a side-street, the anti-fascists pulled up the cobblestones as weapons; the inhabitants of the little street dragged out their furniture to make barricades, and in the end the march was called off.

Things begin to improve

Support for the Communist and Fascist Parties made it look for a time as if the slump might drive us to change our political system, but

The police dismantle a barrier built to prevent the fascist march down Mile End Road, October 1936.

after 1933 things began, very slowly, to improve. Trade and investment improved throughout the world, and our trade improved with it. We were beginning to give more thought to the best use of machine tools, and increased our output per man hour; this enabled us to produce our goods more cheaply and compete better in foreign markets. Also, after 1934, the dangerous behaviour of Hitler made us begin to rearm. Although rearmament in the long run does not make a happier or safer world, it does in the short run provide jobs.

By 1939 we were still a long way from the affluent society which we enjoy today, but we seemed to have turned the corner.

The royal family and the abdication of Edward VIII

George V, grandfather of the present Queen, reigned until 1936. In the spring of 1935 he celebrated his Silver Jubilee, having reigned twenty-five years. This celebration showed how much the British people like having a royal family, for besides the grand official processions and speeches, the citizens showed their enthusiasm by organizing events on their own.

Every street was decorated, festoons of bunting almost hid the sky, and at street corners children were given Jubilee Teas at flower-decked tables. Women wore red, white and blue dresses, and Jubilee mugs were given out.

One of the most popular members of the royal family was Edward, Prince of Wales. Even when he was a man of forty, he still kept a boyish look. People liked his enthusiasm and courage; they knew that he had wanted to share the dangers of the soldiers in World War I, and that when he visited the idle, derelict Welsh mining valleys he had said 'Terrible. Terrible. Something will be done.' But it was also noted that he had Nazi-German friends, and it was thought wrong for an English king to take too active an interest in politics.

When George V died in 1936, the Prince of Wales became King Edward VIII. He at once set about streamlining the monarchy, and caused disapproval at Buckingham Palace by cutting down the number of court officials and the amount of court ceremonial. He had perhaps too individual a character for a present-day king of England and he was much criticized by people in the know who soon discovered that he planned to marry Mrs Simpson, an American lady who had been involved in two divorce cases. Mr Baldwin, who had become Prime Minister in 1935, begged the King not to marry her. The British Press knew all about the matter, but printed nothing, even blotting Mrs Simpson out of photographs in which she appeared in the King's company. So the public were astonished when the truth came out.

What could be done? The Church and government thought that Mrs Simpson was quite unsuitable for the position of queen. The King thought that because of his own popularity and the fact that the coronation was all prepared and was only a few months off, he could get his own way. He was wrong. He overestimated the power of the

Stamp of Edward VIII, issued in 1936. The crown is in the top right-hand corner, to show that Edward had not been crowned.

king in this country and underestimated the power of the Church and government. They would not agree to the marriage and since he would not give it up, he abdicated and his younger brother, the father of Elizabeth II, came to the throne in his place, as George VI.

The abdication crisis showed that the royal family is now in a very different position from that of, for instance, the Tudor kings and queens, or even Queen Victoria. Now the king or queen must obey the elected government.

Steps towards war   1936–9

The approach of the war makes foreign events the most important in our history during these years. We were faced all the time with the questions – should we resist Hitler, or hope that, if he were given a little, he would be satisfied? Should we support the League of Nations and stand together for international law, or act independently to defend our interests?

Peace movements

We had suffered so much during the First World War that we were very anxious to avoid another. The supporters of the League of Nations formed the 'League of Nations Union', which had the same kind of purpose as the United Nations Association of today. Friends of the League of Nations Union organized a 'Peace Ballot'. They went round from house to house and asked people whether they were in favour of disarmament by international agreement, whether they thought that the manufacture and sale of arms by private firms should be forbidden, and whether they thought that, if one nation attacked another, the other nations should combine to stop it by:

(a) Economic and non-military measures?
(b) If necessary, by military measures?

Over 11,000,000 voted 'yes' to the first question, and even on the difficult, second question three-quarters of the people who filled in the form answered 'yes'. This was a tremendous vote, and showed that the British people were prepared to support strong action to prevent war.

There were also people who were convinced of the wickedness and uselessness of all wars. One hundred thousand of these joined the Peace Pledge Union, and swore,

I renounce war, and never again will I support or sanction another, and I will do all in my power to persuade others to do the same.

Those who took this oath were called 'pacifists'; according to their belief it is wrong to arm for, or to fight, any war. Many members of the Labour Party were pacifists, including their leader, George Lansbury, who was one largely because of his Christian beliefs. He

George Lansbury, the pacifist Labour leader, and his wife.

The gay side of the thirties. Dance bands of this period began to play swing.

was very much respected and loved; it was remembered that in 1929 when he was leader of Poplar Borough Council, he had insisted on giving higher poor relief rates than the law then allowed. He and twenty-nine fellow-councillors went to prison rather than obey this law, and as a result the law was altered so that the rich boroughs, which had a high income from the rates and few people who needed help, gave towards the poor boroughs like Poplar. Higher payments then became possible.

Clement Attlee becomes leader of the Labour Party   1935

The Labour Party was split between Lansbury pacifists on the one hand, and those who wanted to rearm to support the League of Nations on the other; as a result the party was divided on foreign policy, and sometimes demanded at the same time that we should disarm *and* fight the fascist aggressors. In 1935 there was a dramatic scene at the Labour Party Conference when Lansbury was ousted from the leadership. Lansbury made a speech in favour of pacifism, which ended:

I would say in the name of the faith I hold, the belief I have, that God intended us to live peaceably and quietly with one another; if some people do not allow us to do so, I am ready to stand as the early Christians did, and say, 'This is our faith, this is where we stand, and, if necessary, this is where we will die.'

Ernest Bevin, a prominent trade unionist, was not moved by the tremendous applause which followed this speech. He stumped up to the platform in his slow, heavy way, and attacked Lansbury for being sentimental and unpractical. Bevin was not liked for this speech, which put an end to the career of George Lansbury, but the conference thought he was right and voted his way. As a result Lansbury resigned and Clement Attlee became leader of the Labour Party.

Trial run for the Fascist armies

The Spanish Civil War   1936–9

In 1936 the Spanish Republic was governed by a 'Popular Front' alliance of Liberal and Socialist Parties. The army leaders and right-wing parties feared that Spain might go further left, and therefore made an armed rebellion under General Franco to set up an extreme right-wing government. Franco was helped by Hitler and Mussolini, so that the war was a kind of dress-rehearsal for the world war which was to follow. Russia helped the Republican government, but, to the extreme bitterness of the Republicans, she did not help them much; this was probably because Spain was geographically the wrong place for the Russians to fight Hitler, and they were not yet ready to fight. You will see in the next chapter how this war was useful to Hitler; here we must say something of its effects on Great Britain.

The 'Non-Intervention' Agreement

Mr Baldwin and his government feared that intervention by other powers might lead to the war spreading and becoming general, and Britain therefore supported an agreement that no country should interfere in Spain or send help to the Spanish armies. The agreement was made, but it was a racket from the first, for Germany and Italy had no intention of keeping it; all they did was to call their soldiers in Spain 'volunteers' and pretend that they had come on their own. In Great Britain, Liberals and the Labour Party opposed 'Non-Intervention'; they thought that we should help the Republican

'Guernica', a painting by the Spanish artist Pablo Picasso. Guernica, a historic Spanish town, was, in 1937, suddenly bombed to ruins by German planes. Innocent civilians were killed. For the first time, the effects of bomb attacks were

86

seen. 'In the painting on which I am now at work, which I shall call "Guernica"...' Picasso explained, 'I am very clearly expressing my horror at the military caste which has plunged Spain into a sea of suffering and death.'

government in the ordinary way, since it had been properly elected, and they were very angry that our government would not undertake to defend our merchant ships in Spanish waters from 'anonymous' submarines, which were really of course Italian or German submarines putting in a little useful practice. They read with delight of a British merchant captain, known as 'Potato Jones', who said that he did not give a hang for submarines; he intended to run his cargo of potatoes through to the hungry Spanish people.

Some young men felt that fascism was wicked and dangerous, that it must be halted at all costs, and Republican Spain must be saved.

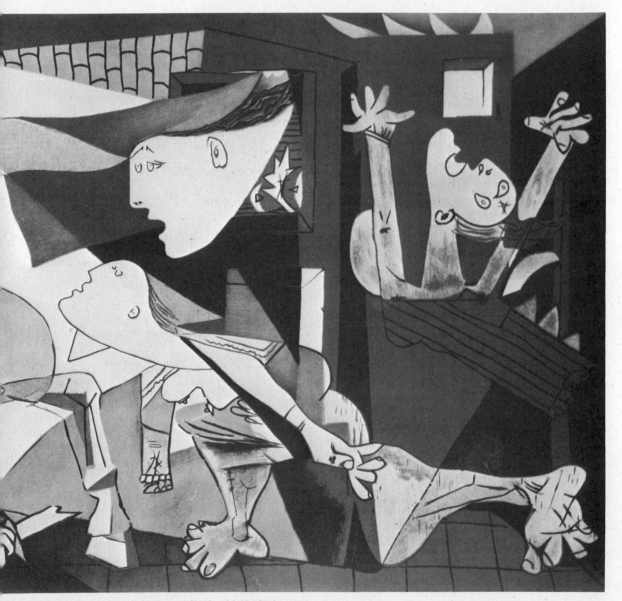

On extended loan from the artist to the Museum of Modern Art, New York

They formed the 'International Brigade' to fight on the Republican side. Men from Great Britain, refugees from Hitler Germany, anti-fascist Italians, and individuals from almost every country fought. Numbers of them lost their lives.

Their heroism could not defeat German and Italian troops and arms; Franco won, and leading Spanish Republicans were executed, imprisoned, or fled abroad. Many people in England felt as if they had been defeated themselves, for they realized the tremendous strength of the German-Italian alliance, which now had in Franco's Spain an ally right out on our Atlantic sea route. When Churchill learnt that Franco's victory was inevitable, he said 'The dark waters of despair overwhelmed me'.

Chamberlain and appeasement   1938–9

Most British people look back upon the years of appeasement and the beginning of World War II as amongst the most tragic and mistaken in our history. But it is easy to be wise afterwards; we know now that appeasement failed, and it is difficult to remember how it looked to people who lived at the time, who thought that war was the most terrible thing that could happen, and who hoped that by giving to the fascist dictators something they wanted we could stave it off.

What was appeasement? It was the policy of trying to prevent war by giving the dictators what they demanded and trying to make businesslike agreements with them. One of the dangers of this policy is that it can be taken for weakness, and by Hitler it was so taken.

Unfortunately, Hitler wanted a war. The fascists believe that wars (provided they are won) are good for a nation, so appeasement was useless from the start, and our only hope was to nip his efforts in the bud, or ring him round with alliances which would give him no possibility of victory.

Germany's drive towards war

Hitler was very cunning, and he approached his war for the mastery of Europe with a series of brilliant successes which put him in a good position for the final struggle.

Practice for German armed forces in Spain   1936–9

We have described how he used the civil war in Spain, where fascist forces under General Franco were trying to overthrow the government, as an opportunity to give his forces practice in warfare. His air force tried out its bombing on the little town of Guernica in Northern Spain.

German troops reoccupy the Rhineland   1936

It had been agreed by the treaties of 1919 that Germany should not send any armed forces into the Rhineland; this part of Germany was to remain peaceful, so that it could not again be used as a springboard for attack on France or Belgium.

German boys of the 'Hitler Youth' march with their banners.

Almost everyone in Germany was organized and marched in a military uniform. Here, Hitler (with his back to the camera) salutes a tremendous demonstration of workers who are lined up with their shovels.

88

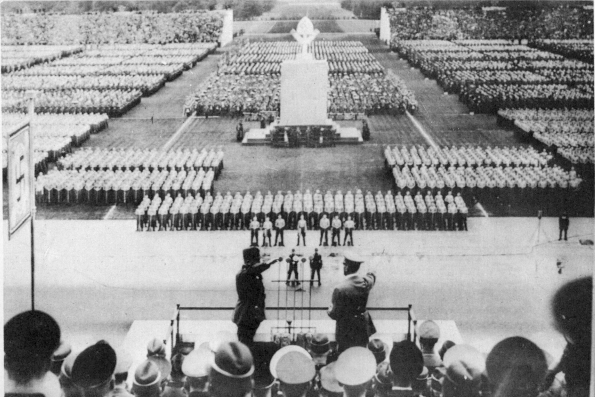

Hitler began his aggressions by sending his troops into the Rhineland. This act of defiance of her conquerers led to wild rejoicings in Germany, and Hitler became more popular than ever.

Should France and England have sent an army to turn the German soldiers out of the Rhineland? They had the right to do so by the treaties. They were still stronger than Germany and could have defeated her then with ease. Churchill thought that Britain and France should have acted together at once. But both Britain and France failed to realize the extent of the danger from Germany, and were demoralized by the sympathy which many of their influential citizens felt for Hitler. After all, we thought, the Rhineland is part of Germany; it was humiliating for her not to be allowed to send troops there, and we should not go on humiliating our enemies many years after the war had ended. Hitler said 'We have no territorial demands to make in Europe', and we preferred to believe him, although in his book, *My Struggle*, he had said that the Germans must win more living space in Europe for themselves.

Having succeeded in his first step he proceeded to the next one.

Union of Germany and Austria   1938

It was proved that Hitler had lied about his ambitions in Europe two years later when his troops marched into Austria, and set up a stooge Nazi government there. The citizens of the great, civilized city of Vienna had to watch whilst Nazi Storm Troopers persecuted and humiliated Viennese Jews. The rest of the world did not act; we were on the slippery slopes of appeasement.

Czechoslovakia: The useless sacrifice   1938–9

Hitler said that Czechoslovakia was 'a revolver, pointed at the heart of Germany'. Churchill pointed out that with Austria as well as Germany in the hands of her Nazi enemies the position of Czechoslovakia was critical. You can see from the map on page 91 the reason for these opinions.

Czechoslovakia was a free, democratic country. She was prosperous and civilized, and valued her happy way of life and was prepared to defend it. Small though she was, she had one of the most efficient arms works in Europe, the Skoda factory, and she had built magnificent fortifications along her German frontier. She had also made treaties of 'mutual assistance' with France and Russia, so that if she had to fight she would not have to fight alone.

Hitler was determined to break these fortifications and destroy this little stronghold of democracy which lay across his route to the Balkans and the Mediterranean.

Hitler demands the Sudetenland   1938

One-fifth of the people of Czechoslovakia were German-speaking and had German ancestors. They were treated politically as equals by the

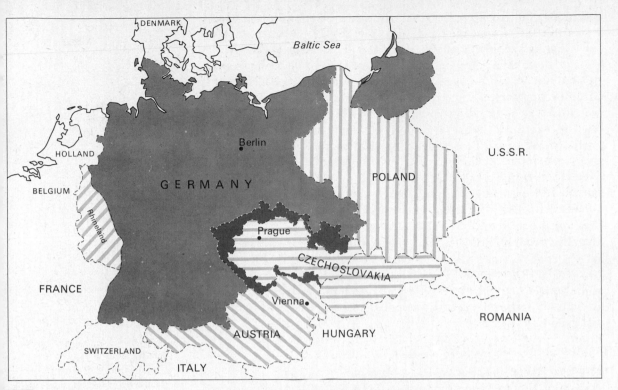

Lands which Hitler added to Germany, 1936–9.

Czechs, most of them had been born in the country and were loyal citizens, but the fact that they were there gave Hitler a chance to make trouble. First he sent in agents to organize a movement amongst them to demand reunion with Germany. Then he made speeches supporting this movement, saying that he could not tolerate that Germans should have to live under foreign governments, and demanding that the parts of Czechoslovakia where the Germans lived should be handed over to Germany. You can see from the map the parts where more than half the people were German, the 'Sudetenlands' which Hitler claimed.

This demand was really an attack on Czechoslovakia. What were France and Russia to do? Russia said that she would carry out her promise to support Czechoslovakia *if France would do the same*. France said that she would carry out her obligations *if Great Britain would support her*. So it all depended upon our government. This is where the tragedy begins.

First Neville Chamberlain, the British Prime Minister, tried to persuade the Czechs to give up their Sudetenlands, and when they refused, he offered to visit Hitler to discuss the matter with him, and try to make a peaceful settlement.

In his usual dark clothes, carrying the usual umbrella, he set off to Germany, and many people in Great Britain and abroad thought that here at last was a man who would stand up to Hitler. But when he came back it was clear that he had not stood up to him. As Lloyd George said in the House of Commons, 'The trouble is that our Prime Minister thinks that he is a match for these crafty, ruthless dictators, but we know that he is not.' Chamberlain told the French Prime Minister that we would not think of supporting Czechoslovakia unless she gave up the Sudetenlands. The French and British ambassadors called on the Czech Prime Minister to persuade him to agree to this.

At two o'clock in the morning, after hours of discussion and pleading, the wretched Czech Prime Minister yielded. He knew that his small country would be defeated if she had no allies, and he hoped to save the rest of her lands by handing over the Sudeten parts.

In the end things were worse than this for Czechoslovakia. Hitler did not even pretend to keep the agreement which he had made with Chamberlain, and demanded much more than the Sudeten parts of Czechoslovakia. Should we fight over this? In the House of Commons Chamberlain, haggard with anxiety, was telling the story of his efforts for peace when a message was brought in to him. His face lit up with joy, and he said that Hitler had offered to meet at Munich the heads of the various countries concerned with Czechoslovakia, except Russia, to discuss a settlement of the question. Once again he got in an aeroplane and flew to Germany.

Munich: 28 September 1938

The fatal agreement was made at Munich. Chamberlain gave Hitler everything he asked for. Hundreds of thousands of Czech citizens and the magnificent defences of their frontier were handed over. The Germans themselves were amazed when they saw the strength of the fortifications.

It was not only Czechoslovakia that was ruined. We and the French had lost a good cause and our good name; we had lost a well-armed ally on Germany's southern frontier, and the chance of resisting Germany in alliance with Russia. All we had got in return proved to be one year of peace. We rearmed during this year, but not to equal the Czech arms which had been thrown away.

Chamberlain did not realize the disaster he had helped to cause. When he got out of the aeroplane on his return from Munich he held out a bit of paper, his agreement with Hitler. 'This', he said proudly, 'means peace in our time.'

Nor did the British people realize at once what had happened; they were so thankful not to have war that crowds cheered Chamberlain. But soon they began to listen to other voices, such as that of Churchill, who said:

We have sustained a total and unmitigated defeat . . . And do not suppose that this is the end. This is only the beginning of the reckoning. This is only the first sip, the first foretaste of a bitter cup which will be proffered us year by year unless by a supreme recovery of moral health and martial vigour we arise again and take our stand for freedom as in the olden time.

Munich Agreement, 1938. When Chamberlain returned from his meeting with Hitler, people believed that war had been averted.

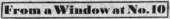

News headline from the *Daily Herald*. Immediately below this article is another headline, a small voice of protest: 'Czechs Cry "We want to Fight".'

The First Lord of the Admiralty resigned as a protest against Munich. In six months he, Churchill, and the many other people who agreed with them, were proved to have been right.

Hitler occupies the whole of Czechoslovakia   15 March   1939

On 10 March Chamberlain said that 'Europe was settling down to a period of tranquillity'. On 15 March, scarcely bothering to make any excuse, Hitler sent his troops to take over the rest of Czechoslovakia. The people of Prague watched the German tanks drive down their streets and knew that they had become the enslaved subjects of Nazi Germany. The whole world realized that war was unavoidable. Appeasement had been useless.

We promise to defend Poland   1939

Perhaps it was because we felt so strongly that we had been wrong not to defend Czechoslovakia that we now promised to help Poland if she were attacked by Hitler, although you can see from the map that she was as difficult for our troops to reach as Czechoslovakia had been. Lloyd George said, 'If war occurred tomorrow, you could not send a single battalion to Poland . . . I cannot understand why . . . we did not secure beforehand the adhesion of Russia . . .'

We refuse to ally with Russia 1939

But even then Chamberlain refused the offer of an alliance with Russia, which would have given us an ally on Germany's eastern frontier and halved the number of troops Germany could have used against us in the west. Russia was afraid of having to fight Germany alone. She thought, since we were unwilling to ally with her, that France and ourselves would stand by idly whilst Hitler sent his formidable armies to occupy the cornlands of the Ukraine which he coveted. She determined to see to it that Germany attacked westwards first; therefore she made with Germany the Russo-German Pact. She knew that it was only a truce, but it gave her two more years, during which she strained every nerve to rearm. All was now set for war between Germany and Western Europe.

Were we justified in making the Munich Agreement? Here are some of the arguments for and against it.

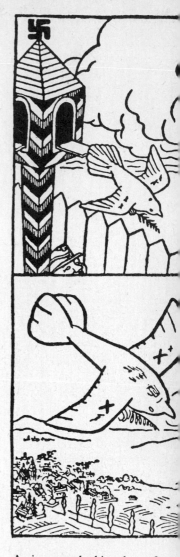

An innocent-looking dove of peace, flying out of the Nazi hutch, becomes a destructive weapon of war. From a Swiss newspaper, 1934.

For	Against
We could not resist Hitler without arms, and our armaments were weak at this time. Therefore we had to put off war at any cost.	We and the French were quite strong enough to fight Germany in 1936 and should have stopped her then.
	We would have been better off fighting in 1938 with the Czech armies and fortifications than we were in 1939 without them.
	The Russians would have fought too, if we had fought in 1938.
The treaties after the 1914–18 war had been harsh on Germany, and it was reasonable that she should demand back the German lands which had been taken from her.	If they were given back, it should have been to the peaceful German government before 1933, and not as a result of Hitler's threats.
It was no use relying on the Russians as allies; their government was weak and their armies unreliable.	Even if the Russians were poor allies for us, it was doubtful whether the Germans would again make the mistake of undertaking war on two fronts at once.
Hitler was a barrier against Russia and Bolshevism; it was to our interest to support his government.	It was dangerous to our interests to help him, because he would soon have demanded our colonies.
In 1938 the Commonwealth was not yet convinced of the necessity to resist Hitler and might not have supported us, as it did in 1939.	The Commonwealth countries would probably have come to our aid in any case once we were involved in war against Germany.

94

For

Our government had no right to risk the lives of its subjects for the sake of a few million Czechs, whom Chamberlain described as: 'a far-off people of whom we know little'.

It was a terrible sacrifice, giving away Czechoslovakia, but worth it for the sake of peace.

Because of the position of Czechoslovakia, landlocked in the centre of Europe, we could not have helped her.

Against

It was immoral to support a power which persecuted the Jews and preached race-hatred, and destroyed her weaker neighbours.

It is in the interest of everybody to prevent powerful nations from bullying little ones; otherwise we can never hope for peace.

We made the sacrifice for nothing since we did not get peace; many intelligent people at the time saw that it would be useless, and it is the duty of our government to give us wise leadership.

In that case, why did we promise to help Poland, which was at least as difficult for us to reach?

Things to do

1 Find out what plans we have now to deal with any unemployment.
2 Find out what workers pay for unemployment insurance, and what benefits they can claim.
3 Was there widespread unemployment in your area during the slump? Ask your grandparents, and other elderly people about this, and look in the files of local newspapers for information of what your area was like during the great slump.
4 If you had £100 to invest, what concern would you put it in, and why?
5 Find out what fascist governments still exist.

Things to discuss

How would you have voted in the 'Peace Ballot' of 1934?

Books to read

B. J. Eliot, *Hitler and Germany*, Longmans
D. B. O'Callaghan, *Roosevelt and the United States*, Longmans

Chapter 5
The Second World War 1939–45

1 September 1939–June 1940 Hitler succeeds everywhere

It seemed at first as if nothing could stop the relentless thrust of the German armies.

Defeat and partition of Poland

They began by marching into Poland, on 1 September 1939. The gallant fighting of the Poles was useless against the formations of heavy tanks, and all that Great Britain could do was to declare war on Germany. A few hours later France too declared war. We could not send any soldiers, or any other kind of practical help.

Russia divided Poland in halves with Germany (see map on page 91), and set to work to organize this extra space for defence. She also demanded the use of some strategic positions from Finland in order to enable her to defend the approaches to Leningrad; when Finland refused these, Russia defeated her in a short war and took them.

We watched these events in Poland and the Baltic without power to intervene, but we had some important successes in sea warfare.

We defeat the magnetic mine

Throughout the war our scientific work was better than that of the Germans, which was perhaps one of the chief reasons why we and our allies won in the end.

Hitler had been hinting darkly at a secret weapon which he had and to which there was no answer, and we found to our dismay that ships were being blown up in home waters which had just been thoroughly swept for mines. Why was this? Then someone saw heavy objects being dropped into the sea by parachutes. One of these fell into shallow water on the mudbanks of Southend; our experts recovered it and discovered its secret. It was a magnetic mine, which lay on the bed of the sea, out of the reach of the tackle of mine-sweepers, and exploded in response to a metal ship overhead. Having found the secret, we found the answer to it; merchant ships were 'degaussed', which means that they were demagnetized by having electric cables put round their hulls. So we were saved from being starved out by the destruction of merchant shipping approaching our shores.

We lose the Royal Oak and sink the Graf Spee 1939

We had a great loss and a great success at sea during the first year of the war. The disaster was when a German U Boat commander sailed his submarine right into Scapa Flow, the headquarters of our Grand Fleet,

People at home had to organize themselves against Hitler's bomb attacks. A key man was the air-raid warden, equipped with gas mask, sand bucket and stirrup-pump, seen here in his shelter with its 'blackout' curtain. From his equipment one can guess what his duties were.

and sank the battleship the *Royal Oak*. This is what a German wrote about it:

On October 13, at 4 a.m., our boat was lying off the Orkneys. At 7 p.m. – Surface; a fresh breeze blowing, nothing in sight; looming in the half-darkness the distant coast; long streamers of Northern Lights flashing blue wisps across the sky. Course West. The boat crept steadily closer to Home Sound, the eastern approach to Scapa Flow. A narrow passage through the swirling waters. The shore was close. A man on a bicycle could be seen going home along the coast road. Then suddenly the whole bay opened out. Kirk Sound was passed. We were in. There, under the land to the North, could be seen the great shadow of a battleship lying on the water . . . near, nearer – nearer – all tubes clear – no alarm, no sound but the lap of the water, only the low hiss of air pressure and the sharp click of a tube lever. 'Fire' – five seconds – ten seconds – twenty seconds. Then came a shattering explosion, and a great pillar of water rose in the darkness. The U Boat waited some minutes to fire another salvo. Tubes ready. 'Fire!' The torpedoes hit amidships, and there followed a series of crashing explosions. H.M.S. *Royal Oak* sank, with the loss of 786 officers and men . . . U 47 crept quietly back through the gap.

But the hunting down of the *Graf Spee* was a splendid success for us.

The hunting of the Graf Spee

The *Graf Spee* was a German pocket battleship, designed brilliantly to be a destroyer of merchant ships. She could sail faster than any ship which had heavier guns than her own 11 inch ones, and she had heavier guns than any ship which could outsail her. At the beginning of the war she stole across the Atlantic and lurked in wait for ships with cargoes for British ports. The first we knew of her being there was when she sank a British liner.

This was such a serious matter for us that we organized a hunt for her with eleven ships.

Our commander guessed that the *Graf Spee* would sooner or later go to the River Plate, where the richest prizes awaited her. He was right. The *Graf Spee* fled from the site of one of her kills to the River Plate, and there three of our ships were waiting; they were cruisers, two with 6 inch guns, and one with 8 inch guns. At first Captain Langsdorff, commander of the *Graf Spee*, thought that he had only small ships to deal with, and steamed towards them at full speed, until not only were they within reach of his guns, but he was within range of theirs. When Langsdorff realized his mistake he threw out a smoke screen, turned under the cover of it and made for the river mouth. But by then it was too late to flee; the *Graf Spee* was attacked from three sides at once, and had to fight for her life. She succeeded in knocking out many of the guns of our cruisers, and fought her way into the neutral port of Montevideo, where we could not attack her and where she had the right by international law to stay for three days. Our hunter ships, reinforced by other vessels by now, lay in wait for her outside.

Winston Churchill, taking up his appointment as First Lord of the Admiralty, at the outbreak of the war.

The German government told Langsdorff to try to break out, and to destroy the ship if he failed.

. . . during the afternoon of 17 December the *Spee* transferred more than seven hundred men, with baggage and provisions to a German merchant ship in the harbour. Shortly afterwards Admiral Harwood learnt that she was weighing anchor. At 6.15 p.m., watched by immense crowds, the *Graf Spee* left harbour and steamed slowly seawards, awaited hungrily by the British cruisers. At 8.54 p.m., as the sun sank, the *Ajax*'s aircraft reported: *Graf Spee* has blown herself up.

Although he had full authority from his government to blow her up, Langsdorff was heartbroken at the loss of his ship, and he shot himself shortly afterwards.

Germany invades Norway and Denmark   April 1940

When the spring came, the real war started for us. Germany invaded Denmark, which did not resist, and Norway, which did resist. (Map on page 103.) Britain sent forces to help Norway, but they failed to make any difference to the German occupation; and our failure in Norway led to the fall of Chamberlain.

He was attacked by all Parties in the House of Commons for having been weak with Hitler when he should have been firm, and of now fighting in a place where he could not resist Hitler with an army too small for the job and without the necessary air support. Lloyd George spoke against him with all his old eloquence, and a Conservative quoted against Chamberlain a speech of Cromwell's saying, 'You have sat too long for any good you have been. Depart I say, and let us have done with you. In the name of God, go.' Chamberlain was forced to resign, and Winston Churchill became Prime Minister. Churchill had always opposed appeasement. He had the energy to direct a global war, and the courage to inspire our will to resist through the months when our situation seemed almost hopeless.

Germany invades Holland, Belgium and Luxembourg   May 1940

This was done rapidly and brutally. In four days of ruthless bombing, during which the lovely town of Rotterdam was completely flattened, Holland was forced to surrender. Then the German soldiers and the Gestapo (the dreaded secret police) came in, and, as in all the lands occupied by Germany, prominent Jews, liberals and socialists were rounded up and sent to German labour camps to be worked until they died. You can read in the *Diary of Anne Frank* the kind of things that happened to some Jewish people. Brave people in occupied territories hid Jews at risk of their own lives, and when the Gestapo ordered the arrest of Jews in Denmark, many of them were smuggled across to Sweden by their Danish friends.

Fall of France   June 1940

The Germans did not stop at Holland and Belgium; they swept on to

July 1940. Invasion was a very real threat. This announcement in a newspaper was from the Ministry of Information.

What do
I do . . .

if I hear news
that Germans are
trying to land,
or have landed?

I remember that this is the moment to [ ] like a soldier. I do *not* get panicky. I *stay* [ ]. I say to myself: Our chaps will deal with [ ]m. I do *not* say: "I must get out of here." [ ]emember that fighting men must have clear [ ]ds. I do *not* go on to the road on bicycle, [ ]car or on foot. Whether I am at work or at [ ]me, I just *stay put*.

[ ]t this out—and keep it!

France. The famous Maginot Lines of defence which the French had built proved to be useless. Lines of defence had been useful during the 1914–18 war, when the fighting unit was the infantryman, and horses were still used to pull guns. Movement was slow then. But by 1939 we were in the age of great heavily armed tanks, and of bombing planes which could smash up the supply routes of the defensive lines. It was a war of movement. The tanks, travelling faster than an army had ever moved before, drove round the Maginot Line, which for some queer reasons did not stretch all the way to the North Sea, and the German air attack created panic and confusion. The French army was demoralized; the roads of France were choked by civilian refugees, fleeing westwards with their most precious possessions piled on to carts and motor-cars.

The British army which had been sent to France found itself caught between the German armies and the coast; it was outgunned and out-numbered, and had practically no air support; so that the Germans could bomb it at their pleasure. The only thing was to get the men to the coast if possible and transport them to England; all equipment had to be abandoned.

Dunkirk   May–June 1940

One of our generals described the journey to the coast:

There was little possibility of sleep that night, as the 3rd Division were moving past, and I repeatedly went out to see how they were getting on. They were travelling, as we had so frequently practised for our night moves, with lights out and each driver watching the rear of the vehicle in front of him, which had the differential painted white and a tail-light under the vehicle . . . However, with the congestion on the roads, roadblocks outside villages, and many other blocks caused by refugees and their carts, the division was fre-quently brought to a standstill. The whole movement was unbearably slow; the hours of darkness were slipping by; should daylight arrive with the road crammed with vehicles, the casualties from bombing might well have been disastrous.

Our army reached the coast at Dunkirk. An SOS was sent out for every boat in the south-east of England which could cross the Channel to go and fetch them home. Eight hundred and sixty boats went out on the job, boats of all kinds, sizes and shapes. They included pleasure boats which had never done anything more serious than a picnic before, barges which were really unfit for the open sea, and all kinds of cargo boats. Fortunately the weather was fine, but they had to face the German bombers overhead.

In his history of the war Churchill describes what it was like:

On the beaches, among the sand dunes, for three, four or five days, scores of thousands of men dwelt under unrelenting air attack . . . The bombs lunged into soft sand, which muffled their explosions. In the early stages, after a crashing air-raid, troops were astonished to find that hardly anybody had been killed or wounded. Everywhere there has been explosions, but hardly

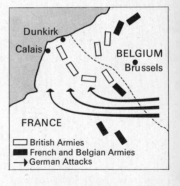

Dunkirk. The Germans divided the French force and drove the allied troops, including the British, to the sea.

'Withdrawal from Dunkirk',
by Charles Cundall, one of the
official war artists.

anyone was the worse. A rocky shore would have produced far more deadly results. Presently the soldiers regarded the air attacks with contempt. They crouched on the sand dunes with composure, and growing hope. Before them lay the grey, but not unfriendly sea. Beyond, the rescuing ships and – Home.

Dunkirk was a wonderful achievement, but as Churchill said, wars are not won by brilliant withdrawals, and our position was desperate. Our only ally, France, was utterly defeated; part of it was occupied by the Germans, and the rest was put under a Quisling* government.

* Quisling was the name of a Norwegian politician who helped the Germans when they invaded Norway. It became the word used to describe any politician who co-operated with his country's enemies.

Britain alone   June 1940–June 1941

When you look at the map on page 103 you may think that Britain might as well have surrendered at this point. The whole of Europe was under German control. Our army and air-force were very small; the sea was not the defence it had been to us in the past because of the formidable power of air attack. Our only support was that America showed her sympathy by giving us 'Lend-Lease', which meant that she lent us goods to enable us to live and arms to carry on the struggle.

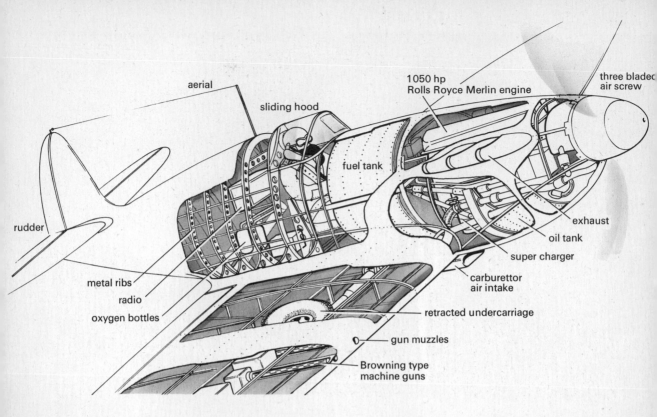

aerial

sliding hood

1050 hp
Rolls Royce Merlin engine

three bladed
air screw

fuel tank

rudder

exhaust

oil tank

super charger

metal ribs

carburettor
air intake

radio

oxygen bottles

retracted undercarriage

gun muzzles

Browning type
machine guns

The Battle of Britain   August – September 1940

'Never in the field of human conflict was so much owed by so many to so few.'
(Churchill, speaking of the crews of our fighter planes.)

Germany now set to work to deal with us. We believed that she meant
to invade us, for during August the bodies of forty Germans were
washed up at different parts of our coast, and the government thought
that they had been practising embarkation. Also, our reconnaissance
learnt that ships were massing in the ports of Northern France, Belgium
and Holland. Germany prepared for her land-sea attack by massive
bombardment from the air of our factories, air-fields and centres of
communication.

Every night, and sometimes during the day, sirens went and people
took refuge in air-raid shelters, tube stations, railway arches, and
cellars, whilst great flights of bombers, 300 or 400 at once, went over to
bomb London and other 'strategic' areas. The night skies over London
were almost as bright as day with the huge fires which the bombing
started. The bombers flew too high for our anti-aircraft guns to reach
them, but our fighter planes took off to engage them, and our fighter
pilots, more than anyone else, were the men who won the war for us.

The newspapers reported daily the number of German planes
brought down. During the week which ended on 17 August 1940, we
were told that we had brought down 236 German bombers for the loss

The Spitfire fighter plane. The
German High Command
greatly admired it. It is
unlikely that the Battle of
Britain could have been won
without it. *Below:* stamps
showing the twenty-fifth
anniversary of the Battle of Brit

hostile to Germany

Germany

allied to Germany

controlled and/or occupied by Germany

neutral

The German position, 1941–2. During the first part of the war, Germany had immense military success.

of 96 of our fighters. It was a desperate business, because we had very small resources in planes and trained pilots and could not make good our losses quickly enough; in the end we were sending up pilots who had not finished their training.

We were nearing the end of our ability to continue the battle when suddenly the Germans gave up the attack. They were losing too many planes and decided that they could not, in the face of our fighter opposition, bomb us into surrender. Bombing continued all through the war, but never again on the scale of the Battle of Britain.

The Russians come into the war   June 1941

Russia knew that when Germany was securely in control of Europe she would turn her armies east to break her dangerous socialist neighbour, and take the rich cornlands of the Ukraine for colonization by the German 'Master Race'. The Russian government used the time bought by the Russo-German Pact (page 94) for an urgent rearmament programme, and massed Russian armies on her western frontier.

After the failure of his bombers in the Battle of Britain, Hitler decided to put off breaking us until he had dealt with the danger of being attacked in his rear by Russia.

On 22 June 1941, the Panzer (tank) divisions struck eastwards across the Russian border.

Ever since the revolution of 1917 our governments had most of them been hostile to the U.S.S.R., and many influential people hoped secretly that Russia and Germany would exhaust each other in war whilst we stood by, neutral. But Churchill was not prepared to make peace with the Nazis; he was prepared to welcome any ally, socialist or capitalist, to help him to defeat them. Therefore, on the evening of 22 June he came to the microphone and made a speech declaring our decision to continue the war as Russia's ally. He expressed sympathy with the Russian peoples, fathers, wives and mothers in the sufferings they would endure at the hands of the brutal Nazis, and added:

Any man or state who fights against Nazidom will have our aid. Any man or state who marches with Hitler is our foe. That is our policy. That is our declaration. It follows then that we shall give whatever aid we can to Russia and the Russian people. We shall appeal to all our friends and allies in every part of the world to do the same.

We were no longer alone; the main front was now in Eastern Europe, and the greatest struggle of modern times took place in Russia. You can see from the map the vast areas of Russia which Germany occupied. So far as possible the Russians evacuated these lands; children and factories were moved eastwards, railway lines were pulled up and bridges destroyed behind them, but even so 12,000,000 Russians, 5,000,000 of them civilians, lost their lives. Finally the Germans were defeated at the decisive battle of Stalingrad in November 1942. The Germans were halted in the vast spaces of Russia, at the end of long lines of communication, in the stress of the merciless winter weather of the steppes. The Russians and their winter had defeated Hitler as they had defeated Napoleon.

We helped the Russians by sending supplies in convoy to Archangel.

America enters the war   December 1941

Six months after Russia entered the war, we gained another powerful ally.

The Japanese were allied to Germany, but had taken no part in the war. They were making their plans, and their spies were telling them of the careless, unprepared behaviour of the American crews at the naval base of Pearl Harbour, where no-one expected attack and most of the officers and men spent most of their time ashore. On 7 December, without declaring war, the Japanese struck. They sent fleets of bombers to Pearl Harbour, burnt and sank many American ships, and crippled American naval power in the Pacific at one blow.

The news was brought to Churchill whilst he was having dinner and he realized instantly that America would at once declare war on the German-Japanese alliance. In a few minutes he was speaking to the American President, Franklin Roosevelt, on the transatlantic telephone. 'We are all in the same boat now,' Roosevelt said. Now, for the first time, we could reasonably expect to win the war.

It was a war of tanks and rapid movement on the hot, sandy coast of North Africa.

Battle of El Alamein.

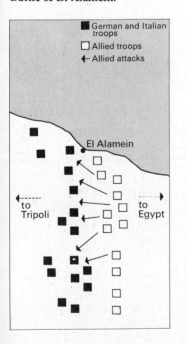

■ German and Italian troops
□ Allied troops
← Allied attacks

El Alamein

to Tripoli

to Egypt

Victory at El Alamein 1942

You can see from the map that the Germans held part of the North African coast. There was the danger that they would strike eastwards and conquer Egypt, which we were occupying. This would have brought them down to the Red Sea and the Indian Ocean.

In August 1942 General Montgomery was given as his first big job the task of defeating the German forces in North Africa.

First we had to build up an army and its supplies in Egypt. An immense amount of material was needed. For instance, *one* armoured division needed 70,000 gallons of petrol and 350 tons of ammunition for *every day* of fighting. Everything had to be sent round the Cape of Good Hope, because the Germans held Crete and Greece and we could not use the Mediterranean routes.

Montgomery pretended that he was going to attack in the south of the German position. He set up numbers of dummy fuel depots and dummy tanks. Trucks, which appeared to be transporting men and goods, buzzed round all day at high speeds, leaving swirling plumes of dust behind them. A map, which contained false information, was allowed to 'fall into' German hands. The Germans were deceived, and when Montgomery opened his attack with a tremendous bombardment on the north of their defences, they could not resist it. Our assault troops which followed the guns broke through, and the Germans were defeated. The desert was littered with the ruins of their burnt-out tanks, they lost all their stores, and we took 60,000 prisoners.

It was, said Churchill, the turning point of our military fortunes.

War on the home front

In modern wars not only the young men are mobilized; everything and everybody that can be useful is controlled by the government. No longer could men and women with private incomes live idly at home. They all had to register, and if they were healthy, they had to do useful work.

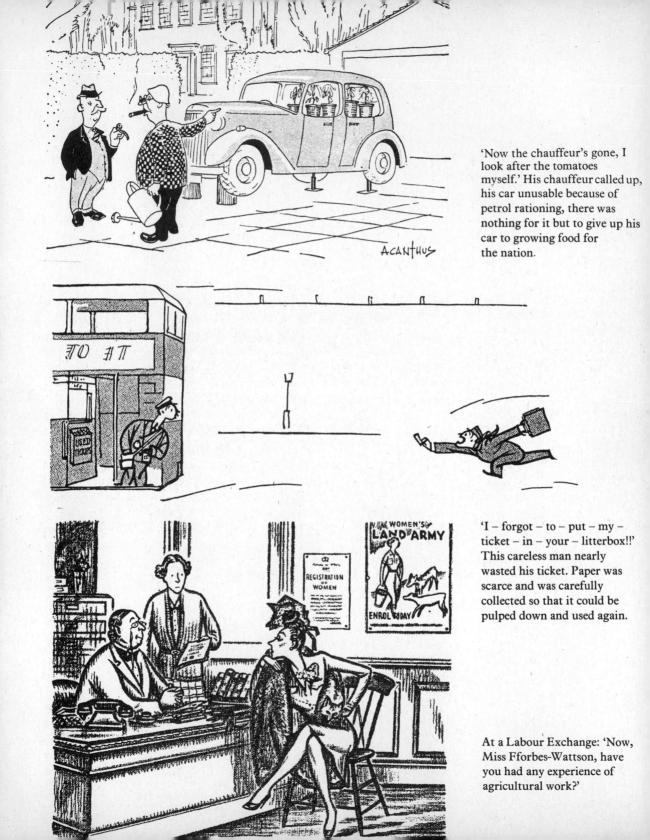

'Now the chauffeur's gone, I look after the tomatoes myself.' His chauffeur called up, his car unusable because of petrol rationing, there was nothing for it but to give up his car to growing food for the nation.

'I – forgot – to – put – my – ticket – in – your – litterbox!!' This careless man nearly wasted his ticket. Paper was scarce and was carefully collected so that it could be pulped down and used again.

At a Labour Exchange: 'Now, Miss Fforbes-Wattson, have you had any experience of agricultural work?'

Citizens responded to such appeals as the 'Dig for Victory' campaign which urged them to turn their lawns and flower-beds into vegetable patches. We had learnt during World War I that rationing was necessary to see that everyone got their fair share of short goods, and during World War II rationing of all kinds of things was excellently organized. Petrol, food, clothes were all rationed, and one's ration book, which contained pages of coupons which were cut out whenever one bought rationed goods, was one's most valuable possession. A 'shell-egg' (a real egg in a shell) became a rare luxury, and housewives had to make do with packets of dried eggs.

The curious result of rationing and controlled prices was that the people as a whole were better fed and clothed than they had ever been. The rich had less, but nobody had too little. All schools were ordered to provide very cheap midday meals, partly to make sure that growing children got extra food, and partly to free the mothers for work outside the home. Children helped to keep up our essential goods by collecting waste paper and other kinds of scrap, so that it could be reprocessed and used again.

At the time of the Battle of Britain we feared invasion. All the sign-posts were taken from the roads, and the names were taken off post-offices and railway stations. People were told not to give the Germans any useful information if they arrived.

As you have read, the Germans did not arrive. But their bombs continued to fall. When the warning sirens went, families went to the air-raid shelter, and the men and women air-raid wardens went to their duty posts. One of the chief dangers was of fire from fire-bombs, and people had to take turns to spend the night at the buildings in which they worked, so that any fire-bombs which dropped there could be quickly dealt with.

Children were evacuated from the dangerous areas, and country dwellers were asked to give hospitality to refugees who had been bombed out of their homes in the towns.

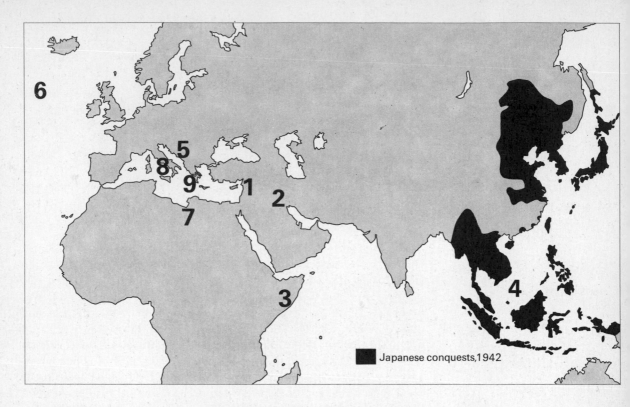

Japanese conquests, 1942

In the later part of the war we sent fleets of bombers to attack Germany. Every evening people who lived near the east coast would hear the slow rhythm and deep roar of flights of heavily laden bombers setting out over the North Sea. In the small hours of the morning they would be heard, one by one, rattling back at tremendous speed with empty bomb racks and almost empty petrol tanks. They did damage to German cities more than equal to what the Germans did here, but it is not now thought that the bombing of cities made much difference to the fighting power of either ourselves or Germany; it was a useless destruction of civilian life and property.

The defeat of Germany

You can see from the information given on the map how widely forces were engaged, and what serious defeats we had suffered, for instance, in the Far East. But by 1943 the Germans were becoming exhausted, and our strength, aided by Russian victories and American supplies, was increasing. The Allies had got the upper hand in the struggle for the Mediterranean, and we were preparing to invade France as the first step in the allied advance into Germany.

We prepare to invade France

The invasion was a triumph of careful planning and cooperation between the Intelligence services and the fighting forces. The invasion

Key

1   Syria and Lebanon 1941
Allies drove out French Quisling forces which held these countries.

2   Iraq 1941
We drove out a pro-German government and set up a pro-allied government.

3   Italian Somaliland 1941
Occupied by British (South African) forces. Abyssinia and Somaliland freed from Italian rule.

4   South-East Asia 1941–2
Japanese conquered Burma, Malaya, Hong Kong, Singapore, the Philippines. British battleships *Prince of Wales*

and *Repulse* were sunk off Malaya.

5 Yugoslavia
1943
We dropped parachutists and aid to guerillas fighting against German occupying troops.

6 Battle of the Atlantic
1941–4
Struggle against U-boat attacks, chiefly on the 'North-West Approaches', the seas north-west of Ireland.

7 North Africa
1940–1
General Wavell drove the Italians out of Egypt and Libya.
1942 June
The German general, Rommel, defeated us at Tobruk and drove us back to El Alamein.
1942 October
Victory at El Alamein.
1943
Allied forces under General Montgomery defeated Rommel and the Italians.

8 Italy
1940
She declared war on Britain and France. Britain won naval victories against her at Taranto (1940) and Matapan (1941).
1943
Allies invaded Sicily.
1944
Allies landed at Salerno, and began to fight their way northwards.

9 Greece and Crete
1941
The Italians failed in their attempt to invade Greece. Later in the same year the Germans drove the allied forces out of Greece and Crete.

demanded that 700,000 men, with tanks, weapons, and other equipment should be got across the Channel in a fortnight. Amongst other things, we had to decide the exact landing points, and we had not got charts and maps which gave us enough detailed information. So the government sent out a request to the public to send in its holiday photographs taken abroad; any sort of photographs were wanted, but on the back must be written the *exact* place. Some of these gave the information we wanted, by showing such things as Mummy paddling and Daddy standing up to his waist in water ten feet farther out. This showed how steeply the beach shelved. Another problem was that we had to be able to bring transport ships close in shore, and we could not use existing ports because they were heavily defended. We decided to build floating harbours which we would tow across the Channel. Churchill wrote about this plan:

The Prime Minister to the Chief of Combined Staffs.
30 May 1942.
. . . They must float up and down with the tide. The anchor problem must be mastered. Let me have the best solution worked out. Don't argue the matter. The difficulties will argue for themselves . . .

These harbours were called 'Mulberries', their code name in official papers.

The invasion forces piled up in the ports of southern England. Altogether 6,000 seacraft were collected, and 15,000 aircraft were ready to support them. Every patch of trees in the southern counties hid ammunition dumps and trucks. Every train and lorry was ready to take them to embarkation points at the chosen moment.

'D' Day   6 June 1944

On 6 June the die was cast and the huge plan was set in motion. This is a description of what it was like in a little town in Kent during that morning:

I went out to shop, but soon gave up all thought of getting anything to eat. The main street was just a solid stream of tanks and army trucks full of soldiers, all driving south. The police pushed civilian traffic into the side streets. The noise of the engines was deafening, the soldiers were singing and we civilians on the pavements cheered and shouted. People threw the soldiers cigarettes, and even flowers, which were hung on some of the tanks. Oh, how I did wish I had something to give. Then I remembered my sweet coupons in my handbag, and there was a little sweet shop behind me, so I ran into it, bought all I could, and threw the bag into one of the trucks. The traffic went on like this all day . . .

That evening Churchill announced what had happened in the House of Commons:

I have to announce that during the night and early hours of this morning the first of a series of landings in force upon the European continent have taken place. In this case the liberating assault fell upon the coast of France. An immense armada of upwards of 4,000 ships, together with several thousand smaller craft, crossed the Channel. Massed airborne landings have been successfully effected behind the enemy lines, and landings on the beaches are proceeding at various points at the present time.

The fire of the shore batteries has been largely quelled . . . Complete unity prevails throughout the Allied armies . . . There is complete confidence in the Supreme Commander, General Eisenhower, and in his lieutenants, and in the Commander of the Expeditionary Force, General Montgomery. The ardour and spirit of the troops, as I saw myself, embarking in these last few days, was splendid to witness.

Germany surrenders   May 1945

This invasion began the campaign which was to end a year later when the Russians from the east, and ourselves and the Americans from the west, were converging on Berlin. Hitler at that moment of failure and despair committed suicide, and Germany surrendered unconditionally.

The discovery of the concentration camps

When the Allies occupied Germany they discovered the full horror of the Nazi dictatorship. They found the camps where the Nazis had imprisoned people from the occupied countries whom they had conscripted for 'slave labour' in their factories, and worked until they were too weak to be of any more use. And worse, the camps where

Belsen, one of the worst concentration camps, was liberated in April 1945. This man was found sitting among the clothes and bodies of the dead, too dazed by starvation and ill-treatment to enjoy his freedom.

Jewish people, including children and babies, were sent to be exterminated in gas chambers. Terrible crimes have been committed in the past, but never before has a government in cold blood organized a crime so monstrous or on such a huge scale. The Allies tried some of the most prominent ministers and officials responsible for the camps, and in 1965 the German government, deeply ashamed of what had happened, is still continuing to arrest and try war criminals.

New weapons of World War II

Radar   One of the reasons why German bombing did not defeat us was that we developed radar for spotting and tracking approaching aircraft. For some time the Germans could not understand how it was that our fighters located their bombers so successfully; we put abroad the story that we had improved the night-sight of our fighter-pilots by giving them lots of Vitamin C, and there were great piles of raw grated carrot on the tables of air-base messes to support this story.

V Bombs   But Hitler had his secret weapons too, and during the later part of the war London was attacked by two new kinds of bombs.

The first of these were the flying bombs. They were bombs fitted with an engine which was set to go a certain distance in a certain direction. The bombs were very hard on the nerves of Londoners, and the people of other towns, such as Portsmouth, against which they were aimed. People would hear the curious, unmistakable noise of the engine coming nearer and nearer; so long as it went on the listeners were safe; when the engine cut out and there was silence, they knew that the bomb was coming down, and they dived down cellar entrances, under the tables of cafés, anywhere they could hope for a bit of shelter, until they heard the sound of the explosion. When the Allies overran the launching sites of the flying bombs in northern France, this attack ceased.

Then there were the V-2s. The V-2 was a rocket with an explosive warhead. There was no defence against them because they went so fast and there was no warning of their approach. It would have been serious for us if Hitler had had more of them, and used them earlier in the war. This was the beginning of rocket weapons. These rockets were minute in size and range compared with the ones which could be made now.

The atomic bomb – Hiroshima and Nagasaki and the defeat of Japan

But, of course, the most tremendous change in weapons, the discovery which has made everyone think and feel differently about war, is the atomic bomb.

It is possible that if Hitler had not dismissed Jewish scientists, and offended other scientists by the cruelty and stupidity of his anti-Semitism, he might have got the nuclear bomb first. Famous Jewish scientists, such as Einstein, were dismissed or resigned in disgust, and

The Germans pioneered new techniques in warfare. Here, a V-2 rocket is launched.

Nazi second-raters took their jobs. A brilliant Danish physicist, Niels Bohr, was asked by the Germans when they occupied Denmark to work on atomic bombs for them, but he preferred to escape to England and work for the Allies.

At the time of the fall of France, a French scientist, Joliot-Curie, knew of the possibility of this new kind of bomb, and he knew that 'heavy water' would be necessary for making it. All the 'heavy water' then available was in twelve sealed aluminium containers in France. Joliot-Curie and his friends set about burning all information about work on nuclear fission, and plotted to get the 'heavy water' to England. One of his friends tells the story:

One night we deposited our valuable consignment for safe-keeping in the State Prison at Riom. The place in the prison which was most secure from intrusion was the death cell, which was cleared for the time being to make room for our 'water bottles'. The dislodged convicts under sentence of death themselves carried the heavy containers to the cell.

In the end the 'heavy water' got to Bordeaux, and was put aboard the British collier *Broompark*. An enterprising carpenter on the boat built a stout raft, onto which the aluminium containers, and $2\frac{1}{2}$ million pounds sterling worth of industrial diamonds were strongly fastened. The scientists in charge were resolved that if the ship struck a mine or was bombed, they would get the raft away and stick to her in the open sea. However, the *Broompark* reached England safely, and Joliot-Curie tricked the Germans into believing that the 'heavy water' had been put aboard another ship which left Bordeaux about the same time and which was sunk.

We and the Americans make the atomic bomb

It was decided that American and Canadian money and resources were needed for atomic bomb research, but we in England had the scientists who were necessary for the job. We agreed that they should go to America and work on the bomb as a team with the Americans.

We drop two bombs on Japan

Germany had surrendered in May 1945, but Japan was not yet defeated. After May, we carried out heavy bombardment of her from the sea, and the Russians, in fulfilment of their promise to help against Japan after the surrender of Germany, were moving troops eastward. In July 1945, Japan was in chaos and on the verge of collapse. She was actually negotiating with the Russians for surrender.

On 6 August the Americans, with the agreement of our government, dropped an atomic bomb on Hiroshima, and three days later a second on Nagasaki. 60,000 people lost their lives at Hiroshima. 40,000 died at Nagasaki.

Why did we do it?

Churchill has written: 'It would be a mistake to suppose that the

The city of Hiroshima after the atomic bomb had been exploded.

fate of Japan was settled by the atomic bomb. Her defeat was certain before the bomb fell, and was brought about by overwhelming power.'

The world was horrified when it discovered what these bombs could do, and many of the scientists who had worked on them were conscience-stricken when they learnt the use to which their work had been put. They had urged that trial bombs should be dropped in the sea, and used as a warning to our enemies of what could happen if they did not surrender.

After Hiroshima, the American government sent Japan an ultimatum threatening to drop a second atomic bomb, this time on Nagasaki, if she did not surrender.

The effects of atomic bombs on warfare

Atomic bombs are not merely bigger than the older kind of bombs; they are different from them in two ways which completely alter our outlook on war.

Firstly, they do not only kill those whom they wound or burn at the moment when they explode; they also kill many who die later from

---

the effects of radiation, and particularly from 'fall out', the radioactive dust which comes down after an explosion. Years after the war, Japanese people were still dying as a result of the bombs on Hiroshima and Nagasaki, and it is possible that those who have survived exposure to radiation may be likely to have deformed children, or unable to have children at all. Through exploding these bombs we poison the earth upon which our descendants must live. Earlier kinds of warfare did not do this.

Secondly, these bombs can cause such complete and widespread destruction that even for the victorious side, war is not now worth fighting. Everything which people love at home, and which they think worth defending, would probably be destroyed if atomic bombs were used.

As a result, we must think more seriously about keeping peace between the nations than we have ever done before.

The cost of World War II

If you compare World War II with World War I, it may seem to you that the first one was much more grim. And for the people of the British Isles this was so. Even the rations were much better in World War II than they had been in World War I, and, despite air-raids, our sufferings and anxieties were much less. We had many fewer casualties and much better generals than we had had in the first war.

One young French volunteer on her way to join the resistance forces in August 1944.

This difference was chiefly because during the 1914–18 war the French and British had done most of the hard fighting against the Germans, whilst in 1939–45 the weight of the struggle was borne by the Russian armies and the peoples of the countries occupied by the Germans. The Russian armies did the hardest fighting, and in occupied countries life was grim, hungry, and, for people who resisted the Germans, very dangerous. Many European people risked their lives to shelter our airmen who came down near their homes, and we got valuable information from underground resistance movements. The Poles, for instance, told us the exact position of important German war factories, which we therefore bombed successfully. If you visit France, you may see tablets set in the walls of houses, giving the names of brave Frenchmen, and the date on which they were arrested by the Germans and taken away to be shot for their part in the resistance. Twenty million people lost their lives in World War II, and most of them were Europeans.

What did we fight for?

In the first place the Allies fought because we had to resist Nazism and the domination of Europe by Germany. But during the war we resolved to make a better and safer world for the future.

The Atlantic Charter and the 'Four Freedoms'

After America had entered the war, Churchill crossed the Atlantic

114

CASE RESERVED
FOR THE BIG ONE
THAT WON'T GET AWAY

Sorry can't
come this
weekend
Good luck
Joe

LOW

Churchill and Roosevelt enjoying a peaceful 'fishing holiday'.

secretly in the battleship *Prince of Wales*; Roosevelt pretended to be going on a fishing holiday in the yacht *Potomac*, and the two leaders met at sea. They did not talk only about problems of winning the war; they also discussed problems of future peace and human happiness. The 'Atlantic Charter' of human rights was issued after their talks. In it America and Britain declared that they did not intend to claim any more lands as a result of victory and that they would struggle to secure for the peoples of the world the 'Four Freedoms' –

FREEDOM FROM FEAR
FREEDOM FROM WANT
FREEDOM OF THOUGHT AND EXPRESSION
FREEDOM OF RELIGION

They also planned to reform the League of Nations, which had not been able to prevent the outbreak of war. Roosevelt was determined to replace it by an organization of states which would be stronger than the League, and which, unlike the League, should include America and Russia.

The United Nations Charter   1945

The new organization was set up by the United Nations Charter in 1945. It was signed by the representatives of fifty-one states, and consisted of an Assembly, at which every state had a vote, and a 'Security Council' of eleven states, including permanent representatives of five great powers, America, Britain, France, Kuomintang China* and Russia. The Council decides on any action which the United Nations takes, and all members of it must agree to any decision. This means that any one of five nations can always prevent anything being done, and has a 'veto' on action. This may seem a weakness of the U.N., and has been very irritating, but it may have been a good idea, for it prevents the United Nations voting for action against any of the great powers, action which it might be impossible or dangerous to carry out.

Despite this limit on its powers, the United Nations has done important work to keep peace both by discussion and by sending forces to danger spots in the Suez Canal area, the Congo, and Cyprus. There is trouble now in many parts of the world and we may hope that the U.N. will be useful in preventing it from spreading. Whether or not the U.N. will be able to solve the problem of keeping world peace depends upon the support which governments can be persuaded to give it.

The U.N. does many things besides trying to keep peace. It has a World Health Organization, a Food and Agriculture Organization and there is the United Nations Educational, Scientific, and Cultural Organization. These do so many things to promote human welfare that there is no space to describe them here, but if you write up to the Council for Education in World Citizenship office in London you can get illustrated information.

* Kuomintang China is the island of Formosa. America would not recognize the new, communist government of China, and insisted that the legal government was that of General Chiang Kai Chek, who rules only this island (1965).

Dates to remember

1939–45	World War II
1940	Fall of France Dunkirk
	Battle of Britain
1941 (June)	Russia enters the War
1941 (December)	America enters the War
1942	Battle of Stalingrad
1944	'D' Day Invasion of France
1945	Surrender of Germany
1945	Surrender of Japan

Things to do

1 Find Kuomintang China (Formosa) on the map, and discuss the reasons why it represents China at the United Nations (1965).
2 Which nations have joined the United Nations since 1951?
3 Ask people to tell you about fighting in different parts of the world during World War II, and about life in Britain during the blitz.
4 Borrow war-time heirlooms and souvenirs from your relations and friends for an exhibition in the classroom.
5 Write to the Secretary, The Council for Education in World Citizenship, 93 Albert Embankment, London, SE1, and ask for

information about the work of the United Nations, and the bodies connected with it such as F.A.O., W.H.O., and U.N.E.S.C.O.

Things to discuss

1 Why did we drop atomic bombs on Japan?
2 What is the meaning and importance of the Four Freedoms?
3 Which nations do not enjoy some of them?

Books to read

K. Bruckner, *The Day of the Bomb*, Burke
W. Churchill, *The Second World War* (Blenheim Edition), Cassell
Anne Frank, *Diary of Anne Frank*, Pan Books
D. Holman, *The Man They Couldn't Kill*, Heinemann
W. Hornby, *The United Nations*, Macmillan
R. Jungk, *Brighter Than a Thousand Suns*, Penguin
R. Jungk, *Children of the Ashes*, Penguin
G. Martelli, *Agent Extraordinary*, Collins
J. Welch, *Famous Sea Battles*, Barker
E. Williams, *The Wooden Horse*, Collins

A cartoonist reflects on the evolution of man. With the atomic bomb, a new era has begun in human history.

117

Chapter 6
The welfare state

May 1945 saw the end of the war in Europe, and the end of the war in the Far East in sight. The British people could throw away their blackout curtains and dream of the piping times of peace when there would be no more food or clothes rationing. An election was called for the beginning of July. It was the first election for ten years.

The Conservative posters showed the portrait of Winston Churchill, with the caption 'Let him finish the job'. He was indeed the hero of the hour. The Labour Party hoped for more votes than they had had in 1935, but they did not dare to hope that they would beat the Conservatives. However, on 26 July, as people huddled round their radios to listen to the results, they heard what became almost a monotonous chant of 'Labour Victory'. The most unlikely places, country towns, London suburbs, had gone Labour. No one was perhaps more surprised at the size of the majority, 146 against all the other parties combined, than the victors themselves. Ernest Bevin was said to be speechless, a most unusual condition for him. When Attlee, the leader of the Party, drove to Buckingham Palace to kiss his sovereign's hand, even King George could not conceal his surprise. Some people were shocked. Had the country shown ingratitude to Churchill, who had carried it through the war?

Election Result   1945

Labour	393
Conservative	208
Liberal	12
Communist	2
Others	25

What caused this landslide?

The vote of the soldiers was largely responsible. At the end of the First World War only twenty-five per cent of the soldiers had voted, after the Second World War the number was sixty per cent. Unlike the soldiers of the 1914–18 War, who had been cut off from life at home, and had lived in their own world of the trenches, the men in 1945 were well informed. They had been kept in touch with events at home by radio. The Army Bureau of Current Affairs had sent regular bulletins to all units; there had been talks and discussions. Every army had its newspaper which published letters and criticisms, and some of these were so bold that soldiers of the First World War might have been courtmartialled for writing them. There had been a difference in the relations of the generals with their troops. The men knew their commanders. Field-Marshal Montgomery had said, 'Every single soldier must know before he goes into battle, how the little battle he is to fight fits into the larger picture, and how the success of his fighting will influence the battle as a whole.' The soldier in the past had not been required to think. In this election the officers were told to persuade their men to use the vote.

1945. Bombed houses contributed to an acute housing shortage. On the other hand, they enabled city planners to build new houses in the place of old.

118

The younger soldiers could remember the depression years, the dole queues and the unemployment. They had heard tales from their fathers about the end of the First World War, how the ex-officers had gone round from door to door selling bootlaces and notepaper in a desperate attempt to make some income. One woman said as she voted, 'My son wrote to me and said I must vote Labour, or else he would be out of a job.'

The people were also prepared for change. They had often been warned that a Labour government would want to take away their freedom. But they had had controls in war-time and had appreciated that the rationing and controls were fair. Every child had had orange juice and cod liver oil. Rich and poor alike had had the same rations. Dinners had been provided at cost price for all schoolchildren. Then too, stories about Russia could no longer frighten them. Russia had been our war-time ally and the defence of Stalingrad had passed into legend. It surely could not be such a bad country if its army could fight so magnificently.

Changes, everyone knew, were coming. The war-time government had passed a bill which said every child was to have the chance of a secondary education. A civil servant, Sir William Beveridge, had been asked to prepare a report on social insurance, and he had brought out a comprehensive plan to defeat what he called the 'enemy poverty'. There was also a scheme on hand to provide more free medical treatment.

The electors rejected the party which they associated with the years of unemployment. It was not ingratitude to Winston Churchill which caused the swing to Labour. They preferred the policy of change which the Labour Party promised.

Labour takes over   1945

The new Labour members trooped into Westminster on the first Wednesday in August, like a lot of new boys on their first day at school. Many of them had never been inside the House of Commons before. They still felt a little dazed by their victory.

When Winston Churchill came in, he was greeted by a rousing cheer from his party, who began to sing 'For he's a jolly good fellow'. Someone from the Labour side began to sing the 'Red Flag'. The effect of this was rather spoilt by the fact that some of them did not know the words. However, a small gallant band managed to sing two verses. The Speaker of the House (who is the Chairman) said good humouredly that he did not know he was expected to conduct an orchestra. The members then retired for six weeks, and the new Cabinet planned its programme.

There was plenty of planning necessary. Six years of war had either destroyed or badly damaged 5,000,000 houses. As you walked through the towns you could see huge gaps left by the bombs of war-time. Families who had been evacuated now hastened back to the cities; in London alone 1,500,000 people returned during the first year after the war. Nor was housing the only problem. We had suffered shipping losses of

19,000,000 tons. Our railways stock was wearing out, and everywhere machinery needed replacing.

Finance

Amidst all the rejoicings from the Labour side, few noticed the remark of Attlee 'We shall have a hard time'. During the war we had withdrawn nearly all our investments from abroad, and had carried on with the help of the Lend-Lease agreement from the United States. On 2 September the American government announced that this agreement would be ended. How then were we to get the money to buy the much needed raw materials, chiefly steel? The United States made us a loan of 3,000,000,000 dollars and we hoped that this would last until 1950, and enable us to recover our export trade. Of course a loan like this is not paid in money, but in goods. Soon after it was made the price of goods rose in America, so that the actual amount we received was less than was expected. In order to repay we had to produce the goods which America or some other country needed.

Our factories were quickly restored and attractive goods once more were placed in the shops, but alas, they were marked for 'export only'. We could not buy them, and rationing had to go on. In fact it became more severe, because we could not spend this precious loan on foods like dried eggs, which had been our standby during the war. One other disadvantage of this state of affairs was that we lost a certain amount of independence. When you owe money to a country you cannot carry out a policy to which that country might object. So when the Labour Party set about transforming the country, it had to work with a heavy load. It was rather like trying to push a car uphill with the brake on.

Out of the army into civvy street

Men were released from the Forces in the order 'First in, first out'. This plan worked smoothly partly because there were plenty of jobs for the newly released soldiers to take. Each one was issued with a 'demob' suit, a pair of shoes, two shirts, a ration book and instructions about where he could find employment or further training. Many men had had their education interrupted by the war; they wanted to return to the universities, and these were soon overcrowded. The technical colleges were also filled, so we established training schools for twenty different trades, and many employers also had their own training schemes for their employees. The 6,000,000 workers in war industries were quickly absorbed into the factories turning out goods for export. You read earlier in this book about the disastrous unemployment which had followed peace in 1918. This time the reverse was true. Although women who had worked during the war were kept on, there was plenty of work for their men also.

'As far as I'm concerned, I don't care if I never see another uniform!'

The mines and railways

The Labour Party had declared that it would nationalize the important

industries. To nationalize is to take the ownership out of private hands
and give it to the State, as is the case with the postal services, for
instance. The government decided to nationalize the coal mines because
the mines needed a great deal of money spent on them and private
investors would not lend it; also, a generation before this, a government
commission had recommended sweeping reforms in the mines which
could only be carried through with government control. In 1946 the
government bought out the mine owners and set up the National Coal
Board. On 1 January 1947 flags fluttered proudly from the pit-heads
bearing the initials 'N.C.B.'. In Wales, triumphal arches were set up in
some places to mark the historic occasion.

Nationalization of the mines was very expensive, because the mine
owners were generously compensated, and huge sums were spent on the
pits to bring them up to date. Conditions of work improved, and strenuous efforts were made to increase the output of coal on which our
industry depended.

In 1947 the railways were nationalized. They also needed a great deal
of money spent on them, and the shareholders were compensated.

In the past both these key industries had often had strikes and bitter
disputes and the government hoped that with fair treatment and better
wages, there would now be peace. Some of the old grievances of the
workers were done away with. The hated Trades Disputes Act of 1927
was repealed and the workers could feel that they had a government

Moment of change: hoisting
the new flag of the National
Coal Board.

Waterloo Station, 1 January 1947. All railway companies were united under one name, 'British Railways'.

which was on their side. However, nationalizing these two industries did not help to make that 'dollar gap', as it was called, any smaller. Because of the amount of replacement of machinery which was necessary it would be a long time before the country felt any financial benefit from having bought the mines and the railways.

The freak winter

The poet Burns warned us a long time ago that our best-laid plans can go wrong. In 1946, as winter approached, there was concern because our stocks of coal were running low. On 16 December the winter began in earnest, rather earlier than usual. Sudden spells of cold weather are common in this country. But this was different. It was not a short spell. It went on unrelentingly into the New Year. During January snow fell every day. On 29 January half the people who normally came into London every day to work, found they were unable to travel. All over the country, from Land's End to John o'Groats the roads had snowdrifts, some of them ten feet deep. The railways were paralysed, the points frozen, and neither people nor coal could be moved. There was talk of a return to the Ice Age.

The chief problem was to get the food around. In one area a man had to walk sixteen miles to fetch food for his village, struggling all the way through snow. Hospitals were the first charge and every effort was made to keep them supplied, but for other concerns and private people heating

123

was reduced, and gas and electricity supplies were frequently cut. Women could be seen pushing prams from the railway depots, not with babies inside, but with lumps of coal. Some streets were without water because the main pipes under the roadway were frozen. The radio, which was listened to every evening with the fervent hope that it would announce the possibility of a thaw, brought little comfort. Most of the news was an account of the villages which were cut off. A children's home with twenty-four babies in it, at one time had only a day's supply of food. Rescue work was carried out on Dartmoor and on the Yorkshire moors where there were isolated farms and hamlets.

People worked on without grumbling. This was a catastrophe which affected everyone and it brought back some of the warm, communal feeling of war-time.

It was certainly much to the credit of the organization that no single village was left quite without food, but the animals suffered. One-third

In Charles II's time, an ox had been roasted whole on the frozen River Thames. In this cartoon, the Minister of Food roasts a modest potato.

A lorry, caught in a blizzard, February 1947.

of the sheep died and 30,000 cattle. In March a thaw started and then just when hopes were rising, the snow came again. This time Scotland was cut off from England by the worst storm ever recorded. The railway line was buried under thirty feet of snow. In one area people used a pneumatic drill to dig out parsnips.

After the frost when the snow thawed, the flood came. The Severn, the Thames and the Fen district were the worst hit, and in London part of the Underground had to be closed. Householders gazed forlornly at their ruined furniture as the waters swept through their houses. The troops were used to help with the floods and experts came over from Holland to advise.

As a compensation there was a marvellously fine summer after this winter. But the winter disasters, the loss of sheep and cattle and the destruction through flooding, not to speak of the millions of broken water pipes, all that meant that we should have to struggle harder than ever to close that dollar gap. People were urged to work hard by the posters put on the hoardings 'we work or want'.

Housing

The British people at this time had enough food, although it was still rationed, but they had not nearly enough houses, and the houses they had were many of them old, without bathrooms or indoor sanitation.

The problem was urgent. Men came back from the forces, married and wanted homes. Those with a little capital might buy a house, but the demand had sent the prices rocketing so that houses cost roughly three times as much as before the war. The best that most people could do was to rent a furnished room or small flat. Every town had its housing list, some with as many as 30,000 names. No wonder those at the bottom of the list felt despondent.

During the war the government had passed an Act making it illegal to raise rents, and had set up tribunals to which tenants could appeal if they thought the landlord charged too high a rent for furnished rooms.

After the war, Aneurin Bevan, a Welsh miner, became the Minister of Health and Housing. He arranged to lend money at a low rate of interest to local authorities for house building. Unfortunately the shortage of material forced the Government to restrict the number of new houses to 200,000 a year (except in 1948, when more were built). There were so many urgent claims, for schools, for hospital extensions and for new factories that priorities had to be carefully considered. The authorities too were hampered by the poor organization of the building industry. There were thousands of small building firms which put up houses in the traditional way, brick by brick on the site. This was slow work at the best of times, and stopped completely in bad weather. We were still working in the way the Romans had done, 2,000 years ago.

In September 1946 the government was given a shock. Quietly and with determination groups of homeless people marched into the disused army huts which were scattered round the countryside. They carried their belongings with them and just stayed put. In London a more spectacular movement arose. One Sunday about 700 people moved into luxury flats in Kensington, where the owners had not yet returned. They ensconced themselves with their children, their bedding and crockery before the police realized what had happened. Their stay was short and not very comfortable as they were without heat or lighting, but friends sent them up food in baskets which were lowered down from

Squatters in luxury flats in London, September 1946.

the windows. This gave publicity to the plight of so many families. Though they were finally moved out of the flats, the government now took over unoccupied houses and let them to families on the housing list. Also they speeded up the building of 'prefabs', small houses built of steel or aluminium, intended to be just temporary and to be pulled down when proper houses were built. These prefabs were the beginning of modern house-building methods in this country.

The new towns

All this was only touching the fringe of the problem. The population was increasing fast and even if a target of 500,000 houses a year could be achieved, it would take twenty years before the needs were satisfied.

Silkin, Minister of Town and Country Planning, decided that entirely new towns should be built. In the thirties when a number of council estates had been put up on the outskirts of the big cities, it was found that the people who moved into them from slum areas found the life dull. There were rows and rows of neat houses, equipped with good kitchens and bathrooms and with little gardens round them. But it was not a community. There were no cinemas, often the shops were far away and worst of all there was no 'mum' round the corner to give a hand with the children, for the old people had been left behind in the town. The idea behind the new town scheme, was to build a whole community,

A modern housing estate in London, 1961. Tall flats provide homes for many people, and wide spaces prevent a sense of overcrowding. Compare this with housing estates of the 1930s.

factories, houses, shops, at the same time, so that these new towns would not be just rows of houses where people slept and went a long distance to work every day, but a place where they not only lived but to which they belonged. It was exciting for the architects. For the first time since the Romans were here a town as such was planned. The old towns in England had grown up haphazard. When more people came to the town the streets were just stretched out further into the country. Now the architects, knowing beforehand that they were to plan a town for 50,000 or for 100,000 inhabitants, could design it for convenience and beauty. Did people want separate houses? Did they want flats? Did they want shopping areas where no cars were allowed? Playing places for children, and community halls were all to be provided. The first of these new towns was Stevenage in Hertfordshire; others were Crawley, Harlow, and Hemel Hempstead.

Unfortunately not enough of these towns were built. Material was wanted for factories, offices and schools. The programme of rearmament used up not only our steel but our manpower. As fast as slums were cleared, new ones appeared, as the older houses slid into decay. No government since the war has been able to satisfy the needs of the people for enough houses.

Fair shares for all

When the country voted the Labour Party into power they expected that the good things of this world would be more equally distributed. They thought that the rich should not have all the advantages. What were the great advantages that the rich had over the poor? They had security. They did not need to fear poverty in old age; they could educate their children for whatever profession they wanted. When ill they could afford to send for a doctor and be treated in a private nursing home.

The Beveridge report promised to give everyone that precious thing, security, and the Labour Party accepted the principle of the report. The Minister of Pensions widened the scope of the Old Age Pensions Act to include everybody, so that what in future was to be called the retirement pension would be given to all women when they were sixty, and men when they were sixty-five. This was a continuance of Lloyd George's scheme of old age pensions, but it was much more comprehensive. *The Times* wrote, 'The people had joined together in a single national Friendly Society for mutual support.' There was no longer to be a pauper class of old age pensioners who were regarded as objects of charity. There was also a difference in the application of the law. Also children's allowances were granted for every child except the first. The Ministry ordered the Public Assistance Boards (no longer called the Poor Law) to give people what they needed with as little trouble or inconvenience to the applicant as possible. This was different from the attitude of the authorities when the Means Test had been applied during the 1930s.

'Please can I have my tooth – or does it belong to the government?'

Bevan and the doctors

Perhaps the most successful measure of the Labour Government was the Health Act, yet it was the most hotly contested. During the war there had been agreement in all the parties that there must be more free medical care. It had been a Welshman, Lloyd George, who had first introduced medical insurance for workers and it was a Welshman, Aneurin Bevan, who was made Minister of Health in the 1945 government. He was sometimes criticized for his violent speeches (as Lloyd George had been) and it was complained that he was tactless with the doctors.

Bevan had seen his father die of silicosis, that dread disease of miners. As a boy he had sold threepenny raffle tickets to buy a pegleg for a man injured in a pit accident. He was determined that all, rich and poor alike, should have first-class medical treatment.

The situation was then that the general practitioners, called G.P.s for short, bought their practices and charged fees for their attendance. Seaside places were popular with doctors because there were plenty of rich people there who could pay well, and the more crowded areas were often short of doctors, because the work there was harder and the financial rewards less. The worker himself, under the Lloyd George Act, could get free treatment as a panel patient, but for his wife and children he had to pay. This meant that many people went without the advice of a doctor because they could not afford it. People all had to pay for dental treatment and for spectacles.

There were two kinds of hospitals, the municipal ones run by the local authority, and the voluntary ones which carried on from private subscriptions, helped out by flag days. The consultants, who were then called specialists, used to give their services free to the voluntary hospitals, usually the first thing in the morning and then made money from private patients whom they could attend to in their own consulting rooms.

With regard to the G.P.s Bevan proposed to abolish the sale of practices and to pay the doctor so much a year for every patient whom he had on his list. Everyone in the country, whatever his income, would have the right to register with the doctor of his choice and to get free treatment and free medicine.

The reaction of the doctors to these proposals was at first one of violent opposition. A campaign was started to urge the doctors not to agree to enter the scheme. When a vote was taken two thirds of them said they would have nothing to do with it. They said it would destroy the old relationship of patient and doctor, that they would become civil servants and would be ordered about by laymen.

We have to understand their training and tradition to understand the reactions of the doctors. At that time it cost about £1,000 to become a doctor. Except for the favoured few who could get scholarships, only well-to-do men could train their sons for a medical career. So it was a middle-class profession. Then, too, there was something special about

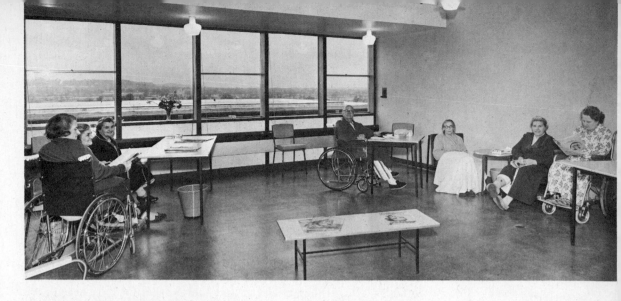

their work. They had a knowledge which set them apart from other people. They seemed to hold in their hands the keys of life, and many of their patients believed they had almost miraculous powers. The older G.P.s particularly resented the idea that laymen, who knew nothing of medicine, should plan a bill which would determine how they should work. The younger men who had not yet bought practices looked on the bill with more favour.

Recovery ward in a modern hospital.

Bevan found allies among the consultants, largely through his friendship with the head of the illustrious College of Physicians, and won their support by such concessions as allowing private beds in hospitals for those who could pay. As a result he got his scheme accepted by the medical profession, and only four per cent of the doctors stayed out of it.

Bevan successfully resisted suggestions that those with money should be asked to pay for medical services; he thought that this would result in two kinds of treatment being given.

In July 1948 the *Daily Mail* summed up the situation very neatly:

On Monday morning you will wake in a new Britain, in a state which takes over its citizens six months before they are born, providing free care and services for their early years, their schooling, sickness, workless days, widowhood and retirement. Finally it helps defray the cost of their departure. All this, with free doctoring, dentistry and medicine – free bath chairs too if needed – for four and elevenpence of your weekly pay packet.

Of course there was plenty of criticism of the way the Act worked. There were screaming headlines in the papers about the 5,000,000 people who had been given spectacles, and the long queues at the dentists. This proved, said the supporters of the Bill, not that people were asking for dental treatment for the fun of it, but that millions of people had needed treatment for a long time and had not been able to afford it.

The propaganda put out by the doctors against the Bill had had some effect. One man wrote to the papers and expressed his surprise that when he had to call in the doctor he found the doctor behaved just as usual.

The cost of the Health Bill was higher than the planners had reckoned. This was because prices everywhere were rising. All the provisions were therefore not carried out. Health centres which had been part of the scheme were not built.

Schools

We need brains as well as brawn if we are to keep up our trade and our position in the world. If we could not afford to have a nation which was not fit, neither could we afford to waste the abilities of our children.

Just as there used to be two kinds of medical treatment, so there had been two kinds of education. The one sort you paid for, the other was free. At the top of the scale of the first kind were the 'Public Schools'. These were very expensive and practically all of them were boarding schools. They had all the advantages of small classes and good equipment, and also they were the schools from which men were appointed to the best posts in the Civil Service, the professions and in industry. So wealthy parents sent their sons to a Public School, partly because the education was good, and partly because they wanted them to have a good chance when they left school. The Labour Government did not touch these schools. They thought they would probably decline because of the high fees which so few could afford, but in fact this did not happen. People found ways of paying the fees by forming trusts which were free of tax, so the Public Schools became more successful than ever.

Then there were the Grammar Schools, to which the majority of the middle class sent their children. Their fees were low, and anyone who could pay them could provide his children with an education which might take them to a university, or any of the professions.

Lastly there were the free schools, in which all children of the working classes began their education at the age of five. Most of them stayed in these schools, elementary schools for the younger children and senior ones for older children, until they reached the school-leaving age of fourteen. But ever since the Balfour Act of 1902 (see Chapter 1) some children won 'scholarships' which gave them free places at the Grammar Schools. Before World War I fifteen per cent of the places in Grammar Schools were held by scholarship winners from the elementary schools.

The Butler Act 1944   'Secondary education for all'

The Butler Act of 1944 said 'secondary education for all'. This could not be done by waving a wand; schools had to be built and teachers found. The Labour Minister of Education promptly set up emergency training colleges for would-be teachers, where they had a shortened course. The school-leaving age was raised to fifteen, with a promise

that it should be raised to sixteen as soon as possible. All fees were abolished and grants were given to boys and girls who wanted to study at a university.

Now that all fees were abolished the question arose, who should go to the Grammar Schools? It was open to any parent now. But clearly most would choose a Grammar School, because they had better buildings, playing fields and were altogether more attractive. So the scholarship examination was kept and only those who passed it were allowed to go to the Grammar School. The others stayed in schools which were now called 'Secondary Modern'. Both types of school, according to the authorities were equally good. The official phrase was that they had 'parity of esteem'. The parents did not believe this. Ambitious parents who could afford it, had their children coached to pass the 'eleven plus' which began to loom large in the life of the child. The education authorities explained that the Secondary Modern type of school was right for those children who were not what is called 'academic'.

Shephalbury Secondary Modern School in Stevenage, opened in 1959. Older schools had been built in cities; the new schools were set in open spaces.

132

Many teachers challenged this idea that children could be divided up in this fashion. Some of the Secondary Modern schools began to send their pupils in for the G.C.E. examination, and when successes came in, the question was asked, why should these children have been labelled at the age of eleven as 'non-academic'?

There was more and more criticism of a system that decided the future of a child by an examination lasting one day at the age of eleven. One solution was to follow the American pattern and have one common school for all children when they left the Junior school. The pros and cons of this have been hotly debated by both teachers and parents. One fear often expressed is that the brightest children would be held back if they were not in separate schools from the others. Questions like this can only properly be answered after experiments have been made. The London County Council built some large Comprehensive schools, which are schools to which all the children go without taking an examination. Coventry and a few other places have also done this, and interesting variants of it are being carried out in different parts of England.

There still remain in most parts of Great Britain, however, the two types of school, Secondary Modern and Secondary Grammar. It is still possible for parents to buy themselves out of the state system by sending their children to private fee-paying schools of their own choice. The new schoolbuildings in England which have been built since the war are the admiration of Europe, but in spite of the fact that £1,000,000,000 has been spent on constructing them, many old out-of-date buildings remain, and classes are still too large. Compare the new school shown opposite with a nineteenth century one in your district.

The Festival of Britain   1951

The Labour Government planned to have an exhibition exactly one hundred years after the famous one designed by the Prince Consort which was held in the Crystal Palace. This time the site was fixed on the south bank of the river Thames, in Battersea. Just as the first one was fiercely attacked, so this plan came in for a great deal of criticism. People complained that labour and material were being used for decoration, when more houses were needed, and when they thought the labour could be more usefully employed. Architects and town planners, who had always regretted that the south bank of the Thames looked so sordid and dreary, and compared it to the attractive banks of the Seine in Paris, were enthusiastic at the idea of brightening and improving the appearance of London.

During the war and for some years after, life had been drab and it was invigorating to see the new buildings going up. There was a very high slender tower, called the Skylon, and Battersea Park was laid out as a pleasure ground and fun fair. There were little tables in the

Stamp issued in 1951.

133

The Skylon towers
above the Royal Festival
Hall, and an ingenious
fountain attracts
spectators.

refreshment pavilion with brightly coloured striped umbrellas over them, a fashion copied from the cafés of France and Italy. The whole effect was one of gaiety and lightness. It was opened on 1 May and continued all through the summer. This time the word exhibition was not used; it was called instead the Festival of Britain. In it were displayed all the new materials, different kinds of plastics, steel furniture and all the man-made fabrics. Other rooms showed scientific inventions. When, at the end of the season the buildings were pulled down, one was left, the Festival Hall, which is now the best hall for concerts in London.

The end of Labour rule   1951

After the five years were up, in 1950, an election was held. This time Labour was returned with such a small majority (5) that Attlee could not bring in any important measure. In a desperate effort he tried to close the dollar gap by cutting expenditure; he put a charge on spectacles and dentistry. This caused Aneurin Bevan and Harold Wilson to resign from the Cabinet. The following year another election brought back the Conservative Party and Churchill became Prime Minister. In the succeeding elections of 1955 and 1959 the Conservative Party remained in power. Churchill gave place to Sir Anthony Eden in 1955. He, in turn, resigned in 1957 and Mr Harold Macmillan became Prime Minister.

Election Result   1950

Labour	315
Conservatives	298
Liberals	9
Others	3

Election Result   1951

Conservatives	321
Labour	295
Liberal	6

Coronation of Queen Elizabeth.
In 1952, George VI died. The
following year, on 2 June, his
daughter was crowned in
Westminster Abbey Elizabeth II.

Edmund Hillary and 'Sherpa'
Tensing, members of a British
expedition led by John Hunt,
conquered the world's highest
mountain, Mount Everest, on
29 May 1953. This photograph
of Hillary on the summit
was taken by Tensing.

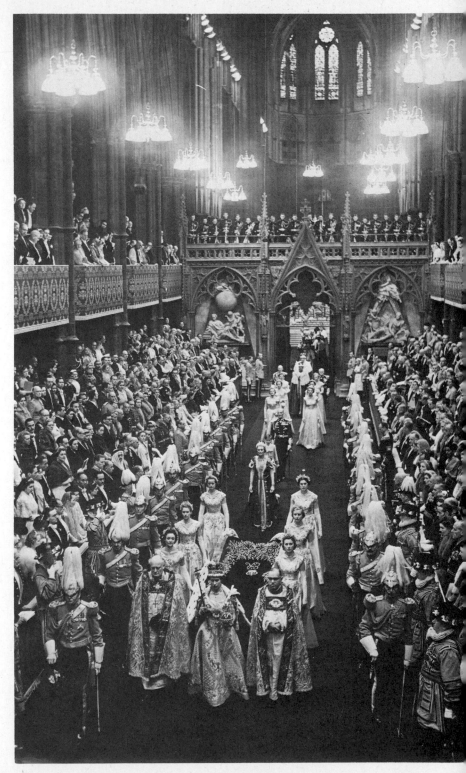

Why did the Labour Party lose popularity? The country had had such high hopes in 1945 and some Labour supporters had seemed to think Paradise was just round the corner.

Life had become a great deal better than it had been before the war. The bogy of unemployment had been laid. Boys and girls leaving school at fifteen easily got jobs; the nightmare of the dole queues had gone. There was a free Health Service, free secondary schooling and generous grants for those who wanted further study. The Insurance Act brought benefits to an enormous number of people.

Housing was probably the greatest disappointment. In spite of the blocks of flats which were soaring up to the sky, and the apparently endless miles of new Council estates, the demand for houses was as great as ever. If, argued some people, a government can't find us a home, why vote for it? The continued restrictions on consumer goods were irksome. It was noticed that other countries had a less rigidly controlled economy.

The main support of the Labour Party was amongst the trade unionists, and there was some unrest and anxiety amongst them. The miners and the railway workers said there was little difference in their lives after nationalization. They saw that, for example, the motor-car workers were better paid than they were. In fact private enterprise seemed to give better rewards than public enterprise.

Income tax on the rich was very high, but some tax was evaded through expense accounts, which were free of tax. Old-fashioned socialists thought there was not enough sharing out of the profits made. Also during this period prices were continually rising, so that one quarter of the old age pensioners had to ask for extra money from the Public Assistance Board. Colossal sums were being spent on rearmament, and some critics of the government queried this and thought the money would be better spent on housing and hospitals.

The Conservative government   1951–64

After six years of war and six years of peacetime reconstruction the economic situation had improved, and people did not want further great changes. The Conservative government did not reverse what the Labour government had done, except in the case of road transport, which was transferred back to private companies and individuals. Steel was also denationalized.

The affluent society

Trade was in a healthy state. Goods flowed out of Britain and there was no fear of unemployment. At last people really began to taste the fruits of victory.

Things which had once been considered luxuries now became commonplace. The housewife expected to have a washing machine and a refrigerator. Television aerials (unfortunately not beautiful objects) appeared on the housetops. The number of cars on the roads

Real Earnings, 1946–63

1946 average wage 165s. a week

1951 average wage 176s. a week

1963 average wage 258s. a week

These figures show the growth of the affluent society, because 'real' means the amount that the money will actually buy.

The affluent society. Hire purchase encourages people to buy, because of the low deposit and small repayments made over a long period of time.

Amount of money spent on consumer goods

electrical appliances, washing machines, television, etc

1947	£224 million
1954	£354
1963	£487

cars

1949	£82 million
1954	£354
1960	£586

increased. The shops were full of attractive wares which were no longer earmarked for export.

There had been a restriction on the amount of money which could be taken out of the country, and this had prevented people from travelling far afield. The government now increased the foreign travel allowance. Holidays with pay and higher wages (particularly for those in the motor-car and aircraft industries) enabled thousands to go abroad for holidays. Before this time workers in the north had thought only of going to Blackpool for a week. Now coachloads of happy people went off for a fortnight to the Mediterranean or the Adriatic. This affected the rather conservative feeding habits of the English; foreign foodstuffs appeared in the shops, and foreign restaurants were opened.

Universities and colleges

There was a big increase in the number of university students now that government grants enabled boys and girls to grasp the opportunity of further education. New universities were set up at Sussex, Canterbury, York, East Anglia, Colchester, Lancaster and Warwick.

We realized that advanced technical training was needed by thousands of young men and women. Many new technical colleges were built in our industrial cities, while others were expanded.

This expansion of education brought its problems, as all changes do. There was an acute shortage of teachers because the new universities

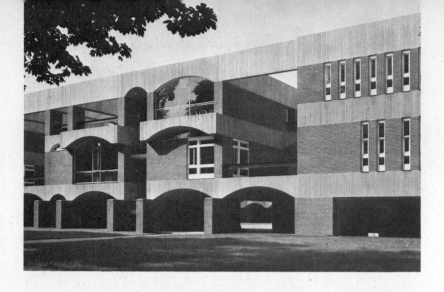

The first new university, that of Sussex, opened in 1961. Its designer, Sir Basil Spence, repeated the shape of the Sussex Downs in his recurring arches.

and colleges needed them, because boys and girls were staying longer at school to get better qualifications, and because there were so many good jobs in industry that people chose industrial work instead of teaching.

The Rent Act   1957

The Conservatives kept up the average of 300,000 new houses a year, and gave far more permits for private building. But there were still people without homes and people living in houses which were old and unsuitable for modern life. The old houses should have been replaced, but since any home is better than none, they had to be kept in some sort of repair.

The government thought that rents should be allowed to go up. The reasons for this were, firstly, that the controlled rents made landlords unable to afford the essential repairs. Bad landlords made this an excuse for doing as little as possible, and let their property fall into a disgraceful condition, but even good landlords could not do what was needed. The second reason was that the government hoped that higher rents would ease the housing situation by making people take in lodgers, or move into smaller houses.

Therefore an Act was passed which freed from rent control houses which paid more than £40 a year in rates. It also said that new tenants moving in after the Act was law, could be charged any rent the landlord asked.

This last point led to 'Rachmanism'. Rachman was a London landlord who owned big, old houses which he let out in rooms to many families. His tenants were poor and their rents were controlled. Rachman (and many other landlords of the same kind) set to work to get rid of these tenants. He did this by such means as letting the stairs get into a filthy condition with overflowing garbage bins, or putting into some of the rooms tenants of bad character, or people who were paid by him to make life impossible for the other inhabitants. When he had driven out the tenants, he could put in new ones at uncontrolled prices.

The Elections of 1964 and 1966

In the general election of 1964 the Conservatives were defeated after being in power for thirteen years. Harold Wilson became Labour Prime Minister with a slender majority (5). In 1966 he held another election and was voted a substantial majority.

In the twenty years since the end of the Second World War great social changes have taken place. The Welfare State has been established and a generation is growing up which takes free medicine and free education for granted. But the continual rise in prices means that the benefits granted under this system are in many cases inadequate. Moreover all sections of the community are asking for more improvements, for example a better medical service and better schools.

Economists say we must bring industry up to date if we are to sell our goods at competitive prices. That means we must train more technicians and use the most modern machinery. Changes like this, however necessary, bring problems with them. We cannot carry out a programme of modernizing industry without this affecting the policy of both management and workers.

Find out from the papers how the government is dealing with the questions of the Health Service, education, and the organization of industry.

Dates to remember

1947 Coalmines and railways nationalized
1948 National Health Act passed
1951 Festival of Britain

Things to do

1 Make a list of all the schools in your area, infant, junior, and secondary. What plans has your Education Committee for re-organizing the Secondary Schools? Do you think there should be a choice in each area of mixed schools or single-sex schools?
2 Make a plan for an ideal new town, choosing the site, its industries, its arrangements for housing, shopping centres, schools, and entertainments.
3 Do you think buying goods on hire-purchase is a sensible way to save? What are the dangers of this method?

Books to read

A. Hancock and R. A. Robinson, *Our Society*, Longmans
A. Sillitoe, *The Loneliness of the Long Distance Runner*, W. H. Allen
Stephen King-Hall, *Our Times*, Faber
Geoffrey Smith, *News and Newspapers*, Johnston and Bacon

Chapter 7
The cold war

The Yalta Conference
The allies agree   1945

In February 1945 Churchill, Roosevelt, Stalin, and their advisers met in the glittering Livadia Palace in the Crimea, one of the most splendid of the residences which had belonged to the Tsars of Russia. They met to plan the post-war world, because, although fierce fighting was still going on, they knew by then that nothing could save the German army from destruction.

The victorious nations would have to deal with destroyed cities, and the likelihood of the outbreak of disease in areas of malnutrition and damaged water supplies. They would have to resettle in civilian life millions of people who had been torn from their homes as soldiers, or as forced labour in German factories. There was also the most important problem of what should be done with Germany, and of setting up governments in the countries which she had occupied and ruled.

It was a friendly meeting. When Churchill came back he reported to the House of Commons: 'The impression I brought back from the Crimea . . . is that Marshal Stalin and Soviet leaders wish to live in honourable friendship with the Western Democracies. I feel also that their word is their bond. I absolutely decline to embark here on a discussion of Russian good faith.' Cheers rose from both sides of the House. The speech seemed a good omen for the future. A few months later the press showed photographs of Russian and American soldiers shaking hands amidst the ruins of Berlin.

Yet two years after this the headlines of the papers would read, 'Britain's Firm Stand Against Russia', and 'Stalin's Proposals Rejected'.

The truth is that it was easy for the allies to agree whilst they shared the task of defeating Germany, but once this was accomplished their different interests and ideas for the future came into the open. The United States and Britain disliked communism and feared that it might spread in the devastated countries over which the war had been fought. They were alarmed at the strength of Russia which the war had revealed. Before the war they had not regarded Russia as a serious rival, and had smiled at the shabby clothing and poor housing of the Russian people, but now they knew that Russia was a great industrial power with a rising standard of living. Russia on her side was suspicious of the other allies, and alarmed by the American belief that communism was a wicked system which should be destroyed. Her allies had not

Allies for peace. American and Russian forces meet for the first time: 26 April 1945, in the German town of Torgau on the Elbe. Here, an American and a Russian soldier shake hands.

Communist countries
in Europe.

shared with Russia the secret of the atom bomb, and whilst America
had the monopoly of this weapon, she held the trump card.

The settlement of Eastern Europe

At the Yalta Conference all the allies had agreed that free elections
should be held in the Eastern European countries of Poland, Hungary,
Czechoslovakia, Romania, Bulgaria, Yugoslavia, and Albania, and
that all political parties except the fascist ones should be allowed to
put up candidates. All these nations except Yugoslavia had been
liberated from the Nazis by the Red Army, but, instead of holding
elections, Stalin gave them governments of his own choosing; these
were, of course, communist. Also, he moved Poland further west, by
taking eastern Poland into Russia and giving her the German province
of Silesia in exchange. We protested, but could do nothing to prevent
these actions. On the other hand, Britain intervened with soldiers in
Greece, overthrew a communist government there and restored the
Royal family. When Churchill had visited Stalin in 1945 they had agreed
that the Russian sphere of influence should be in the Balkans, and that
Britain should settle affairs in Greece. So Europe was divided into two
camps, the communist states of the east, and the western powers.

Germany

Germany was the most urgent problem. It is difficult to imagine the

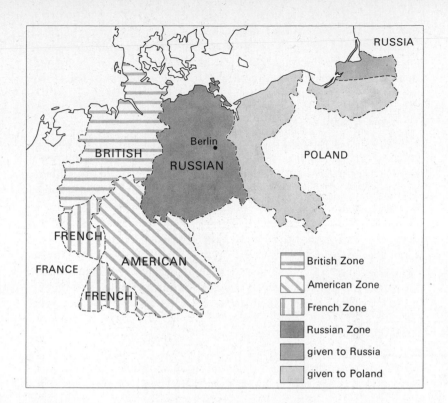

Berlin, 1945.

Germany and Poland, 1945

chaos and misery in that country. Towns, for example Hamburg and Cologne, had been flattened by bombing. Then refugees from Silesia came crowding in so that they could remain under a German government, and added to the numbers of people without jobs or shelter. The concentration camps were opened and the inmates of these, often in the last stages of starvation, had to be looked after, and if possible returned to their own countries. Many of the children in the camps had forgotten where they came from; they had lost their parents and did not remember their homes.

There was also the task of setting up a non-Nazi government, and of re-educating the children and young people, who had for twelve years been brought up on an unmixed diet of Nazi propaganda.

The allies divided Germany into four parts which you can see on the map, the British, American, Russian, and French Zones. You see that the capital city of Germany, Berlin, was in the middle of the Russian Zone. Bevin, the Foreign Secretary, carried out a policy of Anglo-American partnership, and it has been a continuing feature of our policy ever since. None of the allies was prepared to give up the prestige of having a share in the government of Berlin, so this unfortunate city was also divided into four parts, each governed by one of the allies.

Despite these arrangements for dividing our powers and responsibility, disagreements broke out amongst the four powers. It had been agreed at Yalta that Russia should have compensation from Germany in the form of machinery to make up for the destruction of her own industries by the Germans. But the three Western allies complained that Stalin took too much; they feared that they might have to support an impoverished Germany for a long time.

The Berlin Blockade   1948

It looked for a moment as if fighting might break out between the victors over the route through Russian-controlled territory to Berlin. In 1948 the three Western zones of Germany agreed on the issue of a new currency. The Russians objected to the currency reform, which had been made without consulting them, and as a counter action they refused to allow any traffic to come in from the west either by road or by rail. This meant that the western sectors of Berlin were isolated. What was to be done? If we did nothing Berlin would have to buy everything from the east and would fall completely under Russian influence. An American general suggested using troops to force open the road and rail route; if he had had his way, war might have broken out.

We found a third way. We and the Americans mounted a gigantic air-lift. Every plane we could find was used, and the huge city had everything that she needed for life and industry flown into her. Planes came into her airfields at the rate of more than one a minute. After

Berlin air-lift. Transport plane.

Vienna, 1961. President Kennedy of the United States (left) meeting Premier Khrushchev of the Soviet Union

The 'Thaw'

The cold war became less icy because Khrushchev argued that it was possible for states with different forms of government to live peacefully together. He called this 'co-existence'. He also promised an easier time to the Russian people; his policy was to provide more 'consumer goods' such as television sets and cars. People of the East and West began to meet one another; Russian sportsmen, scientists, artists and trade unionists visited this country, and invited their opposite numbers to the Soviet Union. Books which the Russians had not before been allowed to read began to appear in the shops. People spoke of this change as 'The Thaw'.

Khrushchev wanted the leaders of the great powers to meet and discuss their differences, and in 1954 representatives from America, France, Great Britain and Russia met to discuss the German question. There turned out to be no agreement on how Germany could be united, but at least the leaders had discussed the matter, instead of shaking their fists at one another.

The following year they met again, and this time the final peace treaty with Austria was settled.

Khrushchev's speech to the Communist Party 1956

In a speech to the conference of the Communist Party, Khrushchev told much of the truth about the tyranny of Stalin. He explained that

Stalin had got all power into his own hands through the control of the secret police, so that he could have anyone he chose arrested, and no one dared resist. Devoted communists who had given all their lives to Russia and the revolution had been accused of such unlikely crimes as spying for the enemy, and had pressure put upon them until they confessed their guilt. The communists learnt with horror how they had been deluded.

The streets and towns which had been named after Stalin were renamed, and his portraits were removed, but his crimes will not be quickly forgotten.

It would be interesting to know what the history books will say about Stalin in fifty years' time. They may think it important that his cruel, but efficient, rule built the armies which resisted the Nazis. They may say that an ignorant, backward people, such as the Russians were in 1917, cannot manage a democratic government. They may point out that his repressive system discredited communism in the eyes of many people who were prepared to be sympathetic towards it.

Attempt at revolution in Hungary   1956

This was the most terrible event of the cold war period.

In October 1956 the Writers' Association and students of Budapest (the capital city of Hungary) organized a march to demonstrate for 'an independent Socialist Hungary'. This was a daring thing to do, for Hungary also had its ruthless secret police. Nevertheless huge crowds gathered to support the march. When they passed a barracks the marchers called 'Long live the Hungarian Army. Soldiers, join us!' The windows of the barracks opened, and the soldiers threw out small objects on to the street; these were the Soviet badges from their uniforms, and when the marchers realized this, they burst into delighted cheers.

Every citizen of Budapest seemed to be in the street, cheering and singing Hungarian songs, and on an impulse the crowd surged to the twenty-foot statue of Stalin which dominated one of the parks. Ropes were wound round its neck and the people tried to topple it, but it would not budge. Then someone brought welding torches and they melted its knees until the statue crashed to the ground, leaving only the jagged stumps of boots sticking up from the concrete base. The people swarmed on to the prostrate figure with any tool they could find and hacked it into little pieces for souvenirs.

A committee drew up a list of sixteen points which they were going to ask of the government; it included demands that the Russian troops should leave the country and that the secret police should be disbanded. They also wanted more freedom of speech and less rigid control of the economy. The students marched to the radio station to have their sixteen points broadcast. A few of them were allowed in to discuss the matter, and the doors were locked behind them. The rest of the crowd waited anxiously outside – because it was known that many

Fall of the mighty Stalin. From a *Punch* cartoon.

secret police were in the building, and these men did not hesitate at murder. Finally a Hungarian army officer went and knocked and kicked at the door of the radio station. A shot was fired from somewhere and he fell down dead. It was thought that a member of the secret police had done it.

After that there was civil war in the beautiful city of Budapest. The Hungarian people killed the secret police by throwing them from windows or hanging them from lamp-posts, and the factory workers made grenades to knock out Russian tanks. At first the Russian troops withdrew and it looked as if Hungary had won its freedom, but the Russians were alarmed because of the danger that America would use a 'free' Hungary as a base for operations against communism. The Russian troops returned and the revolution was suppressed. Nothing was *quite* the same afterwards; the Russian yoke was not so heavy, and

Civil war in Hungary. Hungarians chip off pieces from the statue of Stalin for mementoes.

On 4 November 1956, at four in the morning, just when the Hungarians thought they had won the revolution, Soviet tanks moved into Budapest. Within a few days, Hungarian resistance had been silenced.

an increasing amount of independence and criticism has been allowed in Russia's 'satellite' states.

The crisis in Hungary showed the dangers of the cold war. Russia had sent in tanks because she feared the West would seize the opportunity to restore a capitalist pro-West government in that country. Some Hungarians who escaped over the border blamed the western powers for not having come to their help. At that time Britain and France were occupied with the Suez crisis which you will read about in Chapter 9, and they did not attempt any armed intervention in Hungary. The uneasy relationship between East and West continued.

Disarmament

Was it necessary for every country to be on one side or the other? Some of them, like Sweden and Switzerland in Europe, and India in Asia, called themselves the 'non-aligned' countries. They remained neutral.

Both parties in England, Conservatives and Labour, rejected this idea. They said that no nation would have any influence at a conference unless it had force behind it, and that the only way to keep the peace was to possess the nuclear bomb, and that fear of the bomb's being used would deter any nation from beginning a war. The word 'deterrent' was used. Only, if we had this deterrent, it was argued, could we be safe.

Scientists became increasingly concerned about this state of affairs. When in 1952 Great Britain tested a bomb in the Pacific, there were protests that the polluted air would cause damage to human beings. It had been found that in Japan, the children of those who had been subjected to radiation were in some cases deformed or mentally retarded. Tests meant that more and more strontium 90 would be present in the air, and it was impossible to reckon what damage this might do to future generations. What would happen if all the other countries began to make bombs? These were the questions which were debated at scientific meetings.

A new campaign 1958

On 16 January 1958 a group of distinguished people met at the house of Canon Collins to found a movement, which they called the Campaign for Nuclear Disarmament, or C.N.D. for short. They wanted Britain to abandon the use of atomic bombs, and to give up the bases which had been leased to the Americans; they did not want to wait until all the states had agreed to destroy the piles of bombs; they said Britain should do it alone. This is called 'Unilateral Disarmament'. A badge was chosen and methods of getting the message across to people were discussed.

A surprising number of people became interested in this new movement. At Easter a march to Aldermaston in Berkshire was organized. Aldermaston was a centre of research for atomic weapons. The march lasted four days and caused considerable interest to the holiday crowds. The following years the march was repeated, from Aldermaston to Trafalgar Square. Bus-loads of young people came up from the North and Midlands to join in. On they tramped, undismayed one year by torrential weather. They carried banners, shouted slogans. There were bands and songs. The majority of the marchers were young, but the middle-aged, even the elderly, also appeared. They slept on the hard floors of schools and church halls. Tired and footsore they gathered in Trafalgar Square for a final meeting.

The campaigners did not succeed in converting either of the political parties to their point of view. They did succeed in bringing the subject

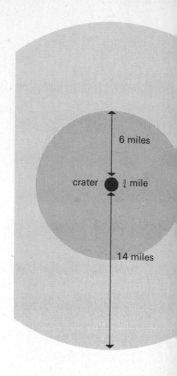

6 miles

crater $\frac{3}{4}$ mile

14 miles

Aldermaston, 1963. The marchers start in good order at the beginning of a four-day hike.

Effects of the explosion of a twenty-megaton nuclear bomb. 6 miles radius from the crater: almost everyone killed. 14 miles radius: most people seriously injured. 'Fall out': the explosion would throw out masses of radio-active dust, which would bring illness or death wherever the wind carried it.

Members of the Committee of One Hundred planned to stage a demonstration outside the House of Commons in April 1961. Police in Whitehall prevented them from getting to Westminster.

to the attention of many persons who might otherwise not have thought about it. They could not be contemptuously dismissed as irresponsible young people. After all, it was not so easy to give up the Easter holiday for a strenuous march. Later some of them grew tired of the slow growth of opinion, and they began what they called 'direct action'. They sat down on the pavements and waited to be dragged away by the police. They tried to enter some of the military bases and deliberately broke the law. This was reminiscent of the tactics of the suffragettes. The main body of the campaigners did not agree with this direct action.

The arguments put forward by C.N.D. were:

1 There is no possibility of safeguarding our people if a bomb is dropped. There would be immediate retaliation.

2 To have bases in this country increases our peril, because if either Russia or America started a war, the first thing they would do would be to attack those bases.

3 The continued manufacture and testing of bombs is a serious threat to the future of the race.

Those who disagreed with them argued:

1 When two powerful countries both have nuclear weapons, the peace of the world is not endangered because neither of them would want to face annihilation.

2 Supposing the attack to come from the East (i.e., Russia), it is imperative that we should be able to strike back from this island.

It is up to the people of this country to decide what is the best means of maintaining peace. What do you think about it? Do we spend too much on armaments?

The Cuba crisis

Cuba is a little island in the Caribbean, not far from the coast of the United States. Like most South American states, it has had a turbulent history, and in 1959 the unpopular dictator, Batista, was overthrown by the handsome, bearded young lawyer, Fidel Castro, who had organized a guerilla army in the mountains. The Cubans set up a socialist government, which the Russians welcomed with an enthusiasm which alarmed the United States.

Many anti-Castro Cubans fled to Florida, where the American government helped them and allowed them to drill and train an army. The exiled Cubans were quite sure that if they landed in Cuba they would be welcomed with open arms by their countrymen, whom they pictured as groaning under the heel of Castro.

In 1961, when they landed at the Bay of Pigs, they had a rude awakening. There was no sign that the Cuban people wanted to be 'liberated'. The invaders were met by a well-equipped army and driven back with ease. But they said that they meant to try again.

In the following year, it was rumoured that Russia was supplying Cuba with arms. Khrushchev denied this. Then the Americans took aerial photographs of Cuba which showed concrete installations for launching rocket weapons. Now the Americans were certain that their cities lay within range of communist-controlled rockets which could be used to carry atomic warheads.

There was some panic in America, and grave anxiety throughout the world. If America bombed Cuba, would the Russians support their ally by bombing America? If they did, World War III would have begun.

Fortunately for everybody the two statesmen most concerned were responsible and sensible. The young American President Kennedy, whose election had been welcomed all over the world, proved that he could act in a statesmanlike manner. He and Khrushchev agreed to a compromise by which Russia undertook to dismantle the launching sites in Cuba and America agreed to withdraw warships from Cuban waters. What is more, Kennedy and Khrushchev agreed to have a special telephone connexion between the White House and the Kremlin so that if there was in the future any sudden scare which might lead to war, they could immediately get in touch with each other to sort things out. This is called the 'hot line' and its existence probably makes us all much safer.

So far as America and Russia are concerned we may hope that the worst days of the cold war are over. There are other threats to peace, and at present there is fighting in south-east Asia.

Fidel Castro, the Cuban leader, addressing a meeting.

The position of Cuba.

Dates to remember

1948   The Berlin Air-lift
1949   First Russian atom bomb
        N.A.T.O. formed
1950   Korean War broke out
1953   Death of Stalin
1956   Hungarian uprising
1961   Attempted invasion of Cuba by Cuban exiles

Things to do

1   Make a list of the heads of government in all the countries of Europe at the present day.
2   What do we mean when we talk of 'trouble spots'? In what parts of the world do we find them today?
3   Can you think of any countries in the world, where people of different races, religions and languages live together peaceably?

Books to read

H. Courlander, *Shaping our Times*, Oceana Paperback
Bernard Moore, *The Second Lesson*, Macmillan
Frances Wilkins, *President Kennedy*, Cassell

Chapter 8
India and Nigeria achieve independence

During this century the 'Empire upon which the sun never sets' became the British Commonwealth of Nations. At the height of our imperial power, Cecil Rhodes, the pioneer who founded the colony of Rhodesia, said 'We are the best race in the world, and the more of the world we inhabit the better.' That kind of language was possible then, for our Empire was based on the strength of our arms and money, and we were proud and sometimes boastful. But the Commonwealth is an association of free and equal nations, held together only by friendship, a shared history and common ideas.

The map on pages 158–9 shows the British Empire in 1939, from which the Commonwealth developed.

The 'White Dominions'

The Commonwealth countries that are best known to us are the 'White Dominions', because these have been colonized chiefly by British people and are in many ways very like Great Britain. Most of us know people who have gone there, and some of you may hope to go overseas to one of them. These are Canada, Australia and New Zealand. We shall not need to say much about them, for during the last sixty years their history has been an uneventful story of steady progress. They have their problems, like all countries, but nevertheless they are rich, happy and successful.

By 1914 they were self-governing in their home affairs, but we still acted for them in their relationship with other countries. So, when we declared war on Germany in 1914, all the Dominions became at war with her at the same time. Canada lost 50,000 men in this war, and the Australians and New Zealanders also lost very heavily. They supported us willingly, but they were determined that in future they would decide for themselves whether they declared war.

Therefore, in 1926, at one of the Conferences of Prime Ministers of the Commonwealth, it was agreed that they should be completely independent in foreign affairs also.

When the Second World War broke out they acted upon this decision. Canada, for instance, did not declare war on Germany until a week after we had done so. Eire, which had the position of a Dominion, remained neutral all through the war; this neutrality cost us ships and lives by preventing us from having anti-submarine bases in Irish ports.

Meeting on equal terms to discuss common problems: Mr Wilson among the ministers at the Commonwealth Prime Ministers' Conference in London, 1965.

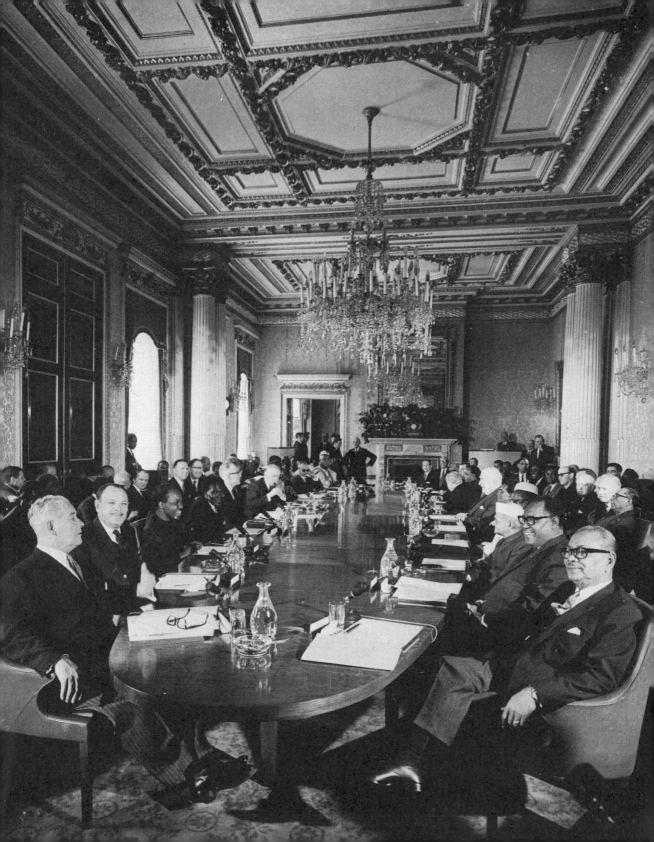

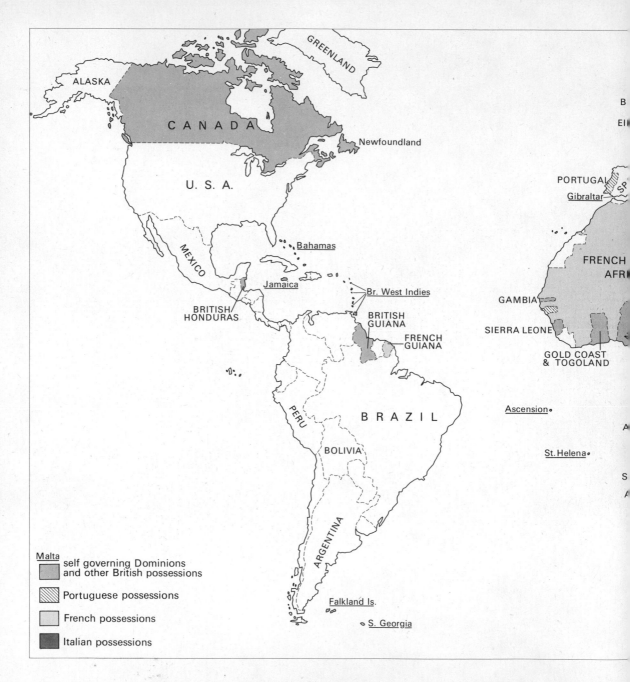

self governing Dominions
and other British possessions

Portuguese possessions

French possessions

Italian possessions

By the Statute of Westminster 1931 the 'White Dominions' were legally established as free and equal states. Their only bond with us now is their goodwill towards us, and the acceptance by most of them of our Sovereign as their Queen. The Queen appoints a Governor-General to represent her in each of the Dominions, but he has no more political power than the Queen herself has in this country.

Empires of the western powers, 1939.

158

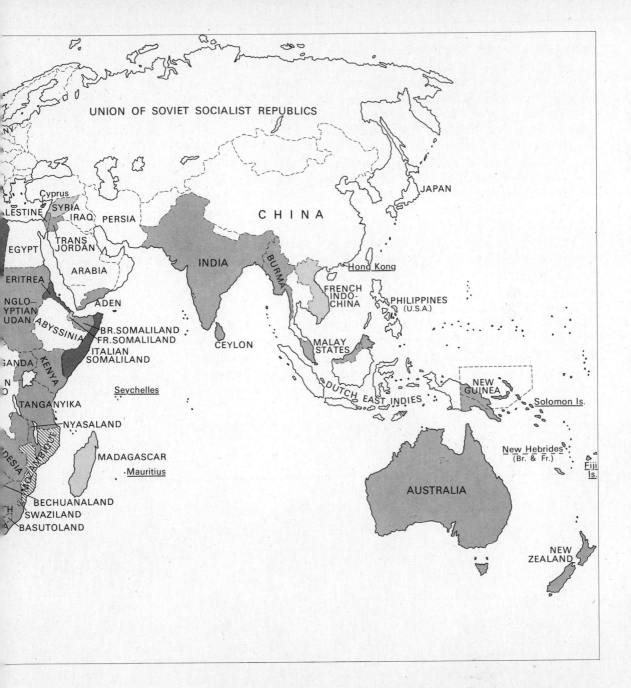

In this book we cannot write about all the Commonwealth, so we have chosen four countries, each of them important in a different way, and we shall tell the history of these countries during the present century. You may like to find out about some of the others on your own. The four we have chosen are India, Nigeria, the Union of South Africa and Ireland.

India

India, with its 400,000,000 inhabitants, was the largest and most splendid part of the British Empire. You may have read in *A History of Britain* SH4 about its teeming population, its rich history of civilization and religion, its great wealth and appalling poverty.

When the story of this volume begins, in 1901, the Indians were already demanding 'Swaraj' – the government of India by the Indians. In theory we were prepared to grant this, but, as always happens in this kind of situation, the Indians wanted self-government at once, whilst we thought that they were not ready for it, and that it should be granted in the future.

The Indians supported us in World War I, and sent some magnificent regiments to fight beside us; but they demanded at the same time that we should recognize their right to freedom and equality and that we should therefore give them self-government. In 1917 we promised to do this, but without saying anything about the exact date at which we would hand over power.

In 1919 we passed an Act which gave the vote to all Indian men and women who owned a certain amount of property, and which gave to Indian ministers in the provinces authority over such things as health and education. But all the powers of the central government remained in the hands of the British, and even in the provinces, finance remained in the hands of the governors whom we appointed. The

The wealth and splendour of Indian princes before independence. Now they have lost their political power, but many are still rich.

Indians bitterly pointed out that, since everything a government does costs money, they really had no power even in the provincial governments.

Nevertheless, this Act was a step forward, and the Indians might have been satisfied with it for the time being, if it had not been for the Amritsar massacre in 1919. Four Europeans had been murdered in Amritsar; the British army officers were angry and tense, and Dyer, the general in command, made the 'crawling order' by which Indians had to go on hands and knees past the place in the street where an English woman had been killed. Then an unarmed crowd collected in an enclosed garden in the town, and did not disperse when it was ordered to do so; Brigadier-General Dyer ordered his soldiers to fire on it, and they fired steadily for ten minutes, whilst the screaming, panic-stricken people struggled to get out through the narrow outlets. Some were trampled to death, others were killed by bullets; altogether 379 were killed and 1208 wounded.

The Amritsar affair enraged the Indians, and made them determined that they would not endure the humiliation of government by the British any longer. They agitated and organized to throw off our authority, and their most important leader in this struggle was the saintly Hindu, Mahatma Gandhi.

Gandhi was a member of a prosperous family. He was sent to England to be educated as a lawyer, and could if he had cared have led a very

The starving poor of India beg for food. Many live in the streets, eating, sleeping and dying on a patch of pavement which is their only home.

comfortable life; but he was more interested in the welfare of the oppressed and the future of India than in his own comfort. He was influenced by the Jains, a sect of the Hindus who believe that it is wrong to take any life or to do violence to any living thing. He thought therefore that political rights must be won without killing, wounding, or causing suffering, and that people had the right not only to life, but also to a good and happy life, and that we are all responsible for one another's happiness. He thought that it was wrong to feast whilst others were hungry, or to wear fine clothes whilst the poor of India had only a few rags with which to cover themselves. He lived according to his beliefs; in order not to destroy animal life, he was a vegetarian; in order not to enjoy luxuries which his fellow-countrymen could not afford, he always travelled third class on the railways, which in India means on unupholstered, wooden seats. He wore the cheapest iron-rimmed spectacles, and when his own teeth came out, he refused to have false ones. He would not drink tea, because he counted it as a 'stimulating' drink. He was a small thin, stooping man, with large, prominent ears, not an impressive figure to look at, and he was a very shy man, a bad speaker. Yet devotion and determination enabled him to play a leading part in the Indian movement against the evils of 'caste', and in the struggle to turn the British out of India.

The Hindu religion has many fine ideas, but it has brought with it the miserable caste system. Caste destroys human communication and happiness. Not only can people only marry within their own caste; the food they can eat and the way it shall be cooked, the places where they may go, the work they may do, the friends they may have, are all of them limited by caste. There are thousands of castes dividing the people of India from one another.

Indian reformers for a long time have argued that caste is not a proper and necessary part of the Hindu religion, but ordinary people could not easily escape from the prejudices and strict caste rules of their families.

Gandhi thought that the way to begin the battle against caste was to defy its rules himself and associate with the 'Untouchables', the members of the lowest rank, below all the castes, condemned to be despised and to do only the poorest kinds of work. He talked and ate with these people, and urged other high caste Hindus to do the same. He joined even in the humblest of tasks, digging and cleaning latrines, to show that even the lowest and dirtiest work is good, and that the people who do it have the right to full human dignity. Many of his family were horrified at this, and his sister was upset because no one would marry her on account of the disgrace. But many agreed with Gandhi and joined with him in associating with 'Untouchables'.

He planned to break down British rule in India without the use of arms and violence, and he maintained that it could be done by arranging for the Indian people to refuse to obey or help the British. This method was called 'passive resistance', or 'non-cooperation'.

A Brahmin, with the marks of his caste on his forehead.

Gandhi at his spinning-wheel
in Calcutta, 1925.

Indian civil servants were persuaded to leave their jobs, and Indians refused to use or buy things made in Britain or with British machinery. Gandhi would not wear factory spun and woven material but instead wore cloth made on an Indian hand-loom, such as the villagers used. He would appear at important meetings, at which everybody was conventionally and smartly dressed, in a homespun loincloth, carrying a homespun bag for his writing materials, and perhaps a few nuts and a little fruit for a meal. Many people laughed at him, but more admired and followed him.

The most important form of non-cooperation was the non-payment of taxes. One tax was the salt tax; the government made salt a government monopoly, so that people were forbidden to collect or buy and sell it on their own, and then put a tax on it. In order to avoid paying this tax Gandhi organized a 200 mile march across India to salt pans on the coast, where his followers collected salt in defiance of the law. On one occasion mounted cavalry charged the marchers, who did not run away, but lay on the ground. On another occasion, when a police car charged and machine-gunned them, seventy people were killed.

When the non-cooperators were arrested, they did not resist; if they were beaten, they did not even raise their arms to ward off the blows. Thousands were put in prison for civil disobedience, but there were always thousands more to take their place.

Sometimes, despite Gandhi's teaching, violence broke out between the non-cooperators and the police. This distressed him very much, and he undertook fasts of penitence. This may not at first sight seem a very useful thing to have done, but Indians learnt with shame and sorrow of these fasts and because of them studied non-violent methods of defying the government more earnestly.

The India Act of 1935 planned a 'Federal India'; this meant an India made up of a number of self-governing states, linked together by a central government. It was the last stage before complete independence, and under it the state governments were to be run entirely by elected Indian ministers.

The way Indians received this Act showed that we could not govern them any longer. There were disagreements and conflicts between different sections of the people and we were no longer strong enough to deal with these conflicts.

If you look at the map you will see that of the provinces of India which we governed ourselves, some were inhabited chiefly by Hindus and some chiefly by Moslems. There were also provinces of India which we did not govern directly, but which were governed by a number of Indian princes with our consent. Of these three sections, only the Hindus agreed to accept the Act and governed their provinces under it. The Moslems refused to accept it because they thought that under it the 'Congress Party', which was mainly Hindu, would have too much power, and the princes refused because they thought their position would be weaker under it.

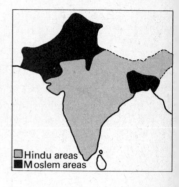

Hindu areas
Moslem areas

The only thing for it was for us to go, and leave the Indians to work out their own problems.

Independence for India and Pakistan   15 August 1947

India and Pakistan received their independence at midnight on 14/15 August 1947.

On that day a huge crowd saw the new flag of India unfurled. The wheel in the flag is 'Asoka's Wheel', the Buddhist sign of tolerance. The crowd greeted it, and their new Prime Minister with the cry 'Jai Hind', which means 'Victory to India'. Their new Prime Minister, Jawaharlal Nehru, made a speech which included these words:

Indian independence flag, showing Asoka's wheel.

At the stroke of midnight, when the world sleeps, India will wake to life and freedom. A moment comes, which comes but rarely in history, when we step out from the old to the new, when an age ends, when the soul of a nation, long suppressed, finds utterance. It is fitting that at this solemn moment we take a pledge of dedication to the service of India and her people, and to the still larger cause of humanity.

He went on to speak of Gandhi, saying:

The ambition of the greatest man of our generation has been to wipe every tear from every eye. That may be beyond us, but so long as there are tears and suffering, so long our work will not be over.

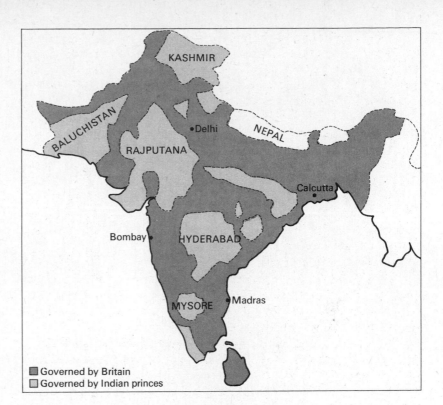

Before independence, India was governed partly by Britain, and partly by Indian princes who had treaties with Britain.

Nehru, a schoolboy at Harrow in 1906.

Jawaharlal Nehru, Prime Minister of India   1947–64

Nehru was to govern India until his death in 1964, and was one of the most admired men of his age.

He had been chosen and trained by Gandhi to be the leader of free India, a strange choice you may think, for Nehru was a wealthy aristocrat, always elegantly dressed, who had been expensively educated at Harrow and Cambridge. His manner when he was young had some of the coldness and insolence which comes from a feeling of superiority, but Gandhi saw behind this a personality which had imagination, sympathy with others, and courage. He and Gandhi worked together with mutual respect and admiration, although Gandhi was deeply religious, and Nehru had no religious beliefs and was attracted to modern ideas about science and progress.

During his struggle for the freedom of India, Nehru had spent nineteen years in British prisons, but the 'Wheel of Tolerance' expressed his own character, for he did not resent these lost years, and remained friendly with the English government and with many Englishmen. It was largely because of his influence that India decided to remain in the Commonwealth, although India, like Pakistan, refused to accept the monarchy and became a Republic.

India and Pakistan become separate states   1947

Tolerance was indeed needed in India. After independence the old

165

conflict between Moslems and Hindus broke out with terrible ferocity in Delhi and the Punjab. Moslems and Hindus were each terrified of being under the rule of the other, so that Moslems fled from Hindu states, and Hindus from Moslem states. In some cases their fears were justified, for in a few places there were horrible massacres of minorities, as happened near this Moslem academy which was in an area which had a Hindu majority:

In August 1947, it found itself engulfed in a sea of angry Hindus and Sikhs to whom everything Moslem, whether man or building, was hateful. All night the teachers and students stood guard, expecting an assault. All lights were out. In a circle around them they could see Moslem villages in flames and Moslem homes burning like torches. Near by is the Jumna river. Night after night they could hear Moslems jumping into the river to escape their pursuers. But the pursuers would jump in after them, and then there was a scuffle and a splash and the victim would be held down till he drowned or gave one last, anguished scream as the knife cut his throat.

When Gandhi and Nehru heard of the danger that threatened the academy they went out and visited it, and after that no-one would have harmed its inmates. But they could not be everywhere. Gandhi went from street to street in the city of Calcutta, pleading for mercy and peace, and he saved this great city from bloodshed.

The struggle was like a desperate surgical operation in which Moslem

East Bengal, 1947. Families fled from their homes as a result of riots between the Moslems and Hindus. These people are waiting for a ferry to take them across a river to safety; they have with them their most precious possessions, which include a musical instrument and a gun.

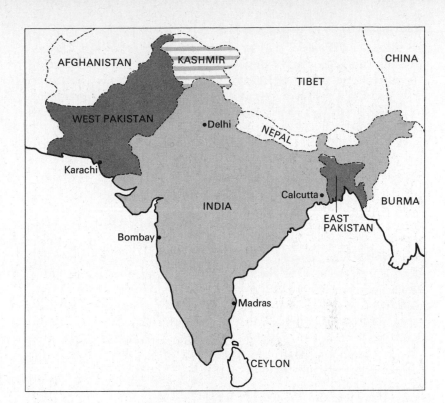

After independence, the states of India and Pakistan were created. Pakistan, divided into two widely separated parts, is difficult to govern.

India was amputated from Hindu India. Three hundred thousand people were killed, or died in the pestilence which followed the fighting, and 14,000,000 people fled to find safety in another state, the largest movement of people that has ever happened.

In the end the dispute was taken to the United Nations, and boundaries for Pakistan and India were agreed, except over the position of Kashmir. You can see from the map how they were divided, and how awkward it must be to govern Pakistan.

The tasks of independent India

Land reform

Nehru believed that the land should belong to the farmers who worked it, and therefore set to work to abolish the big estates, owned many of them by landlords who extorted rents, but did not even live on their land. Acts of Parliament were passed to break up these estates into medium sized farms of less than 30 acres. The government helped the new farms to become prosperous by lending money for such things as irrigation canals, a new pair of bullocks, or a barn.

Five-year plans

Nehru was a socialist who thought that he could learn much from Russia, and, like Russia, India is organizing to increase her production

167

by a series of 'five-year-plans'. The first plan aimed to improve agriculture and increase the food supply, and the second plan concentrated on engineering and industry. Other plans followed, each aiming to improve some aspect of Indian life. Many new factories have been set up and India produces much more than she did, but her population is increasing very quickly, two per cent each year, which is four times as fast as the increase of population in Great Britain. The result is that, even if production of goods increases very rapidly, Indians remain as poor as before, because there are more mouths to feed and bodies to clothe.

Abolition of 'Untouchability'

When India became independent there were 60,000,000 'Untouchables', more than the whole population of Great Britain. Now there are none, for a law has been passed making untouchability illegal. It is a criminal offence to refuse to serve them at a public eating place, or to forbid them to use a public well. They are given grants and scholarships to enable them to get better jobs, and in every government there is at least one 'Untouchable' minister. All the social disadvantages of low caste cannot be abolished immediately by passing laws, but the laws are a necessary beginning, and once untouchability is really abolished, the whole caste system will collapse.

India, Pakistan and the world   1947–64

Nehru became one of the most influential statesmen in the world. When

A primitive method of threshing wheat. These Indian farmers beat it with flails to separate the grains from the husks.

any crisis blew up in international affairs, one of the first questions people asked was, 'What will Nehru do?' This was largely because he refused to take part in the cold war (of which you read in Chapter 7). He was a socialist and sympathized with Russia, but he was not a communist, and believed in our kind of elections and democracy. So he remained friendly with both sides, although the Americans were angry with him for buying Russian fighter planes and for allowing Russia to supply India with atomic power stations.

Pakistan was at the time of partition much more pro-American than India. She joined the South-East Asia Treaty Organization, an alliance which America set up to oppose communist interests in the Indian Ocean area. As a member of this alliance Pakistan is helped with money and arms by America.

India's policy was for peace; she did not believe in war, and she needed all her money and energy for reforms at home. So it was a disaster for her and for the world when war broke out between her and China over the boundaries in Ladakh and Assam on her northern borders. In a short war China showed her greater military strength and took some of the disputed territory with ease. Will this drive India also to take part in world-wide military alliances, to spend her money on arms? Will it mean that she will no longer be the leader of a number of nations who dislike the cold war and will take sides with neither Russia nor America? What is going to be the effect on her future and ours of China becoming a great military power? How will the dispute between India and Pakistan over the state of Kashmir be settled?

Modern India. This up-to-date nuclear power station near Bombay was completed, with Canadian help, in 1960.

Africa

If you look at the map on page 171 you can see how vast Africa is. The maps we usually use make the countries at the equator look much smaller than they really are. Africa is as big as the United States of America, Western Europe, India and China put together. She adds up to one fifth of the earth's land surface. Huge expanses of this land are sun-baked desert, but it also includes some of the most fertile areas of the world; almost every known crop can be grown somewhere in Africa, and every mineral lies under her ground.

Two hundred million people live in Africa. They range in physique from the pale Moors and Egyptians of the north to the dark negroes of the Transkei. They are divided into many nations and tribes, and they speak more than seven hundred languages. In 1960 only one in ten of the African people could read or write, and one of the many jobs of the new African states is arranging for every child to receive education;

Right: Liberation of Africa, 1945–64. Enormous areas have recently become independent of the old European empires. Have any other African countries become free since this book was written?

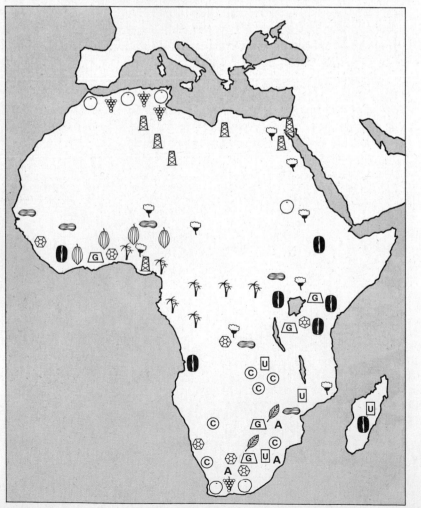

A	asbestos
ⓒ	copper
⬡	diamonds
G	gold
⛏	oil
U	uranium

◯	citrus fruits
	cocoa
	coffee
	cotton
	grapes
	groundnuts
	palm oil
	tobacco

The wealth of Africa.

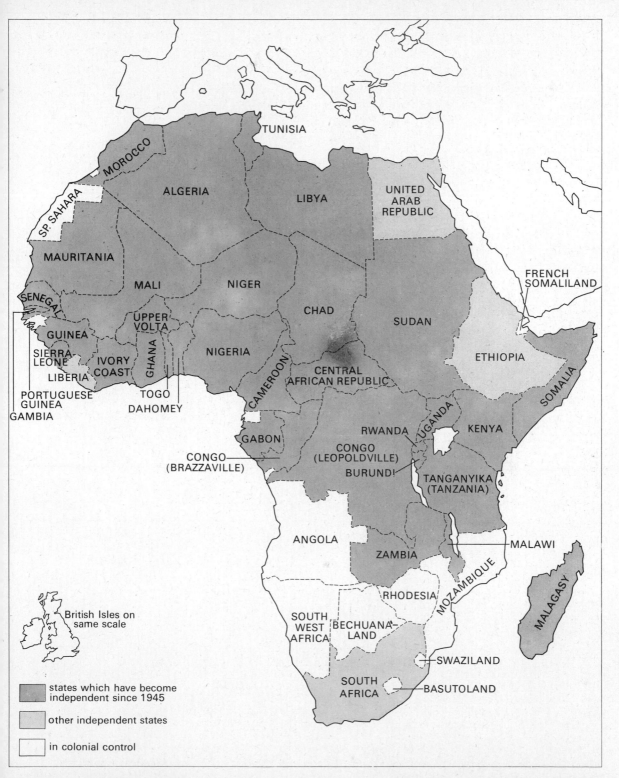

TUNISIA

MOROCCO

SP. SAHARA

ALGERIA

LIBYA

UNITED
ARAB
REPUBLIC

MAURITANIA

FRENCH
SOMALILAND

MALI

NIGER

CHAD

SUDAN

SENEGAL

GUINEA

UPPER
VOLTA

SIERRA-
LEONE

IVORY
COAST

GHANA

NIGERIA

ETHIOPIA

LIBERIA

PORTUGUESE
GUINEA

TOGO

DAHOMEY

CAMEROON

CENTRAL
AFRICAN REPUBLIC

SOMALIA

GAMBIA

GABON

RWANDA

UGANDA

KENYA

CONGO
(BRAZZAVILLE)

CONGO
(LEOPOLDVILLE)

BURUNDI

TANGANYIKA
(TANZANIA)

ANGOLA

ZAMBIA

MALAWI

MOZAMBIQUE

MALAGASY

RHODESIA

SOUTH
WEST
AFRICA

BECHUANA-
LAND

SWAZILAND

SOUTH
AFRICA

BASUTOLAND

British Isles on
same scale

states which have become
independent since 1945

other independent states

in colonial control

and they are helped by the fact that the Africans know that education is necessary for civilized life, and are eager to learn. African children will walk five miles each way to school every day, and be thankful that there is a school to which they can go.

Each part of Africa has its own, different history. Here we have space to write about only two parts of the continent, and we have chosen Nigeria and the Union of South Africa, which are both of them large and powerful states, important in the history of Africa and in the history of Great Britain.

Nigeria

Nigeria is the largest of the negro nations, exciting, interesting, and with an important future. You can see from the map and the pictures that she stretches from the wet coast of the rain forests to the open dry deserts on the edge of the Sahara. There are three main parts of Nigeria, the North of white robed Moslem cattle herdsmen, the East of the Ibo people, who produce palm oil, and the West, the land of the Yoruba cocoa farmers. Altogether more than 50,000,000 people live in Nigeria.

At the end of the nineteenth century the European countries became interested in building empires for themselves in tropical Africa and agreed to share up the continent. Nigeria became part of our share. At first we did not try to govern it, but let a private, profit-making

Yams for sale in Eastern Nigeria.

The tall, long-horned cattle of Northern Nigeria.

Nigeria, composed of three main regions. The Eastern and Western regions cut off the Moslem North from the sea.

172

company, the Royal Niger Company, do the job. The Company was allowed to have a private army to keep order and could make laws and punish those who broke them. This was not very satisfactory, because we were really responsible for what happened, and in 1900 the British government took over from the Royal Niger Company, and trained and sent out civil servants to run the colony.

Above left: Pounding yams to pulp before cooking them.
Above right: Weaving, on a handloom.

Lord Lugard conquers Northern Nigeria   1900–6
Much of our new lands had to be conquered before we could govern them, and one of the greatest of our colonial servants, Lord Lugard, defeated the people of Northern Nigeria. He only had 120 European officers and N.C.O.s, commanding two or three thousand Africans and only five civil servants to help him rule the territory. But with his tiny army, armed with modern weapons, he won victory after victory. He realized that a few men standing in close formation, and firing to order, could mow down vast numbers of horse and camel riders. It was a tricky business, for if he had made a single serious mistake his entire army could have been wiped out. But he never made the mistake and the Emirs of Northern Nigeria became our subjects.

How could Lugard govern a country bigger than England with five civil servants? And not only was the country large; it had no roads, railways, telegraphs; the people in different parts had different ways and ideas, and many of them were hostile to the foreign conquerors. Lord Lugard decided that the only thing he could do was to let the local rulers, chiefs or councils of elders, carry on. The British government would support them, but would insist on certain British laws being adopted, such as the law forbidding slavery. This method of government is called 'indirect rule'.

The provinces of Nigeria united 1914

In 1914 Lord Lugard joined the provinces of Nigeria under a single government, and all of them, from the autocratic emirates of the north to the humble agricultural villages of Eastern Nigeria were ruled by us, indirectly, through local authorities. Lord Lugard had understood that if indirect rule was to be successful we must use the kind of authority the African people of each area had set up and were used to. But the British officials who followed him thought that African people had chiefs, and if they did not have chiefs, they ought to have them; therefore, when the British came upon tribes which were governed by councils of elders, they appointed chiefs, who were called 'Warrant Chiefs' because they held their power by a warrant of the British government. This, as you might expect, was not a success. The elders of the traditional councils disliked having their powers taken from them, and since the people thought of the British government almost entirely as a body which collected taxes from them, they hated the Warrant Chiefs as stooges of the British. The 'Women's War' finally taught us our mistake.

A beggar-boy with a drum to attract the attention of passers-by.

The Women's War 1929

Things were difficult in Nigeria in 1929, as in the rest of the world; the price of palm oil had dropped as a result of the slump, and the villages had become poorer. When a Warrant Chief began to count women, children and animals in his area, the rumour went round that women were to be taxed, and this caused furious indignation.

If the British officers had been ruling through trusted African councillors, they would have known what was going on and the trouble could have been stopped. But the Warrant Chiefs did not know themselves what was happening, so they could not tell us. The British officials in Nigeria were called 'District Officers', and in one place a young District Officer, just out from England, was sent by his senior to a village court-house on business. He arrived to find shouting crowds milling round the huts, and they behaved to him with an insolence which frightened him. He went back to his senior and said that he thought there was serious disorder brewing. The senior District Officer said that he knew the country – it was just a little good-natured noise and meant nothing; the young man was to go back and get on with the job. He went back, but he did not get on with the job. In the meantime the men had got out the long knives they use for cutting grass, and when they saw him they rushed towards him, waving the knives in the air. He turned and fled; some of them were better runners than he was, and soon they were a foot from his heels, slashing down their knives an inch from his back. They could easily have killed him, but they had no intention of doing this; they simply enjoyed terrifying him and chasing him.

This was the beginning. Soon there were riots, almost entirely of women, all over the Eastern Province. They burnt the buildings used as government offices and law courts and the records in them, but they did not kill people. The African men said that Europeans would not kill women, which was one reason why the women took the foreground, but in the end we did kill women. At Opobo the women advanced right up to the soldiers to take the rifles from their hands, and the soldiers fired to prevent this. Some women were killed by shots, but more were drowned by being pushed into the river in the stampede which followed the shooting.

The 'Women's War' taught us the importance of knowing and respecting the opinions of the people we govern. Also, it shows how difficult the task of District Officers was. A District Officer might be stationed forty miles from the nearest European; he was responsible for law, order, tax collection and road making in a huge area, inhabited by people whose language he might not understand.

Nigeria in World War II

The war did much to speed-up Nigeria's approach to independence.

Thousands of Nigerian young men enlisted and served in British armies overseas. Their war experience taught them many things besides fighting. They learnt to handle trucks and other machinery; they learnt that not all Europeans were masters – many were ordinary soldiers like themselves – and further, they learnt that in Malaya and the Philippines European armies had been beaten by non-Europeans. This gave them confidence that they, too, could take an equal position. Also the war led to Africans, both the soldiers and the civilians at home, making up their minds that they must learn to read and write.

When a Nigerian soldier wanted to write to his family he had to dictate the letter to one of his officers, and when the family got the exciting envelope they had to take it to a professional letter-writer to read, and had to dictate to him the answer. The subject-matter might be private, and letter-writers could be gossips. How much they wished that they could write themselves.

As a result of this wish, in some places District Officers organized 'Mass Literacy Campaigns'. The people of the villages clubbed together, paid a penny or two each to get a teacher and some blackboards. Then the whole village would meet for education. Grandparents, children and grandchildren, and could be heard spelling out together such sentences as 'We walk ten miles to the market'.

We can see from this the energy with which the Africans are learning the ways and skills of the modern world. They are interested in new things and are prepared to take up new ways. This song from Bida, a place north of the Niger, shows their delight with new opportunities, and now,

An African carving showing an African hunter bringing home his kill. The artist has shown the fierce movements and expression of the hunter, and the sad, beautiful head of the dead antelope. A cat rubs himself against the leg of the returned hunter.

'Mammy-Wagons', so called because many of their passengers were women taking their goods to the market. No laws limited the number of passengers, brakes and tyres were often faulty, and drivers more enthusiastic than careful.

only thirty years after it was written, the Nigerians have universal suffrage, their own universities, parliament and Prime Minister.

Bida Praise Song

'A Bida Drummer' 'Modernization'

A translation of a Nupe praise-song in honour of Etsu Bello's first motor-car. Etsu Bello reigned 1915–24. From S. F. Nadel *A Black Byzantium*, Oxford 1942, pp. 140–1.

The name of Allah is the beginning of all things
Let us speak of the day when *Etsu* Bello bought a new motor-car.
On the day when *Etsu* Bello bought a new motor-car,
The whole of Bida went out to build a road.
Younger brother and elder brother, they went out to build the road.
All the people on the farms went out to build the road.
The young bride, she went out to build the road.
The bridegroom, he went out to build the road.
Why did they all go out to build the road?
It was because *Etsu* Bello had bought a motor-car.
Because of that all the people went out to build a road.
They said: 'Let us build a road on which the car can travel.
Then the man who wants to go to Baddeggi, in this car he will go.
And Zungaru, the man who wants to go to Zungaru, in this car he will go.

And Wuya, who will travel to Wuya, in this car he will go.
The man who will go to Jima, in this car he will go.
The man who will go to Kacha, in this car he will go.
The man who will travel beyond the river, in this car he will go.
Thus he will go', they said, and therefore let us make the road.
Etsu Bello has the money to buy the car.
But the car will benefit all the people of Bida, from the farms and from
   the city,
The great man and the servant.
They thank *Etsu* Bello because he has bought the car.
Etsu Bello who has horses, and who now has a car.
Etsu Bello can say: Though the horse may break his legs
We shall go all the same.
On the day when *Etsu* Bello bought the motor-car,
The bottles of the glass-makers turned into glass beads.
And the kernels of the gomombara grass became necklaces.
All the people were giving thanks to *Etsu* Bello.
Because he gave his money to buy a motor-car,
That motor-car that will become a thing of benefit
To all human beings.

Nigeria becomes independent   1960

After the Second World War we realized that the Africans were
moving fast into the modern world and that we should not be able to

Below left: The new Nigeria. A College of Arts, Science and Technology at Zaria.
Below right: A new building in the old style, home of a rich Nigerian from the Moslem North Province. Lorries and bows and arrows, new emblems and old, are used to decorate the plaster walls.

A public notice in South African (Afrikaans) and English. Africans are forbidden to picnic in the same place as Europeans.

with rights in European towns. They may go to European towns to work, but they may not have their families there; they must live in 'Bantustans', the native areas. They are not to mix with Europeans by sitting in the same cafés, waiting-rooms, compartments of trains, seats in parks. They are not to bathe from the same beaches, go to the same cinemas, play on the same games-fields or in the same teams.

Twelve per cent of the land is left for the Africans to live and farm on, and this mostly dry, poor, mountainous land. Yet the Africans are three-quarters of the people. They are forced to go and work for the Europeans, not only because their lands do not grow enough food to keep them, but also because they must earn money to pay their taxes. Each adult African man has to pay £1 a year poll tax, and ten shillings a year tax for his hut. When they go into European areas to work they are not allowed to do skilled work; they are hewers of wood and drawers of water, and their wage is about one-seventh of what a European would earn for the same kind of work.

If a European employs an African to do skilled work of the kind reserved for Europeans, such as carpentry, both the European and his African employee may be fined £100. Any African who takes part in a strike may be fined £500, and/or sent to prison for three years.

What this means to Britain

You may think that this is all a long way away, and that although we do not like Apartheid, it is nothing to do with us, and that we cannot meddle with other people's affairs all over the world.

Why do so many people bother about what happens in South Africa?

In the first place, if you turn back to page 27 and read about the Act of Union, you will see that Apartheid is partly our fault. There is also the matter of human standards. We are all inhabitants of one world and must have some feelings for one another's welfare. We think that Apartheid is wrong; the Churches think that it is contrary to

One of the shanty-town slums
near Johannesburg.

Christianity and it is absolutely against the Atlantic Charter, which
Churchill and Roosevelt drew up during the war.

Another reason for our concern is that we need the friendship of
the new African nations. If bloodshed broke out between the races in
South Africa, it would have a very bad effect on the relations between
Europeans and Africans everywhere.

'The winds of change are blowing over Africa'

Macmillan, the British Conservative Prime Minister, visited South
Africa, and whilst he was there he made a famous speech in which he
used these words, and said that we must accept a very different position
for Africans in the future. The speech was rightly taken to be a criticism
of Apartheid; it delighted the Africans, and made the white South
Africans (except for the courageous individuals who resist their government in this policy) very angry.

South Africa leaves the Commonwealth   1961

When we criticized Apartheid, and welcomed into the Commonwealth
on equal terms the new African states of Ghana and Nigeria, South
Africa left the Commonwealth. But we still treat her in some ways
as if she were a member, and give her favourable trading terms,
including financial help for her exports of fruit to us.

Many educated Africans were taught by Christian missions, and
some have hoped that Christian ways of peaceful persuasion would
improve their position. The Christian Chief Luthuli was given the Nobel
Peace Prize in 1960 for his efforts. But the government dismissed him
from his chieftainship, and Luthuli said that his methods had failed.
He said, 'Who can deny that thirty years of my life have been spent

New housing for Africans. Clean, tidy, but barrack-like estates are being built in some areas. This one is for bachelors only. The government tries to prevent African women and children from coming to European towns.

knocking in vain patiently, moderately, modestly at a closed and barred door? What have been the fruits of moderation?'

Some Africans decided that Luthuli's methods were useless. They decided that only violence, secret organization and sabotage of government undertakings such as ports and railways, would force a change of policy. An organization called 'Spear of the Nation' was formed for this, and one of its leaders was a lawyer, called Nelson Mandela. He was an athlete, who used to be seen practising running in the streets of Johannesburg before he went to his office. This came in useful, for he was soon on the run in real earnest, and made so many escapes from the police that he was known as 'The African Pimpernel'. But he was caught in the end, in 1964, and tried for treason and sabotage, and was given a life sentence. At his trial he made a speech which included these words:

During my lifetime I have dedicated myself to the struggle of the African people. I have fought against white domination, and I have fought against black domination. I have cherished the idea of a democratic and free society in which all persons live together in harmony with equal opportunities. It is an ideal which I hope to live for and to see realized. But if needs be, my Lord, it is an ideal for which I am prepared to die.

Perhaps the best hope for South Africa lies with the United Nations, which now has many African members, all of them anxious to end Apartheid. Also, countries such as Norway, which has no practical interest in Africa, have urged the United Nations to act in the matter.

At the time when we write this book no one can say what the answer will be.

185

Ireland 1914–24

Although Ireland is quite a small island, which has fewer people living in it than London, her history is important to us. She is a near neighbour, and we have had a stormy relationship because she has never accepted conquest by us. Her history is closely connected with our own, and she is of special concern to us because many of her people live and work in England.

Ireland – The enemy at our back door

At the end of Chapter 1 you read that the Asquith government in 1914 was engaged in the task of giving Home Rule to Ireland.

This was difficult because Great Britain still believed in being an imperial power, and thought that she had the right to govern where she had conquered. With regard to Ireland in particular, the Conservatives thought that as she was part of the British Isles she ought to be united to us under one government; therefore they called themselves 'Unionists'.

But the chief obstacle to Home Rule was the House of Lords who strongly objected to an independent, self-governing Ireland. So when the Liberals in 1912 brought forward a Home Rule Bill to give the Irish control of such things as roads and education, the Lords vetoed it. The House of Commons therefore had to pass it three times before it became law, and this took nearly two years to do. The war broke out before the process was complete.

It was a pity that it had not been settled, for all through 1914–18 we had to keep a garrison in Ireland in case she took advantage of our struggle with Germany to attack us in our rear, and soldiers who were no longer fit enough to fight in the trenches in France were many of them given the miserable task of serving in Ireland, holding down a people who spoke their own language and were closely related to them.

This proclamation was read from the steps of Dublin Post Office on Easter Monday, 1916.

The Easter Rising 1916

During the Easter weekend of 1916, Irish Republicans made a rising in Dublin. It was hopeless from the start; only a few Irishmen fought, and we had thousands of British troops stationed in Ireland. Nevertheless the Easter Rising was important, for after it was defeated the British government held secret court martial trials of the prisoners, and shot those found guilty of organizing rebellion. This caused great bitterness in Ireland, which counted these men as patriots fighting for their country, and thought that they should be given the rights of prisoners of war. The cause of Irish freedom was now watered with the blood of martyrs, and after these shootings nothing short of complete independence would satisfy the Irish. The Home Rule Bill of 1912 was no longer enough.

Sinn Fein victory at the elections 1918

'Sinn Fein' is the Erse for 'Ourselves Alone'. The Sinn Fein party

Easter Rising, 1916. A street barricade in Dublin.

186

POBLACHT NA H EIREANN.

THE PROVISIONAL GOVERNMENT
OF THE
IRISH REPUBLIC
TO THE PEOPLE OF IRELAND.

IRISHMEN AND IRISHWOMEN: In the name of God and of the dead generations from which she receives her old tradition of nationhood, Ireland, through us, summons her children to her flag and strikes for her freedom.

Having organised and trained her manhood through her secret revolutionary organisation, the Irish Republican Brotherhood, and through her open military organisations, the Irish Volunteers and the Irish Citizen Army, having patiently perfected her discipline, having resolutely waited for the right moment to reveal itself, she now seizes that moment, and, supported by her exiled children in America and by gallant allies in Europe, but relying in the first on her own strength, she strikes in full confidence of victory.

We declare the right of the people of Ireland to the ownership of Ireland, and to the unfettered control of Irish destinies, to be sovereign and indefeasible. The long usurpation of that right by a foreign people and government has not extinguished the right, nor can it ever be extinguished except by the destruction of the Irish people. In every generation the Irish people have asserted their right to national freedom and sovereignty; six times during the past three hundred years they have asserted it in arms. Standing on that fundamental right and again asserting it in arms in the face of the world, we hereby proclaim the Irish Republic as a Sovereign Independent State, and we pledge our lives and the lives of our comrades-in-arms to the cause of its freedom, of its welfare, and of its exaltation among the nations.

wanted an independent, republican Ireland, and after it had won a sweeping victory at the 1918 elections, it defied London by setting up a government in Dublin, and recruiting Irishmen into the 'Irish Republican Army' to fight for their freedom. This set going a guerilla war which in three years nearly brought the British Empire, which had fought Germany successfully, to her knees.

'The Troubles'

Visitors to Ireland can still see signs of this war, which the Irish people call 'The Troubles'. The burnt ruins of the houses of the English gentry (nearly all of them destroyed by the I.R.A. during the war) have mostly been removed, but there are still graves by the roadsides inscribed something like this:

PATRICK O'SULLIVAN
I.R.A.
Shot, June 18th 1920

Patrick O'Sullivan had been an ordinary farmer during the day, but at night he took his gun from under a peatstack and became a disciplined soldier of the Irish Republican Army, carrying out raids against the English forces and the Royal Irish Constabulary.

The Black and Tans

The Royal Irish Constabulary were the British/Irish police, nicknamed the 'Black and Tans', after the name of a pack of hounds, and because of the black arm-bands and hats which they wore with khaki uniforms.

At first this force was largely made up of Irishmen, but at the beginning of the 'Troubles' most of the Irish were driven to resign by the boycott organized against them. If they went into pubs, other men turned their backs on them; if they gave a greeting in the streets, they were cut dead; their children in school were ignored by the teachers, and the shopkeepers refused to serve their wives. Few men could stand the loneliness and hostility which this meant. They resigned, and their place was taken by Englishmen. It was a nasty job holding down the Irish, and only Englishmen who did not mind nasty, and sometimes dirty, jobs, would enlist in the Black and Tans.

You can imagine the kind of army which resulted from this situation. American newspapers were filled with stories of its crimes. There were crimes on the other side too, but the world sympathized with the I.R.A. more, because it saw Ireland as a small country fighting a powerful one for independence.

The I.R.A. were helped by an excellent information service. When the British military police studied the notebooks of the I.R.A. leader, Michael Collins, after his death, they found in them many references to a man called 'G'. But they never found out who 'G' was. 'G' worked at the British government headquarters in Dublin Castle, and was able

Arthur Griffith was a leading Irish journalist, whose ideas had led to the founding of the Sinn Fein party. In May 1918, he was 'in jail for Ireland', because he and other Sinn Fein leaders had refused to join the British Army. While imprisoned in England, he became a candidate in the Cavan by-election. This dramatic poster enabled him to win it.

to tell the Irish the names of British spies and informers. One night the Sinn Fein rounded up fourteen of these and shot them, some of them in the presence of their wives. Michael Collins' secretary wrote of this night:

One of them got shot next door to me. I had got out of jail the night before, and gone to a house for a good night's sleep. Next morning I was brought to my feet by shots, and there was one of the British being shot in his pyjamas in the back garden.

Immediately after this, the Black and Tans broke into a football ground, fired into the crowd, and killed fourteen people as an act of vengeance.

The man whose photograph could not be found

The I.R.A. had some brilliant leaders. One of these was Michael Collins.

He lived under the noses of the police in Dublin, and yet, although he was known by sight to thousands of Irishmen, had a price on his head, and never wore a disguise, they never caught him. This was perhaps because the police could not get hold of a photograph of him. There were plenty in existence, but his family and friends were well organized, and hid the lot successfully. 'An air of innocence is the best disguise,' he said, and strolled around with a casual air, armed with nothing more deadly than his fountain pen.

His escapades became legendary. Secret rooms and hiding places were built, as they had been in England for priests 300 years earlier. He specialized in organizing prison escapes for Irish nationalists; he got de Valera out of Lincoln jail by getting a wax impression of the priest's key smuggled out, having keys made in its pattern, and smuggling them in inside cakes sent to the prisoners.

Irish Free State   1921

The war dragged on for two years before both sides were prepared to admit that they could not beat the other, and were willing to negotiate.

It was difficult to agree upon a treaty, because the Irish wanted a united Ireland, including Ulster, completely outside the British Empire. Ulster is the northern part of Ireland, where most of the people are Protestant, and do not wish to be under the Irish government. The British, on the other hand, wanted to keep Ulster as part of the United Kingdom, and to make the rest of Ireland into a Dominion of the British Empire, in a similar position to, for instance, Canada.

In the end the British government got most of its own way, and the Irish delegation went back with a Treaty which gave Ireland self-government, but kept her within the British Empire, and made it necessary for her ministers to swear that they would 'obey His Majesty King George V'. The Irish Parliament, or 'Dail', passed this treaty, the British troops marched out of Dublin, and the Irish Free State was set up.

Ireland, 1922.

189

Civil war in Ireland   1922–5

This all sounds like a happy ending, but really the situation was tragic. Many Irishmen thought that their struggles had been wasted by a treaty of this kind, and civil war broke out between Irishmen who would accept the treaty, and those who rejected it.

The civil war was worse than the war between England and Ireland, for it divided families and friends, and was fought with treachery and murder. No one knew whom he could trust. Collins' intelligence service was now useless, for he did not know which of his countrymen were on his side.

The struggle cost Ireland some of her most devoted patriots, amongst them Michael Collins, who was shot when he was ambushed.

The Sovereign Democratic State of Eire   1936

Those who were in favour of the treaty won, and proved that it was right to accept it, for under their determined Prime Minister, de Valera, Ireland obtained complete independence in a few years without further bloodshed.

The abdication of King Edward VIII and the scandal which went with it were a heaven-sent opportunity to de Valera, for it gave him an excuse to pass a law abolishing the oath of obedience to the crown. Finally, de Valera drew up a constitution for Ireland which never mentioned the name of Great Britain, and the English name of the Free State was changed to the Irish name of 'Eire'. Since the British government did not want another war with Ireland, it accepted these changes, and even agreed to abandon the right to keep military forces for the defence of the British Isles in some of the Irish ports.

At present, although Englishmen count as foreigners in Ireland, we allow Irish people to come to the United Kingdom as if they were members of the Commonwealth. The one grievance left to the Irish is that the six counties of Ulster do not belong to Eire. It is difficult to know what should be done about this, for most of the people who live in Ulster probably want to remain under the government of Great Britain.

A stamp commemorating the Easter Rising.

The disaster of Suez   1956

Our reputation as an imperial power received a great blow in 1956, over the affair of Suez.

The Suez Canal had been under our control from the time when Disraeli had arranged for Great Britain to buy more than half the shares in it. Egypt had since then become independent of European interference in her affairs, but the Canal, which ran through her territory, remained in our hands.

Egypt, under President Nasser, was by 1956 developing into a modern state, and as part of her plans for progress she was building the Aswan

The Suez Crisis. The Anglo-French and Israeli forces attack the Egyptians.

dam to irrigate part of the desert. America and Great Britain were to have lent the money for this, but America withdrew money because she thought that Egypt was spending too much on arms from Russia. We supported America and withdrew our money also. Nasser 'punished' us by nationalizing the Canal and declaring it Egyptian property. He had the right to do this, provided compensation was paid to shareholders; other countries had nationalized foreign-owned industries, but it was humiliating for us, and we were alarmed for our oil supplies which came to us through the Canal.

We prepared to deal with Nasser by building up an invasion force in Cyprus, and when it was ready the Israeli army advanced into Egypt.

How did the Israelis come into the matter? Israel and Egypt had always been enemies, because the Arabs disliked the Jewish state having been set up in Arabic lands, and Nasser had threatened to destroy Israel. The Israelis hoped to overthrow him by attacking him with the help of the British and the French.

How did the French come into the matter? They also were anxious for an opportunity to overthrow Nasser, because he was helping the rebellion of their colonies in North Africa.

When the Israelis advanced we and the French said that we must act immediately in order to stop the war; we bombarded Egyptian ports and sent an army to the Canal Zone, between the Israeli and Egyptian armies. Naturally, all the world believed that we had arranged the invasion with the Israelis beforehand, and that our statement that we had sent our troops to prevent a war was an excuse to cover up our intention to overthrow Nasser. It was said that it was not in any case our job to intervene on our own; the United Nations should have been asked to do it. The Americans, and most of the members of the Commonwealth, were angry with us and refused to support us.

In the end a United Nations force was sent to the Canal Zone, Nasser kept control of the Canal, we and the French had to withdraw. Our good name and our power in the area from the Nile to the Euphrates dropped sharply. Russia lent Egypt money and technical aid for the Aswan scheme, and seven years later, in 1964, the Russian leader, Khrushchev, opened the completed dam amongst joyous scenes of Egyptian-Russian friendship.

The Suez venture cost us a lot of money; by cutting off our oil supplies it forced us to impose petrol rationing for some months, and it was a hard blow to what remained of our old-fashioned imperial pride.

Conference of Commonwealth Prime Ministers   1964

A conference of Commonwealth Prime Ministers took place in 1964 in London. It was attended by the learned Eric Williams, Prime Minister of Trinidad, the vivid Jomo Kenyatta of Kenya, the dignified, aristo-cratic President of Pakistan, who had been educated in England to be an army officer, by the socialist Nkrumah of Ghana, and by many other great men who between them rule areas which stretch round the earth. There were deep disagreements of course; for instance, the African members thought that the Africans in Southern Rhodesia should immediately be given the vote and so enabled to take over the government, whilst strong European influences favoured going slow over giving Africans the vote and wanted to maintain for the present government by the minority of white settlers. But this disagreement was prevented from becoming a clash because they worked out a compromise by which there was to be a special conference of the people concerned to decide how quickly the Africans should be given the vote. The problem of Southern Rhodesia may not be settled quickly or easily, but this decision shows that the Commonwealth Prime Ministers can work together. The Prime Ministers know one another well and respect one another; they all speak English, and these Commonwealth conferences are useful occasions for settling difficulties.

The uses of the Commonwealth

There are important reasons why the peoples of the Commonwealth should try to strengthen the bonds which hold it together and increase its power.

The first is that we can increase one another's wealth. Look at a map of the Commonwealth and find out how varied their products are. We, for instance, need to buy sugar, cocoa for chocolate, and palm oil for industry, and the West Indies and West Africa produce these things. On the other hand, we produce machinery which they need but cannot yet make themselves. By large-scale arrangements for buying and selling we can exchange these products in an economical way.

We can also help one another in world influence. We ourselves are no longer the greatest power, and many of the Commonwealth countries are small and weak. None of us alone can hope to sway world affairs, but together we are a tremendous power. The Commonwealth gives us valuable allies amongst the new nations, and we are a friend and supporter of theirs amongst the old nations, able to foster new industries for them and send them technical advisers. The United Nations may play an increasingly important part in world affairs, and the British Commonwealth group of nations should be amongst its most respected members.

Should we join the European Common Market?

Great Britain is at present connected by trade agreements with the seven E.F.T.A. (European Free Trade Association) countries. All of these have a smaller population and less industry than we have, and if we entered the Common Market, our E.F.T.A. partners also would probably have to enter it, since they could not stand on their own. You can see from the map that the union of the Common Market and E.F.T.A. countries would make a very rich and powerful group.

If you look at a map which shows the Roman Empire of nearly 2,000 years ago, you will see that the idea of a united Europe is not a new and wild one. On the contrary, it has a very long history. The Channel which divides us from Europe is not an important barrier, and if a Channel tunnel were built it would scarcely be a barrier at all. Perhaps the movement of our population from the north to south-eastern England is partly caused by the closer trade and social links which we are forming with Europe. But if we enter the Common Market it must be on terms which enable us to keep our links with the Commonwealth.

Dates to remember

1922   Irish Free State set up
1961   South Africa left the Commonwealth

Things to do

1   Collect news items about South Africa from the newspapers, television and radio, and find out about the positions of the Africans in the country.
2   Talk to Irish people you know, and find out their opinions about the position of Ulster. Do we govern it well? Should it be joined to Eire?

Books to read

D. Marquand, *South Africa*, Black
A. Paton, *South Africa and Her People*, Lutterworth

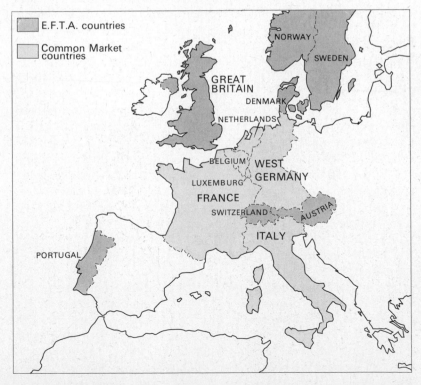

The Common Market and European Free Trade Association. The Common Market countries are larger and more powerful than E.F.T.A.

Chapter 10
Technical advances

The second industrial revolution

This century is the age of the second industrial revolution. The first industrial revolution replaced the power of human and animal muscles by the power of steam. The second one gave us the power of electricity, the internal combustion engine and, now, atomic energy. These new servants have altered almost every moment of our lives. Let us begin by considering the toils of the housewife.

Domestic changes

Ta-ra-ra-boom-de-ay!
Monday is my washing day.

If we could put the clock back and look at any house on Monday morning in the year 1901 we should see in the scullery a large brick structure called a copper. It has a wooden lid and inside is a container made of either copper or a cheaper metal. Underneath is a place for a fire. The housewife must first fill the copper with the water and then light the fire and start the family wash. This in addition to all the ordinary housework and cooking. Every garment is either scrubbed on a board or worked up and down in a tub by a dolly, an instrument with a long wooden handle. Then the clothes are rinsed and finally the white ones are put into the copper and boiled. The fire must be stoked up to keep the water boiling quickly. After twenty minutes the clothes are lifted out of the copper with a wooden stick, and as the lid is taken off, the whole room is filled with steam. Then, if the day is fine and there is a backyard or a garden, the clothes, after they have been mangled are hung out to dry. If it rains, then they must be dried round the kitchen fire. At the end of the afternoon the housewife has an aching back, the kitchen is moist and steamy. The following day there is the work of ironing. Flat irons are used, heated on the fire or possibly on a gas ring. Ironing then was no joke, because garments were much more elaborate than they are now. There were frills and tucks, all of which had to be smoothed out. This ritual of the family wash was repeated every Monday.

One of the first signs of progress on the domestic front was the provision of a copper heated with gas. Then, in the late thirties of this century, washing machines were introduced. They were at first so expensive that few people could afford them, but electric irons became common and they made ironing much easier. After the Second World War, the scene changed. Washing machines became a necessity instead

Above: A mid-Victorian kitchen. Water had to be drawn from the pump, seen at the back of the picture. When the kitchen was cleaned, the table and floor had to be scrubbed, the steel fender polished and the grate black-leaded.

Below: A modern kitchen. How long would it take to clean?

of a luxury and the modern housewife no longer had to dread the back-breaking work of scrubbing the clothes. Further than that, crease-resistant fabrics were put on the market and these required no ironing at all.

The housewife of 1901 had not finished with the wash when it was all ironed. She had then to sew on hooks and eyes, or buttons which had come off, and darn the stockings. Nowadays zip-fasteners have taken the place of hooks and eyes, and nylon, made from coal tar, is used for stockings. Darning is now a forgotten custom. Vacuum cleaners have replaced brooms and brushes. When in 1901 a room was decorated, the paint was difficult to put on and took a long time to dry. The paints on the market now are easy to apply and dry immediately. The new gas or electric cookers are easy to regulate. Gone are the vast kitchen ranges which had to be black-leaded and which were uncertain in performance. Hot water is now supplied by gas or electricity. No longer must the milk be boiled in summer to prevent its going sour. A refrigerator keeps the food fresh. The modern kitchen makes use of plastics and smooth surfaces which can easily be wiped clean. Detergents have largely replaced soap.

Compare the two pictures of an old and a modern kitchen on page 195. Do you agree with people who sigh for the good old days?

Moving pictures

In 1872 the Governor of California had a dispute with a friend. He said that when a horse trotted it had all four feet off the ground. The friend insisted that this did not happen. An English photographer, Mr Muybridge, who was there, was asked if he could possibly take photographs which would decide the question. He placed twenty-four cameras along the racetrack with a piece of thread across the course attached to each shutter. The horse broke the thread and snapped the shutters as it galloped past. In the end, when he had developed the plates Mr Muybridge proved that for a few seconds the horse had all its feet off the ground. The governor had won, though the proof was rather expensive in the use of cameras.

Other people who saw the pictures were inspired to experiment and tried to get a continuous picture. The first real cinema was produced by two Frenchmen, the brothers Lumière. They managed to make eight short films and showed them in a basement in Paris. The show ran non-stop and the queues lined up all day. In February 1896 the brothers brought these films to London and showed them at the Regent Street Polytechnic. The last film was of a train arriving at a station, and when the audience saw this they thought the train was coming straight at them. There was panic, screaming and pushing, and some women fainted. After this the manager hired a nurse to deal with the casualties.

The new invention caught on rapidly and soon there were little cinemas all over the country. They began to take the place of the old music halls. They were cheap, there was no need to book beforehand as

The apparatus used by the Lumière brothers when they showed their first films.

Below left: The famous film comedian, Charlie Chaplin.

Below right: The Keystone Cops. Like Charlie Chaplin, they made silent comedy films.

for a theatre, and as the shows ran on continuously, it did not matter what time one arrived. These first films were very jerky, most of them were like comic strips. A special kind of acting was needed, because although there were sub-titles, the plot and the emotions all had to be shown by action. The most famous of these silent film actors was Charlie Chaplin. His bowler hat, baggy trousers, and big boots were known all over the world.

The jerkiness of the early films was soon overcome and in 1929 the technicians were able to synchronize sound with the picture. This brought great changes. Some actors who had been brilliant in silent films were found to have impossible voices, and a new technique of acting was required for the 'talkies'. The most important centre of this new industry was Hollywood, in California. This place had been chosen because originally the films had been shot out of doors, and there was very bright sunlight in California. Hollywood became a legendary place, more like the Arabian Nights than twentieth-century America. So much money was made out of producing films that the directors could give large salaries to the stars, as they came to be called. It was every girl's dream to be taken on at Hollywood. Lavish sums were spent in production, and besides the actors there was a whole army of stage directors, screen writers and camera men.

Expensively made films were not necessarily the best. Britain and France also made pictures, some of them of very high quality. After the Second World War Italy and Poland produced wonderful films. Unfortunately, the cost of the apparatus for showing sound as well as vision meant that going to the pictures was no longer so cheap. The little old cinemas, the 'flea pits' gave way to large luxurious picture palaces. Recently some of these have closed down, partly because they have had to face the competition of television.

Wireless telegraphy

The first man who overcame the technical difficulties of doing this was the Italian, Marconi. There has probably never been a discovery which caused more quarrels and jealousy between nations than this one. Marconi's claim to be the founder of wireless telegraphy was challenged by the Russians, who declared the credit should go to Popoff, the Germans said it was their Professor Slaby who was responsible, and the Americans supported De Forest. The claims of the British Captain Jackson ought to be included. He made communication without wires between ships two years before Marconi did. Probably the truth is that though several scientists were on the right track, it was Marconi who was first able to launch a company and put his discovery to practical use.

Marconi was lucky in that he had a rich father who allowed him the opportunity to experiment. He came to England with his apparatus in 1896 (accompanied by his mother who was Irish) and obtained a patent. He gave a trial from the General Post Office in London and the message was heard at a receiving station a mile and a half away.

After this he continued his experiments with ships at sea. He was convinced that he would finally be able to send messages across the Atlantic. The scientists thought this was impossible. They said the curve of the earth would direct the messages into space.

Another difficulty in the path of Marconi, besides the disbelief of the scientists, was the jealousy of the cable companies. They saw their monopoly and with it their profits departing. When Marconi built a wireless station in Cornwall and another at St Johns, Newfoundland, in 1901, and transmitted signals from one to another, the indignant cable companies warned him off the territory and said it was illegal to set up such stations. Marconi was destined only to make slow progress until the practical uses of wireless had been demonstrated. Some of the ship-owners had been persuaded to have wireless on their ships. In 1909 a White Star liner was hit in a fog off the coast of Newfoundland and badly damaged. There was a wireless on board, and Jack Binns, the operator, stayed by his set all night, while the ship was sinking, and gave the agreed signal C Q D (come quick danger). The message was picked up by another liner, the *Baltic*, which was guided through the fog by Jack Binns. In the small hours of the morning, in fog and darkness, the crew and passengers were transferred to the *Baltic*.

What really shook the world was the disaster to another White Star liner, the *Titanic*. As the name suggests it was a large ship, actually the largest and most luxurious liner ever built, and as it slipped down the runway at Belfast, the Press murmured the word 'unsinkable'. Every possible comfort and delight was arranged for the passengers, and among the toys for them to play with was the wireless installation, and the two operators were kept busy sending personal messages to friends. It was an unusually cold spring and the icebergs were drifting in the water. On Sunday 14 April 1912 the *California*, a ship sailing west-

Guglielmo Marconi.

An artist's impression of the sinking of the *Titanic* in 1912.

A ship's wireless cabin in 1912. Marconi trained special operators to use them. The wireless cabin on the *Titanic* was in the hands of two Marconi operators.

wards from Boston, wirelessed an iceberg warning to the *Titanic*. Just before midnight when the *Titanic* was making twenty-two knots, racing to win the Blue Ribbon of the Atlantic, she struck an iceberg. Three hours later 1,500 people were dead. The two wireless operators sent out the signal CQD. The Captain told them to alter it to the latest signal SOS (save our souls) and said 'It may be your last chance to use it'. The *California*, which had given the ice warning, was only ten miles away and had wireless on board but only one operator, and he had gone to bed ten minutes before the *Titanic* started signalling. Had they had a round-the-clock wireless all the passengers might have been saved. In a desperate attempt to reach the *California* the Captain ordered rockets to be sent up. These were seen by the crew. They just thought the people on the *Titanic* were having a celebration. It occurred to none of them that the great ship, the *Titanic*, might ever sink. Two other ships heard the call. The *Carpathia*, fifty-eight miles away, arrived in record time to pick up about 700 survivors.

The next morning the *New York Times* printed a photograph of Marconi, and put underneath the caption 'The Real Rescuer'. Before this disaster Marconi shares were a drug on the market; no one would buy them. They now jumped up to ten times their original value. A law was passed in 1914 stating that every ship which carried fifty or more crew and passengers must have a round-the-clock wireless staff so that someone would be listening all the twenty-four hours. It is puzzling to understand why the number fifty was decided on. What happens, asked one of the Marconi men, if forty-nine set out and a baby is born on the voyage?

Perhaps the criminal classes did not bless Marconi. Dr Crippen, a murderer, was arrested when he landed in Canada, because a wireless message had been sent from England to the Canadian police.

Wireless was used for ships at sea, to send warnings and weather reports. As a result of further advances it was able to supply something else – entertainment. On 15 June 1920, a date to remember, from Marconi's station in Chelmsford, the voice of Dame Nellie Melba singing 'Home, sweet home' was heard all over England, in Paris, Rome, Warsaw, and out on the Atlantic. This was the first real broadcasting. Everyone was excited about this except the Postmaster-General, who said sternly that wireless must not be used for such frivolous purposes. Unfortunately for him, people wanted the frivolous service; and two years later, in May 1922, the first broadcasting station, 2LO, was opened, and millions of people were able to hear through their headphones, concerts, talks, drama, and the B.B.C. became a part of British life.

One great benefit came to patients in hospitals, when they were provided with earphones and could listen to wireless programmes, instead of lying bored and listless. Busy mothers thanked the B.B.C. when it provided a children's hour, so that with any luck they might get a quiet hour to themselves.

Dame Nellie Melba, the famous Australian singer, broadcasting from Chelmsford in 1920.

Television

If you ever visit the town of Hastings you might notice a plaque on the wall of one of the houses in Queen's Arcade. It states that John Logie Baird carried out his early experiments there.

John Logie Baird suffered a series of misfortunes. As a boy he made an aeroplane and attempted to fly in it from an attic window; the plane crashed to the ground and Baird was lucky to escape with his life. Then he designed an aerial transmitter, but in a storm the wire blew down and entangled a coachman, who was pulled on to the ground. Baird's father had considerable trouble in trying to soothe the feelings of the coachman, who failed to appreciate the boy's ingenuity. At school, and later at the technical college, Baird's studies were continually interrupted by ill health. When he left school he had a post with the Glasgow Corporation for two years, but what he really wanted to do was to pursue his own studies and he thought if he could make a large sum of money he might throw up his job and devote himself to science. He tried to make diamonds from coal. The only result was a tremendous explosion in which Baird was fortunate to avoid serious injury. He then turned to business and succeeded in making more money than he had been earning as an employee of the Glasgow Corporation. He went to Trinidad in search of health and there he invested in a jam business. This failed and he returned to England with only £200.

He wrote to his sister and asked 'Shall I start to manufacture glass razor blades, or work at television?' 'Razor blades,' was the prompt reply of his sister. Baird rejected this advice. Instead, he rented an attic in Hastings and set to work with a few pieces of make-shift apparatus. He bought a second-hand projector lamp from a bicycle shop, with that and knitting needles, wire and sealing wax, with an old tea-chest for a laboratory bench he began to work. In these unpromising conditions he succeeded in getting a flickering picture on the screen. He was not

The original Baird television apparatus, showing the puppet which Baird used as a model.

The first public demonstration by Baird in 1925.

satisfied with this small result, a picture of only a Maltese cross. He struggled to reproduce a human face. He worked with a marionette puppet, because it was a patient sitter and never got weary of being a model. At last the great day came when this dummy appeared on the screen. Baird rushed to the offices on the ground floor and seized the first boy he could get hold of and dragged him up to his attic. He put him in the chair and proceeded to televise him. When he looked at the screen it was blank. The boy, terrified of all the whirring discs had ducked his head, convinced he was going to be murdered. Baird managed to reassure him and there, unmistakeably on the screen, was the head of Billy, the office boy. He was the first person to be televised.

Baird interested some Members of Parliament in his work, and they induced the B.B.C. to start experimenting with television. The first television service opened from the Alexandra Palace in 1936. Meanwhile, some Americans, who had more money and better conditions of work than Baird, had improved on what he had done and it was finally the American, not the Baird system which was used. Baird went quietly on with his work trying to get colour television until his death in 1946.

Television was stopped during the war and only after the war did it become popular. What a difference it has made to our lives. It keeps people at home much more. It has made the remote parts of the world more real to us. Photographs show a country, but only television makes us feel that a foreign country is real. Then we can see scenes in the street, big occasions are televised, such as the Coronation in 1953 and the Opening of Parliament. Perhaps the sufferers from television are the notable people, who, as they step out of an aeroplane, have to face the battery of television cameras and know that every movement, every gesture will be seen by millions of people. Politicians not only have to speak well, they now have to have what is called a 'television personality'. Perhaps we can sympathize when Members of Parliament say that they do not want the debates to be televised.

Farming

What picture do we conjure up when we think of an English farm? We see a charming old house with a red roof, set amidst trees. In the pastures round the house, the cows are contentedly chewing the cud. We may think of haymaking in summer, or in the autumn, the magnificent shire horse pulling the plough along a straight furrow. Inside the farmhouse there is a large, inviting kitchen, with sides of bacon hanging from the ceiling, and leading off the kitchen is the dairy, where there are great shallow bowls of milk, from which the cream is taken off by a skimmer, and there is a wooden churn for making butter. Your grandparents may tell you they have seen farms like this. It would be difficult to find one now.

The old house remains, as attractive and inconvenient as ever. But the old barns are being replaced by concrete structures. There may also be a high silage tower. The modern farmer can send a sample of his soil to an agricultural institute and he will be told exactly what fertilizer it needs, and how much. Also more attention is paid to the kind of crops to grow. We now have a larger variety, particularly those crops which are used for cattle fodder. Attention has been paid to grasses, with the result that we can now keep five sheep where one was kept in the past. More skilled attention is paid to the health of cattle, and to breeding. Veterinary inspection is the rule, and a greater amount of penicillin is used yearly on animals than on human beings.

The combine harvester carries out four different processes. It cuts, threshes, and winnows the corn. A great improvement on the medieval way of getting in the harvest.

202

'He *loves* feeding the chickens.'

Machines are now used wherever possible. Cows, driven in for milking, go into an electrically-lighted shed, and mechanical milkers are used. All cows have to be tested for tuberculosis, so that when your bottle of milk arrives on your doorstep, it has been pasteurized and cooled, and is guaranteed free from any tuberculosis. The whole process, from start to finish, has been done by machinery.

Lifting potatoes is now done by a machine. Tractors do the ploughing. In fact a farmer need never see a horse. At harvest time the combine harvester, which is a factory on wheels, cuts the corn, threshes it and packs it into bags. Hedges are being cut down to make it easier to move the machinery. The modern farmer has to be a mechanic as well as a man who understands crops and cattle.

Changes have also come in the way the animals are reared. It began with keeping hens in a battery. They stay all their life on one perch, and in the winter artificial light is used in the evening, to encourage the birds to lay eggs. The chickens are hatched in incubators, and the most popular strains are those which develop early and begin to lay when they are young; they only last in this unnatural condition for a year. The cockerels are given food to help them to form flesh early, then they are strung along on a machine, killed and the feathers stripped off, all by machine.

Calves and pigs are kept indoors too, so close together that they can hardly move. Their food is carefully regulated so that they grow quickly. This kind of farming, which is becoming increasingly common, is called factory farming.

Some people object to this as being cruel. The farmers reply that the animals are warm and fed well, that they have never known any freedom so that they do not miss it. They also say that by forcing early growth they get far more meat and it is all-important to increase our food production. Complaints have been made that the meat of these calves and pigs is tasteless. Many housewives insist that the free-range eggs (which are eggs from hens which are allowed to run about) are better and richer.

The animals which still enjoy freedom are the cows. They could not be kept in a healthy state and give milk unless they were allowed to browse in the fields.

These changes in farming methods have many effects on country life. For one thing, far fewer men are needed on the farm. It does not take so long to get in the corn when a combine is used. Also if there are fifty calves standing in a shed, one man pushing a button can send the food into the troughs, but though fewer men are required, they must all have the skills of modern farming and be able to overhaul machinery.

Some people mourn the changes in the countryside. The naturalists and the bird-watchers who will lose the flowers in the hedgerow, and the birds who used to nest in the hedges. Others think that a great deal of the beauty of the English rural scene will disappear with the hedges. All changes disappoint some people.

The motor-car

In Chapter 1 you read how motor-cars began to displace the horse at the beginning of this century. The early cars were expensive and not very reliable. Travelling in them was not comfortable because the roads were not then tarred, and cars stirred up a tremendous amount of dust. Women used to put on special clothes before going out for a drive, protecting their eyes with goggles and wrapping themselves up in veils.

The first cheap cars were produced during World War I by the American manufacturer, Henry Ford. He made cars cheaply by using interchangeable parts, and his mass-produced vehicles were called scornfully 'Tin-Lizzies'.

Motor-cars, motor-buses and motor-coaches have brought great changes to the countryside. Ever since the coming of the railways the country roads had been quiet, and the old coaching inns had decayed. Now once again the roads were lively with traffic. Garages and road-side cafés sprang up. Once-lonely villages were linked up by regular bus services. The attractive byways of the country were now open to picnickers and holiday-makers. Our habits of amusement, work and trade have all been altered by the internal combustion engine. In many ways it has made life much easier; think, for instance, how few patients a doctor could see in a day when he depended on a horse to take him around. But the motor has also given us new problems to solve, problems of preserving peace and quiet, of providing space on the roads for the volume of traffic, and of making the roads safe.

Above left: A 'petroleum carriage' which took part in the first of the Paris–Rouen motor competitions in 1894. It is driven by clutch and gearbox. The first motor-cars were introduced in England in 1895.

Above right: Touring car, 1920. During the 1920s, cars became more popular, and many people made weekend treks to the country or seaside. The wheels have wire spokes.

Below left: Austin 7, 1932. By this time, British cars could be mass-produced, and less wealthy people could afford a small saloon car. It still had a running board.

Below right: Ford Consul Cortina, 1965. Pressed steel wheels and no chassis.

The problem of old cars. Few people want old cars; most want the latest, most fashionable model. Here, a car breaker's yard has been constructed at Waltham Cross to deal with old cars.

The problem of overcrowded roads. Motorways, like this one at Chiswick, temporarily ease the problem.

Flight

For centuries men have gazed at the birds and longed to skim through the air on wings. The first men who really made this possible were the two Wright brothers, Wilbur and Orville, who were born in America nearly a hundred years ago. They had no technical education and when once they were asked how they managed to achieve what they did, Wilbur answered, 'My father always encouraged us to find out things for ourselves.' When Wilbur was ten years old, his father brought him a small toy. He threw it at him and Wilbur expected to catch it but found it floated up to the ceiling. It was a small object made of cork and bamboo and was propelled into the air by a rubber band. Wilbur tried to make others like it, and to make them bigger. He found that the bigger ones would not fly. He had stumbled on the law that when a machine is enlarged its weight is increased more than its strength. Later he and his brother Orville had a bicycle shop. During the winter months, when there was little business to be done, they occupied themselves with designing and building a glider.

They chose what they thought was a good spot to try out flights, Kitty Hawk in North Carolina. Their glider was successful, and they turned to the problem of providing the machine with a petrol engine. In December 1903 the first successful flight was made – lasting for twelve seconds. They were disappointed to find the government of the United States was not much interested in what they were doing, so the Wright brothers came to Europe and found recognition there. Both French and British engineers had been working on the same problem, and soon more ambitious flights were made. In 1909 paper boys in London dashed through the streets shouting 'Blériot has flown the Channel.' Old ladies still murmured 'If God had wanted us to fly He would have given us wings,' but flying had come to stay.

An invention which has a military use is always sure of encouragement in wartime. During the First World War great strides were made

The first flight by an engine-controlled aeroplane was made by the Wright brothers in 1903.

One of the early R.A.F. Bristol fighter planes, used during the First World War.

The Zeppelin, an engine-driven balloon filled with helium gas, was designed in Germany and used during the First World War. But it proved too vulnerable to enemy attack. After the war, both Britain and Germany experimented with airships for transport, but gave them up because of the expense and danger of explosion.

in the design of planes. The R.F.C. (Royal Flying Corps) was founded. Later it became the Royal Air Force. Aeroplanes were used for reconnaissance and also to a smaller extent for dropping bombs.

Although airports were built near the large towns of Europe and regular services were started from London to Paris and other capitals there was little change in design of aeroplanes until the thirties, when once more we had to rearm. This stimulated research into aeronautics. Whittle invented the jet engine, which came into use at the end of the Second World War. With this engine a plane could fly at 400 miles an hour. There was no doubt that during this war we led the world in aeroplane design. When Göring was asked what he needed for victory he replied, 'A hundred Spitfires'.

In this connexion we ought to mention here the work of Sir Robert Watson-Watt who invented Radar, without which the damage done by the Luftwaffe would have been infinitely greater. The Germans at the

London Airport. It has been designed with runways facing different directions, so that they can be used according to the direction of the wind.

V.C. 10 passenger aircraft. From London to New York by sailing ship: six weeks. From London to New York by steamship: six days. From London to New York by air: six hours.

time were working on this but had not got nearly so far as the British. This is an example of how the Germans lost the war, partly through their scientific inferiority.

Since the Second World War flying has become commonplace. Passenger planes have increased in size and roughly 3,000,000 people every year leave for holidays from London Airport. Businessmen find the time saved in flying to America rather than going by sea is invaluable. A jet plane, carrying a hundred passengers, flying backwards and forwards to New York for a fortnight can convey more passengers than could the *Queen Mary* in the same amount of time.

Man invades space

Man's successful invasion of space is the most extraordinary scientific achievement of the century. The first cosmonauts, travelling in spacecraft which cost vast sums of money and the work of thousands of

1

2

3

4

5

6

Six space stamps, two from America: (1) Colonel John Glenn's space flight, 1962; (2) The 'Atlas' Rocket and launching tower, 1964; and four from Russia: (3) Launching of Sputnik I, the first artificial satellite, 1957; (4) Yuri Gagarin, the first 'man in space', 1961; (5) Sputniks, 1964; (6) Leonov taking the first 'walk' in space, 1965.

scientists and technicians, have looked at our turning globe from outside earth's atmosphere.

Every country will be influenced by these new powers of man. New methods of broadcasting may result from them, as well as the possibilities of journeys to the moon.

Automation and computers

Ever since the beginning of time man has made tools. At first they were very primitive ones of stone; later bronze was used, and then men learned to work with iron. But however much tools were improved, man still had to use his hands. Nails had to be hammered in, wood carved, and stone chipped. Every table, every pair of shoes and every yard of cloth was made by skilled and trained labour.

When, at the end of the eighteenth century, steam was used to

Control panel of a modern factory. Only one man is required to take charge.

drive machinery and it was found that, for instance, cotton could be spun by a machine, the need for so much skilled labour declined. The labour force was divided into a small, skilled section and the vast mass of semi-skilled and unskilled.

In the present age we see machinery beginning to perform what used to be done by the unskilled. We can see how this works if we take a motor-car as an example. When they were first manufactured at the beginning of this century, each part was separately made and then assembled by skilled engineers. The first step was made when the complicated process was broken up into separate parts, and each part done by a machine. If you had gone into a factory in Coventry forty years ago you would have seen men (and women) standing in front of a moving belt, and automatically dropping a nail in a hole as it came by. Or else, perhaps, a man would have to give a turn to a screw as it passed him. This work was deadly monotonous and required little skill. Now machines are undertaking this, dropping in the nail and turning the screw. There is much less need for the unskilled labour which used to make up about eighty per cent of the labour force of every factory.

Not only are machines undertaking the work of the unskilled. They are themselves being controlled by electronic computers. These are electric brains, which are so skilfully and intricately designed that they can start an operation, check it, correct an error, and register measurements. It is easy to see one effect of all this. What is to happen to the workers in a factory run by automation? For instance, in 1963 a factory was built in Kent which cost £2,000,000, but it is operated by exactly seven employees. In a motor-car factory, in 1965, 555 things are done to a cylinder block by a continuous automated process.

Automation does not only invade the factory, it is also making a revolution in offices. Computers can do calculations in half an hour which it might take a mathematician or an accountant two years to work out. Many offices have installed computers to do work which was once done by clerks.

More highly trained scientists are needed to design the new devices, more engineers to make and service them, and fewer unskilled workers to do mechanical tasks.

Dates to remember

1896 First cars introduced into England
1909 Blériot flew from Calais to Dover
1922 British Broadcasting Corporation started
1936 First television studio opened
1941 First jet flight
1961 The first man sent into space

Things to do

1   Make a list of the uses of electricity:
    (a) In the home.
    (b) In a hospital.
2   Find out how people amused themselves before they had the cinema, radio, and television.
3   For what purposes are radio and television useful besides amusement?
4   Try to arrange a visit to a farm.
    Take notes on the machinery used on a farm, and find out where the feeding stuffs for the animals come from.
5   Make a list of all the food you eat during one day, and then make a list of all the machinery you think may have been used to produce it.
6   Collect pictures of the newest motor-cars, aeroplanes, sputniks.
    Write under the pictures information about the new characteristics of each one.
7   Find out if there are any automated factories in your district, and try to visit one of them.
    Find out how the method of production has changed as a result of automation.

Books to read

Lawrie Cade, *Pioneer Airmen*, Muller
F. R. Elwell, *Science and the Farmer*, Bell
I. O. Evans, *Inventors of the World*, Warne
Egon Larsen, *Men Who Shaped the Future*, Phoenix House
Egon Larsen, *Men Who Changed the World*, Phoenix House
P. Pringle, *Great Discoveries in Modern Science*, Harrap
W. M. Johnson and Karl Spielberg, *Space Travel*, Oliver and Boyd

Chapter 11
Medical advances

The English used to laugh at the Chinese, who, they were told, used only to pay their doctors when they were well. As soon as they became ill, they stopped payment. That seemed a topsy-turvy thing to do. Here you sent for the doctor when you were ill and paid him to cure you.

But is it a foolish arrangement? After all, we want to be well, and to pay for the blessing of health is only logical. Twentieth-century medicine began to approach the Chinese point of view. Keep people fit. Don't wait until they are ill. More and more the emphasis is now being put on preventing illness.

Vitamins

A Dutch doctor, called Eijkman, was sent out to Java in 1885 to investigate the causes of an outbreak of beriberi in the population there. That is a disease found in the East. It makes people listless and weak, and after a few months ends in death. Ever since Pasteur had shown how germs cause diseases, doctors had come to think that all diseases were spread this way. Dr Eijkman stayed at a hospital in Java and tried to find the germ which he was sure must be present in the patients. One day he noticed in the hospital yard that all the hens were drooping in a lifeless way. This only confirmed him in the belief in the germ theory. Obviously the same germ which had affected the patients was attacking the poultry.

Then the Superintendent of the hospital found out to his dismay that the hens were being fed with polished rice. This was too good and expensive for hens. He ordered at once that they were only to have the cheap, unmilled rice, not fit for human consumption. A day or two later Dr Eijkman saw that the hens had perked up and looked bright and lively. He began to think of the possibility that their different food might be the cause. He went to one of the prisons where the convicts were given unmilled rice and found they were all healthy, while in another where they were given polished rice, there was a high proportion of sufferers from beriberi. Clearly something valuable had been removed from the rice in the process of milling. Later research workers called this substance a vitamin, and named this one vitamin B because it cured beriberi.

Vitamins are substances which play an essential part in the chemistry of the body. Though they are only required in very small quantities, the absence of them leads to illness and possibly death.

Above: Children's welfare clinic in 1911. The girls are being searched for lice.

Below: Children's welfare clinic today. It tries to detect ill-health in the early stages, and has special departments of dentistry, eye-testing, and speech therapy. Many clinics run special educational courses for parents.

212

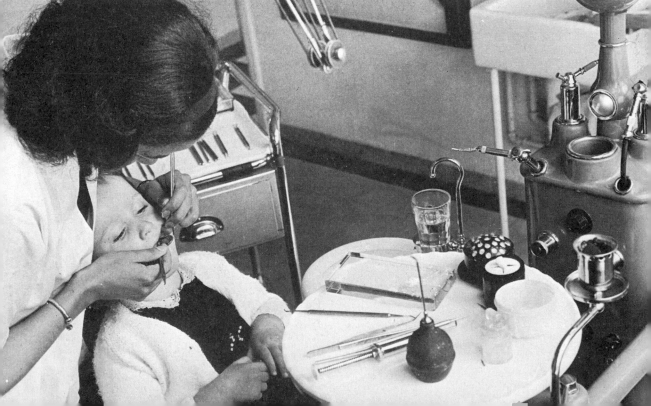

Two chickens hatched out on the same day. The upright healthy one has had Vitamin D added to its diet; the other is the control.

It had been known since the eighteenth century that lime-juice or lemon-juice prevented sailors from getting scurvy, but the scientific reason for it was not understood then. The precious substance in lime-juice was called vitamin C. If Scott of the Antarctic had taken a sufficient quantity of this, the members of his expedition might not have died. The supply ran out too soon, and after three months without any vitamin C their resistance was too low to stand the hardships.

There was a disease very prevalent in England, particularly in the northern towns, called rickets. In fact it was so common there that the Germans labelled it the English disease. Children with rickets often grew bow-legged, or suffered other minor deformities. Here again a knowledge of vitamins came to the rescue. The chemists had worked out what they thought were perfect diets for the human body, the right proportion of protein, starch, etc. Dr Gowland Hopkins of Cambridge worked on feeding experiments, chiefly with rats, which are useful animals for such tests because, like human beings, they are omnivorous. He found that the rats on some perfectly balanced diets were not healthy and did not thrive. When he added a very slight amount of fresh milk each day, they developed at once into sturdy animals. Puppies fed on this *chemically* correct food grew rickety. Again a small amount of milk transformed them. Vitamins A and D are found in milk, the vitamins necessary for bone and growth. When these were provided there were no more rickety children, in fact nowadays one is rarely seen in this country.

A great deal of research was done on these lines, and a whole group of vitamins was discovered. Now they are manufactured in the form of pills, and by ensuring that children have the proper food there has been a tremendous improvement in general health. These discoveries may sound very simple, but in actual fact they involved years of patient work by hundreds of experimenters. An idea may come accidentally, as in the case of Dr Eijkman and the hens. If the Superintendent had not ordered a change of food for the poultry, people might have gone on searching a long time in vain for a germ which caused beriberi.

When a feeding experiment is carried out to test some particular food, or perhaps a new drug, two groups of animals are used. One group, called the control, has the normal diet, the other group has the normal diet plus the substance which is being tested. Great care has to be taken that the conditions are otherwise the same for both groups. The animals have to be weighed and examined every day, and any changes must be exactly noted. When the animals are killed and dissected, any effects which the diet has had on the heart, liver and other organs must be looked for. Only after hundreds of such experiments have been carried out can a scientist feel sure that he can say with certainty what is the effect of a particular kind of food or drug.

An example of patient research is connected with a disease, fortunately a rare one, called pernicious anaemia. At the beginning of this century there was no cure for it. In 1920 it was found that patients suffering from this complaint could lead normal, healthy lives if they every day ate some raw minced liver. It was a most unpleasant remedy. Then the biochemists got to work to discover what exactly it was in the liver which provided what was necessary. Not until 1948 were they able to isolate this vitamin and make it in a form of pill. So those attacked by pernicious anaemia no longer had to rely on a nauseating diet. Behind every discovery is a whole army of backroom boys, sometimes called boffins, who carry out the tests.

The killers

However healthy a person might be, yet he could still be attacked by a number of deadly diseases. How were they to be treated? There were two methods, either to prevent them occurring, or render them comparatively mild and harmless.

Malaria or ague, or the shaking sickness, was an obstinate disease. It was known to occur in damp, marshy places. Sometimes it had been called the Roman fever because it abounded in the marshy country round the city of Rome. In this country it was chiefly found in Kent. Quinine was the only medicine which was any use in reducing the fever. But once a person had one attack of malaria, he never entirely got rid of it; the fever might return, sometimes after many years.

An Englishman, Sir Ronald Ross, discovered that it was carried by one type of mosquito. The insect, after biting a person who had malaria, could carry the infection to the next person it happened to bite. The problem then was to get rid of mosquitoes. They lay their eggs in water, and when the eggs hatch the young rise to the surface to

Above, the emblem of the World Health Organization; below, a mosquito, as symbols of the international campaign against malaria.

breathe. Sir Ronald Ross's method was to drain all the marshy places, and also to pour a small quantity of oil on the pools and ditches. The oil covered the surface of the water; when the eggs hatched the insects died because they could not get to the air. It was by doing this that south-east England was completely freed from malaria.

This was a possible method in a comparatively small area like the marshes of Kent. It was not practicable in a large country. In recent years mosquito control has been carried out by spraying with a disinfectant called D.D.T. In large areas in the East, where the houses have been sprayed like this, the mosquito, and with it malaria, has disappeared.

The other method, that of making the disease harmless, is really a development of the ideas of Dr Jenner. He gave his patients cowpox, because it made them immune from the far more deadly disease, smallpox. The body always sets up a resistance to a germ which enters it. Whether the germ is a mild type or a virulent one, the resistance is the same. Then, argued the doctors, if a mild form of the disease can be injected, the patient will manufacture in his own body what are called antibodies, which will prevent him from having a bad attack.

The fight against malaria is not new. This coin commemorates Empedocles, a philosopher and scientist who lived in Sicily in *c.* 450 B.C. He noticed that malarial swamps bred fevers, and drained several at his own expense.

Left: Spraying for malaria in Iran. Spraying operations have to be quick and thorough, otherwise the mosquitos have time to develop a resistance to D.D.T.

One of the most frequent killers was tuberculosis, then called consumption. In 1908 two Belgian doctors, Calmette and Guérin, took a virulent strain of the tuberculosis germ from cattle, and began to cultivate it on potato boiled in glycerine and ox-bile. The bacteria grew well on this strange diet, but after twenty-five days the two doctors found that the strain had become slightly less virulent. They took some of the tamer germs and grew them for another three weeks, and so on every three weeks for thirteen years and finally they grew a strain so weak that it could not produce the disease. If this strain were injected into a man, he would get immunity from tuberculosis. Millions of lives have been saved by the discovery. This protection is now given to nurses and medical students, to children whose parents have been tubercular, and is called *Bacillus Calmette Guérin*, or B.C.G. after the names of the two doctors who worked on the bacillus unremittingly for thirteen years. Perhaps the most important quality which a research worker should have is patience.

Children can now be protected in this way by 'immunizing' them from diphtheria and whooping cough, and the search still goes on to find means of combating measles, mumps and other afflictions.

At the beginning of this century polio, or infantile paralysis was rare and only a few cases were known. Then there came a remarkable increase. Originally it only attacked children under five, but later older children and also adults succumbed to it. All that could be done was to use artificial means to help a child to breathe, the 'iron lung', while the muscles were paralysed, and to give remedial massage afterwards. The doctors were puzzled that the disease was strongest and most prevalent in countries where there was good sanitation and a high standard of living; they were used to illness caused by poverty or by dirt. Here was something which attacked the prosperous and the active. It seemed that the healthiest children were the ones who suffered. Doctors all over the world worked on this problem, and millions of pounds were spent on research. It was not until 1950, after the electron microscope had been invented, that the virus which caused polio was traced. It then became possible to prepare a vaccine which would provide immunity from this disease. Anti-polio injections are now given to all young babies.

Travelling became much safer. Englishmen who had worked abroad had been open to all sorts of tropical fevers. It was said that there were not enough trees in the Isthmus of Panama to provide crosses for all those who had died of yellow fever, the 'Yellow Jack'. The French could not complete the Panama Canal because the workers died in their thousands. If you go to certain parts of the world now you are inoculated against cholera and typhoid and take pills to prevent malaria. The west coast of Africa is no longer 'the White Man's Grave', and that most terrible of diseases – leprosy – can now not only be cured, but also prevented.

The following figures, for England and Wales, show how increased medical knowledge combined with welfare work has saved the lives of children.

Number of children born alive who died before the age of one year:

	per thousand
1901–10	128
1911–20	100
1921–30	72
1931–40	59
1941–50	43
1951–60	25

'Chance only favours a mind which is ready for it.' Pasteur.

The discovery of penicillin is sometimes said to have been accidental. But is that really true? Are great discoveries really accidents? Dr Alexander Fleming worked in the bacteriology department at St Mary's Hospital, London. During the First World War he was sent to a hospital at Boulogne. Many of the wounded men who were brought in had to have an arm or a leg amputated because they had a gangrene infection, and the only way to stop that spreading was to cut off the affected limb. Many died from blood-poisoning, or septicaemia, as it is called. Now, as you have read in the last volume, when operations were performed in a hospital, scrupulous care was taken to sterilize everything so that no infection would get into the wound, but these soldiers often had deep wounds and had been hours in transit before they came from the base dressing-stations. There was no way of killing the germs which were multiplying in the bloodstream without at the same time destroying the tissues of the body.

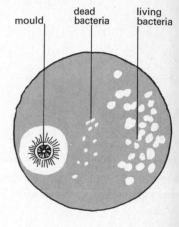

A penicillin mould.

After the war Dr Fleming returned to his laboratory at St Mary's Hospital, and continued in his search for something which would counteract these germs which caused blood-poisoning, boils, and skin diseases. One day in 1929 when he examined the specimens he had in small dishes, he noticed that the lid of one of them had slipped. Into this dish a small mould had floated. You or I would probably have covered the dish again and thought no more about it. Fleming was meticulous and examined it carefully. He found that in a small area round the mould the germs which he was cultivating had disappeared. The mould must have some property which destroyed them. He threw up his other work to concentrate on this mould. He believed that he might have found something important. He made preparations from the mould and found that it worked miraculously on some festering wounds. He published a paper about this mould, called *penicillium notatum*, but no one at that time realized its importance.

Meanwhile, in Germany some chemical substances were discovered which killed germs in the body. The chemical drugs, however, were not entirely satisfactory, and two Oxford scientists, Florey and Chain (the latter a refugee from Hitler's Germany), looked up the earlier work of Fleming and started on an attempt to purify the mould which they produced, a preparation which they called penicillin. At the beginning of the war it was difficult to find the workers, because there was so much essential war work for the chemists to do. However, they managed to get a laboratory in Oxford and cultivated the mould in milk bottles. Harassed British housewives were told they must on no account lose or break a bottle as it would not be replaced. There was much grumbling about the shortage of bottles. The housewives did not know that the bottles were being conveyed to Oxford, where Florey and Chain successfully produced a few grains of penicillin. There was no doubt about the wonderful properties of this product. But how could they make enough when the army and the air force would need so much? They were invited to America and found there scientists who had the possibilities of working on the mass production of penicillin. They searched round for suitable substances on which to grow mould, and a young worker, nicknamed 'Mouldy Mary' one day brought in a canteloup melon, which proved a good breeding-ground. Soon, instead of a bottle containing a pint of culture for penicillin, the Americans had tanks and stills holding 16,000,000 gallons.

During the war penicillin was reserved for the forces. There was only a limited amount available. In the First World War 70 per cent of the wounded limbs had to be amputated, in the Second World War, the number was only 20 per cent. Also loss of sight was reduced by half. This was due to penicillin. A young Scottish army doctor was given injections of it, and knowing how much it cost he murmured as each drop went in 'Tenpence, tenpence, tenpence'. What agony for a frugal Scot! After the war it was released for general use. Doctors began to examine other moulds, and samples of soil from all over the world were tested, to see if the moulds they produced could also be used as germ killers. Now a whole generation of people is growing up who are so used to the idea that sore throats, mild temperatures and boils can be instantly cured by a dose of penicillin that they can hardly imagine a world where it could not be prescribed.

Bottling penicillin in the sealed, sterilized glass cabinet of a modern laboratory. The girls wear dark glasses and rubber clothing to protect them from X-ray lighting inside the cabinet.

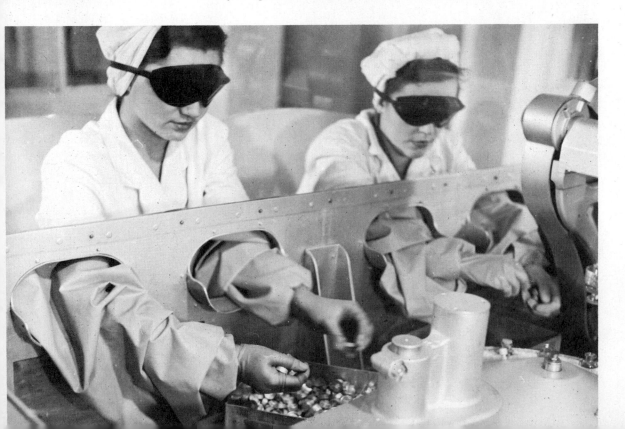

It is possible that some of the early herbalists had known of the power of this mould. In Psalm 51 we read: 'Purge me with hyssop and I shall be clean: wash me and I shall be whiter than snow.' We now know that hyssop contains a mould similar to that from which penicillin is made.

If the lid of the dish in Dr Fleming's laboratory had not been loose, the mould would not have floated in. If one of the other thousand moulds had appeared, nothing might have been noticed about moulds. How far do you think the discovery of penicillin was accidental?

Blood transfusion

There is one killer of which we are often reminded on wireless and television; this is traffic. Every day people are killed or seriously injured in road accidents. One danger the victims run is that they may lose a great deal of blood before they reach the nearest hospital.

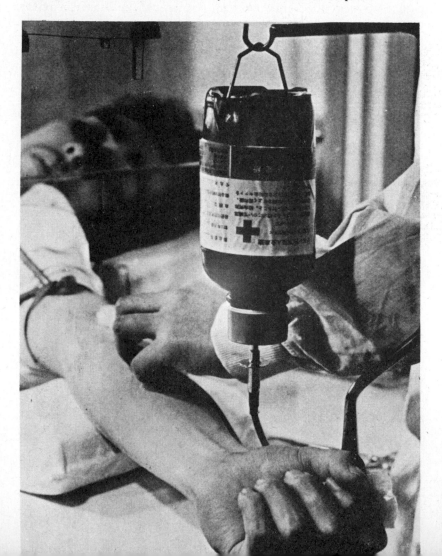

A blood transfusion. A pint of blood is pumped from a vein in the volunteer's arm; it takes about half an hour and is normally completely painless. Volunteers apply to regional blood transfusion centres run by the National Health Service.

There is a curious entry in Pepys' Diary in the year 1666: 'Dr Croone told me at the meeting of Gresham College tonight, which it seems they now have every Wednesday, again there was a pretty experiment of the blood of one dog let out until he died, into the body of another on one side while all his blood ran out on the other. The first dies upon the place, the other very well and likely to do well. This did give occasion to many pretty wishes, such as the blood of a Quaker to be let into an Archbishop and such like: but as Dr Croone says, it may if it takes, be of mighty use to a man, the amending of bad blood by borrowing from a better body.'

There were attempts after this to pass blood from one man into another, but with such bad results that the experiments stopped. Not until the early nineteenth century was blood transfusion tried again. A British doctor had a woman patient desperately ill from loss of blood after childbirth, gave her blood from another human being and saved her life. He published an account of this and many other doctors tried to do the same thing. What puzzled them was that sometimes it was a perfect success, at others for no known reason, a complete failure. The answer was supplied at the end of the century when Dr Landsteiner, an Austrian, demonstrated that there were four different types of blood, and that it was necessary to give the patient blood from the same group as his own. If the right blood were given, success was almost certain.

There was the problem of having a donor at the moment when transfusion was required. In 1922 a method was invented of preserving the blood and hospitals asked for volunteers to give their blood. In this way a supply was always ready.

In the Second World War thousands of lives were saved by this. A story is told of a wounded German officer in a British hospital. After he had been given a blood transfusion the doctor said to him: 'Now you have a pint of good Jewish blood in your veins.'

We often hear appeals on television for more donors. Every hospital now has its blood bank and relies on volunteers to keep up the supply.

A blood bank.

The unknown ray

Scientists working on a problem do not know and sometimes do not even dimly guess what the final result may lead to. Professor Röntgen was a physicist at the University of Würzburg in Germany. Late on Friday, 8 November, 1895, he was carrying on an experiment in his laboratory when he noticed something extraordinary. He had covered an electric bulb with black cardboard, and when he switched on the current he saw little dancing lights on his table. Now the bulb was completely covered, how then could any ray penetrate? On the table there were some pieces of paper which had been coated with metal salts. It was on this paper that the lights were shining. Professor Röntgen picked up a piece of this paper and held it at a distance from the lamp, between it and the lamp he placed a variety of objects, a book, a pack of cards, a piece of wood and a doorkey. The ray penetrated every one of them except the key. This mysterious ray could shine through everything except the metal. He called his wife into the laboratory and asked her to hold her hand between the lamp and a photographic plate. She was completely bewildered by this request, nevertheless she obediently held up her hand for a quarter of an hour, and when the plate was developed there was a picture of the bones of her hand and of the ring on one finger. The ray could pass through the flesh but not through the bone or the ring.

When Professor Röntgen described what had happened at a scientific meeting, he called this new ray 'the Unknown', the X-ray. Doctors quickly saw how this could be used, and soon there were X-ray machines installed in all the big hospitals. At first the doctors did not understand how powerful the rays were and many of them were injured, losing a finger or an arm through exposure, when they were using the machines. The most obvious use for this discovery was to enable the surgeon to see exactly how a bone was fractured. Other uses came later. It was found that these rays could be used to destroy cancer cells, just as they destroyed the healthy cells of the doctors who first used the apparatus. Methods were found out later by which ulcers in the stomach could be located, and the lungs could be X-rayed to show if there was any tuberculosis present. 'Mass X-ray' units are sent round to factories and detect early signs of trouble in the lungs.

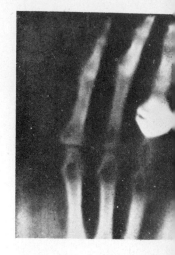

The first X-ray photograph, showing the hand of Professor Röntgen's wife.

A modern X-ray unit.

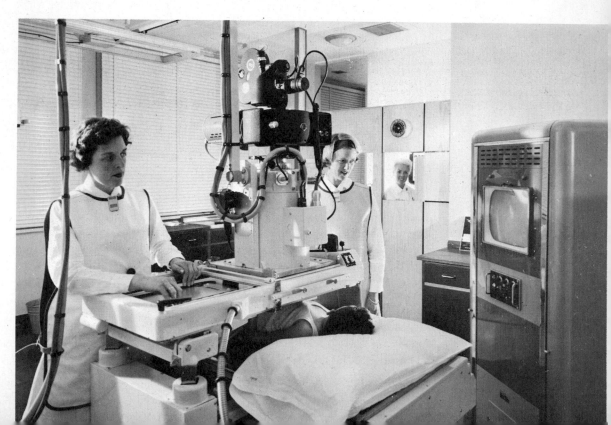

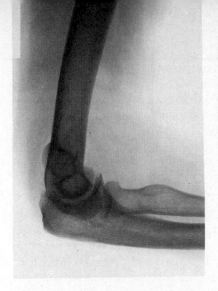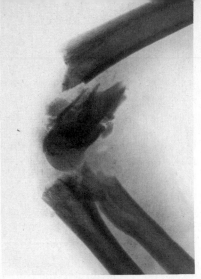

X-ray of a normal arm and X-ray of an arm with complicated fracture (i.e. a fracture which damages other tissues).

It would be pleasant to think that Professor Röntgen, whose discovery did so much for medical science, could have died an honoured man. Malicious people spread the rumour that he had stolen his discovery from a laboratory assistant. He died, poor and neglected in 1923.

Mental illness

We have come a long way in the treatment of mental illness since the eighteenth century when madness was considered something to be laughed at. People used to go for amusement to see the lunatics at Bedlam, who were chained to the wall or kept in cages. One of the first doctors to urge that the insane should be treated in a humane way was a Frenchman called Pinel. A friend of his was confined in an asylum. He managed to escape and was found in a wood, half-eaten by wolves. Pinel was so horrified at the conditions in the asylum, that in 1792 he petitioned the government of the Revolution to allow him to take off the chains which had fastened the inmates to the wall. He was given reluctant permission. From this time onwards he devoted himself to the study of insanity, and to persuading doctors that mad people had rights, just as other citizens had.

In England a bill, piloted by Lord Shaftesbury through Parliament, did away with some of the worst abuses in the treatment of the insane, and all through the nineteenth century there was a slow improvement in the management of the lunatic asylums.

In the twentieth century great advances have been made in the treatment of the insane. No longer do we believe that the only way to treat mental patients is to keep them out of the way, shut up in institutions until they die. Doctors have investigated the causes of mental sickness. New methods of treatment and new drugs are continually being tested. In many cases, which formerly would have been thought hopeless, there is now the possibility of recovery.

Surgery

You will have read in the last volume how surgery was made painless by the use of anaesthetics. Though it was painless it was extremely unpleasant, and there was generally vomiting after the operation.

In this century there has been tremendous improvement in the way gas, or ether, or chloroform is given. The patient is made unconscious before the operation begins by a small injection which acts so rapidly that he is not aware anything is happening. Local anaesthetics are also used. The Peruvian Indians used to chew the leaves of the coca tree and found this made them able to endure fatigue better, and also it produced numbness in the tongue and the lips. From this substance cocaine was made, and an injection of a similar drug is often used now when teeth have to be extracted.

Apart from this, modern surgery has made enormous strides. Thirty years ago it was thought to be impossible to operate on the heart. Now it is successfully done. Attempts are now being made to replace an organ which is worn out by grafting in an organ from another person. It is possible to remove the cornea from the eye of a dead person and use it in the eye of someone who is blind and so restore their sight. It sometimes seems as if there were no limit to what a surgeon can do. You may have seen on television how complicated operations are carried out.

Have we then reached the end of the road? Can everyone look forward to perfect health? Unfortunately, not yet. There are some diseases for which no cure has yet been found, some kinds of cancer, for example. Enormous sums are spent every year on cancer research. Some progress has been made but we are still waiting for the 'breakthrough', although surgery – in some cases – is effective, and so is treatment by X-rays and by a radium needle. Also, there are nervous diseases, the causes of which are unknown. Rheumatism and bronchitis still account for a great deal of suffering.

The progress of medical science brings its own problems. We saw what tremendous benefits were brought about by the antibiotic drugs. But germs, just like human beings, learn to protect themselves, and some of them now do not respond to penicillin; they have become immunized to it. In the same way some mosquitoes now are not affected by D.D.T. Every new advance seems to bring new difficulties. Doubtless they will be overcome, and perhaps fifty years from now there will be a generation of people to whom all these ills of the flesh which we have described will seem remote and strange, as far away from them as the Great Plague of Charles II's reign seems to us.

Dates to remember

1895 Röntgen discovered the X-ray
1899 Landsteiner discovered the different blood groups
1912 Vitamins discovered
1929 Fleming found the properties of penicillin

Things to do

1 Find out how much is spent on medical research by the government and how much money is provided by private donors.
2 Make a list of all the hospitals and clinics in your town. How many have been built or added to since the last war?
3 Increased medical knowledge and care means that people live longer than they used to do. What provision do you think should be made for old people? Should they live in hospitals or homes, or should they have specially designed small flats?
4 What improvements would you like to make in the Health Service? What other countries in the world have a free medical service?

Books to read

G. Bankoff, *Milestones in Medicine*, Museum Press
W. A. C. Bullock, *The Man Who Discovered Penicillin*, Faber
F. R. Elwell and J. M. Richardson, *Science and the Doctor*, Bell
Boswell Taylor, *Medicine To-day*, E.S.A.
Norman Wymer, *Behind the Scenes in a Hospital*, Phoenix House

Children in Taiwan line up for B.C.G. vaccination against tuberculosis.

Chapter 12
Past — present — future

History explains how we have reached our present situation. If we look back a hundred years, we can see that we have come a long way in this time. Life has become easier for most people in this country, and it is not only easier in such things as that people are now cared for if they are ill, can most of them afford enough to eat, and do not have to work all their waking hours in order to keep body and soul together. It is also easier in that people can do more varied and interesting things with their lives. If children are good at school work they can get scholarships and go on to further education, which leads to many kinds of jobs and interests. If young people want to learn to play the guitar, or the piano, or are gifted at painting or dancing, they can get help from their local council or the state to learn these things; they may do it in the evenings as a hobby, or, if they are good enough, study full time for professional qualifications. If people want to go for holidays abroad, before they are married and have children to support, or after their children are earning, they can probably arrange to go. A hundred, or even fifty, years ago, only the few who were rich could think of these things.

In the beginning man survived and multiplied because he was the most intelligent of the animals, but for a long time, many thousands of years, nearly all his energy and ability was given to the basic tasks of getting enough to eat and defending himself against stronger animals. Then he learnt to produce food, to build cities, and he created a number of civilized pleasures and arts. He learnt to make varied and delicious foods, beautiful clothes, books, music, and architecture. He hunted for pleasure instead of from necessity. But these new advantages were only for the few who were wealthy and powerful; the vast majority of humanity led a life of insecurity and toil. Now, in this century, we see for the first time the possibility that all men and women may enjoy the good things of life, and some of the more fortunate nations have almost reached this condition. What kind of world will result from this new prosperity and opportunity?

This book, and the history books dealing with earlier times, tell something of how these changes happened, and of the efforts of the people who brought them about, both famous and brilliant politicians such as Lloyd George, devoted reformers such as Lord Shaftesbury, and the millions of humbler people whose support enabled these men to carry out their reforms. All those who have voted for improvements have played a small part in change; local councillors who tried to improve such things as our schools played their part, so did the men

Headquarters of the United Nations in New York. In the foreground is the Library; farther back, the tall building of the Secretariat, and the low General Assembly in the shape of a loudspeaker.

and women who shared in the struggle against Nazism and so saved us from fascist tyranny.

In this chapter we consider the next steps which we have to take, the problems which face us now, and the history books which will be written in the year 2067 will describe and criticize what we do about them. 'Things to do' are particularly important here, for they are concerned with our problems and it would be useful to begin collecting ideas and information about them now.

What are the problems? What have we not yet achieved? In what ways is our life still unsatisfactory?

We will give some suggestions. You might like to put our list in what you think is its proper order of importance. You may want to add some things which we have left out, or to strike out some of the suggestions because you think that they are not serious problems, or are problems that have been solved since this book was written.

1 Keeping world peace

We put this first, because we must make sure that there will be people alive to have a history, and that all our past achievements are not wiped out in a tremendous war.

We cannot go into the question of ways of keeping peace in detail, because it alters every year as the nations change in power and position, and as new international conflicts flare up and old ones die down. There will probably be rapid changes in the future as new nations come on to the international scene, and the South American, African, Arabic, and Asiatic countries move in to take a more active part in world affairs.

Why did we fail to keep peace in 1914 and 1939? How is the situation different now, and how should we deal with the changed character of war? We have so far adopted the policy of joining an alliance with America called the North Atlantic Treaty Organization (N.A.T.O.) which enabled us to put up a firm front to Russia in the time of Stalin, but many people think that this is not necessary any longer because Russia is peaceful in her policy, and our alliance with a more powerful country like America takes away a good deal of our independence.

Here are some of the possibilities for us:

1 *We could rely upon the strength of America and the N.A.T.O. alliance.* The advantage of this is that the N.A.T.O. group of nations are strong enough to stand up to any enemy. At present, in 1967, Russia and America are the only countries with enough nuclear weapons to fight a big war. Great Britain cannot make enough of them to count against those two, who have enough between them to destroy life on the northern half of the globe.

But relying on N.A.T.O. and America has some disadvantages. Suppose a N.A.T.O. country in Europe was attacked, would the American

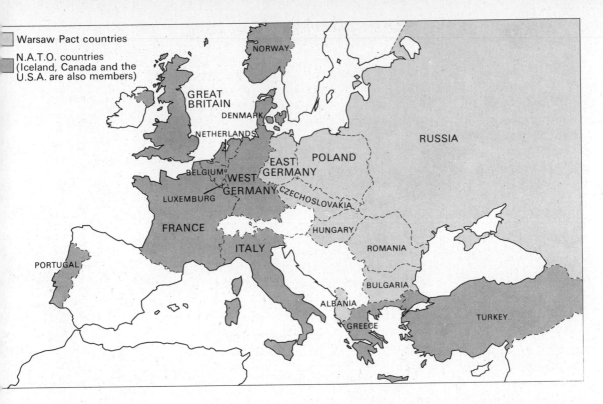

Warsaw Pact countries

N.A.T.O. countries
(Iceland, Canada and the
U.S.A. are also members)

NORWAY

GREAT
BRITAIN

DENMARK

NETHERLANDS

RUSSIA

BELGIUM

EAST
GERMANY
POLAND

WEST
GERMANY

LUXEMBURG

CZECHOSLOVAKIA

FRANCE

HUNGARY

ITALY

ROMANIA

PORTUGAL

BULGARIA

ALBANIA

TURKEY

GREECE

he North Atlantic Treaty
ganization, the alliance of
e capitalist countries which
as dominated by the U.S.A.,
d the Warsaw Pact
lliance, which was dominated
Russia. Fortunately the
stility of these two blocs has
t yet led to a hot war.

President think it right to risk the death of, say, 90,000,000 Americans by involving America in a nuclear war to defend a European country?

Also, the N.A.T.O. alliance means that we run some risk of becoming involved in war started by America in some part of the world in which we have no interests.

Are there now any important enemies which are likely to attack us? In the past other nations coveted our empire, and our armed forces were built up to defend it. Now we have little empire to defend.

2 *We could give up nuclear weapons and nuclear alliances and neither make the weapons nor take any part in plans for delivering them.* We could concentrate instead on 'conventional' weapons, which means ordinary tanks, guns, etc. By this policy we could hope to make it not worth anybody's while to attempt to invade us, and we could be strong enough to defend our commercial interests and defend ourselves against anyone except the nuclear giants.

3 *We could support the United Nations.* We could use our influence to strengthen her forces for putting an end to quarrels which might lead to serious wars. We could work through the United Nations to get the nations to agree to disarmament. This would be a slow business, because neither America nor Russia could be expected to disarm and so be at the mercy of the other. But they could perhaps be persuaded to disarm bit by bit in step with one another.

We live in the tense world of 'balance of terror', which means that America and Russia are too much frightened of one another to start a war. Fortunately at present both the American President, and the head of the Russian government, are determined to avoid war, and have a special telephone line from the White House in Washington (the President's home) to the Kremlin in Moscow, so that the heads of both countries can talk to find a way out and avoid misunderstandings if trouble threatens.

But we shall be in a very dangerous position if we get a more warlike government in America or Russia, or if other countries, which may be more bomb-happy, get control of nuclear weapons.

Things to do

1 Collect information from television, radio, newspapers, and the United Nations Association, and decide which of the possibilities seems to you the best way for Great Britain to remain at peace. Are there other ways by which Great Britain can help to maintain peace?

2 In what parts of the world are there quarrels which are a danger to peace? Find out about them, and find out what the quarrels are about. Remember that it is usually quite easy to find out the British point of view in any disagreement in which we are concerned, but it may be very difficult to find out the point of view of the other side.

Emblem of the United Nations: the world, surrounded by a wreath of olive leaves, symbolizing peace.

II   Movement of people and things

At first sight this may hardly appear to be an important subject. Yet human life and civilization has always depended upon the movement of people and things. Today, if it were not for transport, all but a small proportion of the population of the British Isles would die because there would be neither work nor food for them. Every weekday thousands of tons of food and raw materials must move into our towns and hundreds of thousands of workers must get to their places of work, and hundreds of thousands of tons of goods must be taken to all parts of the world to be sold. Changes in transport during the last fifty years show more than any other single thing how quickly society now alters.

What part will the railways play in the future?

After they were nationalized in 1947 the railways continued to run at a loss. This is partly because they must pay £36,000,000 interest each year to the shareholders who had money in the railways when they were taken over. Some people argue that these interest payments should not continue for ever, and should come to an end after a reasonable time. But interest charges account for only one-third of the railways' loss, and even if it were not for this burden, the railways would find it hard to make a profit; their stations, lines and maintenance staff are expensive, whereas motor traffic has the right to use the roads for the mere cost of a motor-vehicle licence.

In 1962 the government asked Dr Beeching to make suggestions for the proper and economical use of our railways, and the result was the 'Beeching Plan', by which unprofitable minor lines and stations are to be closed. He maintained that country places are better served by buses.

A planned transport system?

In the past we have muddled through somehow over transport. Enormously bulky and heavy goods, which would be more suitable for rail, fill up the roads. On the other hand, expensive and slow stopping trains serve villages which are near good main roads. Once-quiet villages and country towns are filled with petrol fumes, and their inhabitants can hardly cross the road to get to a shop on the other side. In the cities during rush hour, when tired people are anxious to get home, traffic jams slow movement to five miles an hour.

We have reached the point at which we must plan our transport. We must use our main-line railways for certain kinds of long-distance transport; we must plan and build roads to take an increasing volume

traffic jam. A few hours er, that side of the road may empty and the other e jammed.

of traffic, and arrange it so that our cities are not choked with cars, and our villages become peaceful again.

How are we to get the traffic from the outskirts of the cities to the centre? One answer would be to make traffic tunnels underground leading to central car-parks, but this would be terribly expensive. Another answer might be to make people leave their cars at the outskirts and provide monorail lines for the passengers to the centre.

Can you think of other answers?

It is too expensive in time, petrol, wear and tear on the nerves, and the character of our towns.

Things to do

1 Make an ideal plan for traffic arrangements for your town or district.
2 Decide what is the best use for the railways, in goods and passenger traffic.

Things to discuss

1 What part should air transport play in communication between British cities?
2 Should minor railway lines be closed?
3 Would you like a monorail to be built near your street?
4 How long should railway shareholders go on getting interest on their shares?

1 *Middletown* as it is now; noisy, dangerous, uncomfortable. Pedestrians find it hard to cross the street.
Motorists cannot find parking space.

2 *Middletown* as it could be replanned. The through-traffic flows round the central area on clearways. Those who have business in the town can leave their cars in handy car-parks. There is a service road at the back of the shops for delivery vans, etc.

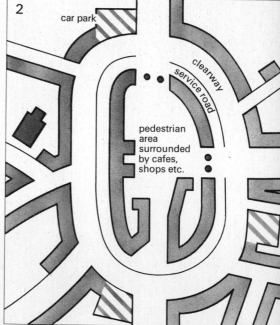

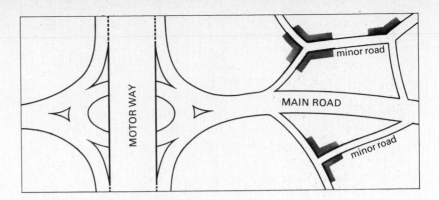

...an of a motorway, showing ...p-roads for joining and ...ving it.

Classified roads should serve the whole country

1 *Motorways* Long distance, fast roads, with ways on and off them only at about ten-mile intervals. At least six lanes of traffic.

2 *Main roads* A network of these should cover the country, linking places and feeding into the motorways. They should by-pass villages. They should carry four lanes of traffic so that overtaking would be safe and easy. No stopping should be allowed on them, but there should be frequent cafés, lay-bys and access lanes.

3 *Minor roads and country lanes,* leading to villages, farms, etc.

III Providing a home for everyone

You have read in Chapter 6 how the government in 1945 recognized the need for many more houses, and started a crash-programme of building.

Twenty years later we can see that the efforts of both the Labour and the Conservative governments did not match up to our needs. We should probably be building 500,000 houses a year, instead of 400,000. Our cities in 1967 still have their long housing lists. Clearly we underestimated the size of the task, and not only have we built too few homes, the kind of building and the planning of our estates has been criticized. It is said that we failed to take account of the new age of the motor-car and twentieth-century ideas of the possibilities of city life.

Why we did not build enough

For one thing, families have been larger than we expected. There was a lot of talk about the 'bulge' in the birthrate after the war. But it turned out not merely to be a temporary increase in the numbers of babies; people have gone on having larger families, as you can see from the figures in the margin of page 234, and now the 'bulge' children are marrying and needing homes of their own.

233

Think about these figures:

1 You can see how the hard years of the slump, and the war, brought down the birthrate with a bump.

2 The birthrate now is very low compared with the rate 1900–20; so why do we talk so much of our increasing population? The answer is that in the bad old days a great many babies died. Now that people are not so poor, and now that we have a Health Service, few babies die. In Great Britain only twenty-two babies die out of every 1,000 born. In India a hundred out of every 1,000 die.

Another reason for the housing shortage is that our prosperity means more households. People are not content to lodge with their relatives if they can afford a separate home, and they marry younger if they have plenty of money.

Also, there is movement from the country to the towns. More money can be earned in towns, and perhaps most people find town life more interesting. Cottages on the hillsides of Wales are left empty, whilst people who move into Birmingham find it difficult to get even a room in which to lodge.

The housing estates have spread out around the industrial towns, covering the countryside with a red rash of roofs, eating up good agricultural land, increasing the distances of rush-hour travel, and making it harder to get to the country for a walk or a blackberry expedition. Look at the picture on page 127 and you will see that these houses, although they can be attractive when the trees have grown round them, are very extravagant in land. We are finding that we cannot afford the space for this 'house and garden' kind of development. The handsome blocks of flats (see the opposite page) save space, but they demand expensive building standards, with deep foundations, lifts and fire precautions. It costs very much more than houses.

Money is the chief difficulty. We can build as many houses as we can afford to build. Local councils borrow money for their building programmes, and the number of houses they can build depends upon the amount they have to pay for the money they borrow. If they have to pay £6 each year for every £100 they borrow, then the interest rate is 6 per cent, and in this case the cost of borrowing the money is more than half the cost of building and running a housing estate. If a council house costs £2,500 to build, you can work out how much the council must pay each year (at 6 per cent) for the money which built it.

The government has to consider not only money, but also the men and materials which we can afford to give to houses, and therefore it authorizes local authorities to build up to a certain number, and limits house-building in this way.

New towns

New towns may be the best way to plan our future housing. Some

The birthrate in Britain

Year	Rate	
1900	27	
1910	25	
1920	24	
1930	16	births pe
1940	14	1,000
1950	15	populatio
1960	16	
1962	18	

A block of flats can house mo
people in a smaller space
than the individual houses
seen opposite, in Cumbernaul
New Town, near Glasgow.

Shopping precinct for pedestrians only, at Elephant and Castle, London.

people think that many of our old cities are already bigger than they should be, and that they are inconvenient, muddled, crowded, and awkward for both pedestrians and motorists. They think that instead of allowing these old centres to go on spreading, we should build new, small, pleasant towns, where the architecture is good, which have pedestrian centres where people can walk and shop in peace, where industry is sited so that it is easy to reach, but does not spoil the view, where the roads are designed so that drivers can get to shops and houses without endangering the people on foot, where trees, grass spaces, and gardens are within easy reach of everyone. Above is a photograph of a centre built in 1964.

The lower photograph on page 235 is of some small modern houses which have been arranged to look out on to a small friendly square, where their inhabitants can meet and their children play. It shows one of the many possible groupings of houses which are better than a row along the edge of a street.

Industries and people have to settle in the new towns at the same time, and the towns need a balance of industry, so that there is skilled work and heavy manual work, and also work suitable for women and girls. This raises the question of how we should make sure that industries are set up in the new towns if employers prefer to buy up old factory space cheap in existing towns.

Should we build our new towns in the north and take steps to prevent the drift to the south-east? Industries no longer need to be near the coal and water power which took factories to the north 200 years ago. Now they want to be near to London and the Continent, and the power which they use is electricity and oil instead of coal and water.

Things to do

1 Find out from your local council:
   How many people are on the Housing List?
   What qualifications are needed to get a house?
   What are the rents of council houses?
   What did they cost to build?
2 Visit local housing estates. Note their good and bad points and think of ways in which they could be improved.
3 Visit the 'Show Houses' of private firms which are building houses.
4 Visit any housing sites where houses are being built by new, 'pre-fabricated' methods. Find out how much these houses cost and how long they take to build compared with houses which are built brick by brick.
5 Make a plan for your ideal council house.
6 Plan a block of flats, making arrangements for laundry, waste disposal, storage of prams, garages, play space for young children and older children.

Things to discuss

1 Should new industries be compelled by the government to go to new towns or to areas of unemployment?
2 What method could be used to persuade industries to go willingly to the places where they are needed?
3 What arrangements should be made for housing old people when we build estates?

IV Enough to eat

Food and shelter are the two things upon which human life depends; health and the number of people whom the earth can support, depends more upon food than anything else, more than upon shelter, which is a simple problem in many warmer countries than our own. Every increase in the available food supplies means life for more people.

In the beginning of history when men were hunters, very few human beings existed. They had to live in small groups and follow the movements of the grazing animals they hunted. Life for them was uncertain, and, perhaps, cruel, for the sick and the old had to be left behind to die. Man had to travel quickly and light, carrying with him little but some skins for tents and his weapons. Even with few and scattered people, the hunting often failed and there was famine. When

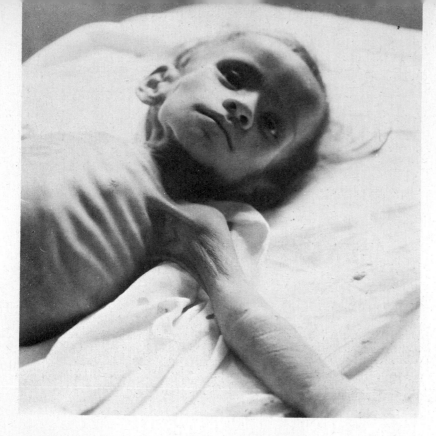

In a country too poor to offer help, this Peruvian child is starving to death. Only the rich nations can help.

man had learnt to grow food and to keep animals in flocks and herds, he could settle in one place, live together in larger numbers, and have more possessions, and when the plough was invented food supplies were so much increased that cities became possible in the fertile river valleys of the Nile and Euphrates.

Farming today enables 2,600 million people to live on the earth, but it does not enable all of them to live well.

The people of Great Britain are amongst those who have enough to eat. Although we are crowded on to a small island, and only four out of every hundred workers are employed on the land, yet we grow a good deal of our food, and the sale of our industrial products enables us to buy the rest of what we need. We are amongst the few countries whose people enjoy more than the 2,700 calories each day which are the necessary minimum for good health. The other lucky ones are most of the countries of Western Europe, the United States, and Russia. Two-thirds of the world's population has less than 2,200 calories a day. Calories are the measurement of the energy given by food.

The terrible diseases of hunger are almost unknown in Great Britain. The common diseases caused by food in this country are those caused by eating too much, especially too much of the more harmful kinds of food, such as sugar. We have bad teeth very early in life through eating sweets, and too much sugar also results in our having a great many

Help comes to some.
Venezuelan children receive
milk from U.N.I.C.E.F., the
United Nations (International)
Children's (Emergency) Fund.
International and Emergency
have now been deleted from
the title.)

cases of diabetes amongst older people. Sweet and fatty foods probably increase the number of heart-failure cases.

The hungry countries

In the rice-eating countries of China, Malaya, Java and Japan, beriberi is common. Tropical Africa has yaws. The maize-eating countries of Italy, Spain and Portugal suffer from pellagra, and Turkey and Yugoslavia have rickets.

The reasons for world hunger

Medicine in this century has reduced the death-rates. Many, who in earlier times would have died in infancy from infections due to dirt, now live to grow up and eat, and have children who also need to eat. The population was once thinned out by, for instance, smallpox and pneumonia, diseases which drugs can now control. So although science has increased our ability to produce food, it has also increased the number of people who consume it. We must produce much more food, and it is especially urgent to produce it in the countries where the standard of living and farming is still very low and the birthrate still very high.

It is difficult for the poor countries to take the first steps towards prosperity. Because they are poor, they cannot afford the fertilizers and machinery which are necessary for improvement. Nearly two-thirds of the world's farmers have no tools or implements except a hoe or a wooden plough. The primitive farmer's hoe is not like the ones we use in our gardens; it is more like a pick-axe with a broad blade, and the user brings it right above his head before bringing it down to break a patch of earth, which is very hard work.

As for the wooden ploughs, they are hardly changed from the ones seen in pictures from Ancient Egypt, and they only scratch the soil instead of turning it as the blades of modern ploughs do. In India 80 per cent of the people, nearly four times as many as in the British Isles, work on the land, and yet India is hungry, and because of their hunger, the average age at which Indians die is under forty. In this country people can expect to live to be seventy-one.

What has it to do with us?

We are now troubled by the problem of hunger overseas, and realize that we are all responsible for it, *because we can do something* about it. A hundred years ago we could have done very little; Asia and Africa were then long journeys from us and we were ignorant of what happened in them; also, those who wanted to help the unfortunate could find plenty of hunger within the British Isles. Now, no nation seems far from us, and perhaps we have wider ideas of humanity and realize that all men are our concern.

Oxen pulling a plough over the parched earth. Only poor crops can be produced by this method.

Emblem of the Food and Agriculture Organization. 'Fiat panis' is Latin for 'let there be bread'.

A F.A.O. specialist in Ceylon teaches agricultural students the advantages of using a tractor.

We especially owe help to the peoples who were in our empire, Indians, Africans and West Indians, because many Englishmen made enormous fortunes from their products, and much money came to this country through the cheap labour of Indians and Africans.

What can be done?

The answer is a different one for every area, and you can get information about many interesting things that are being done from organizations which have been formed to help (see end of this section). Here we have room for only one example.

A scheme carried out by the United Nations Food and Agriculture Organization has helped the people of an area of Thailand which was a shallow swamp. Every summer the swamp dried and many fish died. The F.A.O. experts persuaded the inhabitants to build dikes to keep the water in all the year, and to root out the weeds which filled the pools. Then better kinds of fish were put in the pools, and today this swamp gives 200,000 lb. of fish every year, and also produces water all the year round for the use of the farmers.

Harvesting the sea

We have scarcely begun to make use of the food that the sea could give us. We behave with regard to the sea very much as early man behaved to the earth – we hunt and kill its wild creatures, but we do not farm

it. At present we only get 9 lb. of food per person from the sea, 1 per cent of human diet. The future will perhaps see us farming the oceans. We may plant seaweed crops on the ocean beds where the water is shallow, or we may trawl myriads of small forms of life with fine nets. Or we may pen and breed fish in enclosed waters. There is, for instance, the 'manatee' or 'sea-cow', which grows up to twelve feet long and carries more good meat than a bullock. These creatures could live in sea pens, or in estuaries and rivers, and they have the added virtue that they like eating 'water-hyacinth', a harmful weed which chokes waterways.

These ideas are not wild dreams. Serious work is being done to find ways of getting food from the seas, and since there is more sea than land, we may hope that sea farming will enormously increase our food supplies.

A manatee at the London Zoo is fed with a cabbage leaf.

There are people in Britain who do not have enough

Although we are a rich nation, there are people in Great Britain who do not have enough. The newspapers, during the winter of 1963–4, told of old people who had died because they could not afford enough fuel and food to enable them to stand the cold. When Beveridge made his plan for the 'Welfare State' (page 120) he suggested that pensions and insurance payments should go up and down as the cost of living changed, so that whatever happened to prices, they would always buy the same amount. But this idea was not made law, and because prices have more than doubled since the Insurance Acts were passed, the pensions are now worth much less.

Old age pensions in 1965 were £6 10s. for a married couple, and £4 for a single person.

Some old people who have saved and who have earned pensions from their employers, find that the income which they had thought would be enough, will not keep them at the prices of today.

If they do not have children to look after them the lot of the old can be hard. Often they have to leave their own homes and go to institutions, where they suffer from losing their independence, from having nothing to do all day, and from the feeling that no one cares much what happens to them. Here are two descriptions of homes for the old which were visited in 1962. One of them is well run and has a kind matron; are homes like this the answer to the needs of the old? Or are there other solutions, better than any kind of institution?

A report on an old workhouse ward, still in use in 1962, says:

M Ward consists of forty-two beds in two big dormitories. Each dormitory has been roughly divided into two by . . . putting seven wardrobes (shared by each group of twenty-one women) across the centre. The half farthest from the door was the sleeping compartment, and although the beds were new, with wooden frames, and about half of the mattresses were interior-sprung and not hair, they were only two feet apart, separated by a bedside chair. There were only two thin blankets on each bed, and the sheets were worn and patched and rather grey. There were no lockers. In addition to the seven wardrobes, the twenty-one women shared seven dressing-tables ranged at the far end. The nearer half of the room had been divided into a dining quarter and a sitting quarter . . . The women sleep, eat, and spend the entire day in the one room . . . the room did not have any curtains . . . and the lower windows were made of frosted glass.

The matron of a good home, where the residents have rooms of their own reports:

. . . the residents take over the bare room and furnish it themselves. We have an advantage in single rooms in their being able to have a wireless and do what they want . . . So far as I am concerned, I don't know what time they go to bed, or what they do in their rooms . . . The one or two I'm not sure of at night I go and call on before I go to bed. So many Council Homes don't allow them to lie down in the afternoons, but here the place is quite dead between 1.30 and 3.30.

Where is the money to come from?

It is easy to say what we should like in the way of roads, houses, hospitals, pensions and many other things.

But they all cost money. We spend more each year on social and public services, yet we will want more, and other countries are overtaking us in these things.

A home for old people in 1944. Crowded, dingy rooms, hard chairs, nothing to do, and too few trained staff to look after them. Such institutions still exist.

It all depends upon the amount we can make and sell, and this depends upon two things, labour and capital. From the point of view of labour, it depends upon the amount of work a man does in a week, and this in its turn depends largely upon capital, the amount invested in Great Britain in factories and machinery, particularly the new computer and automatic machine tooling which enables one skilled, highly trained operative to do work which twenty men would have been needed to do twenty years ago.

Things to do

1 Find out how much the old age pension is at the time you read this book. Go into prices and consider whether it is enough to enable pensioners to go on living in their own homes.
2 Write to 'War on Want' and 'Freedom from Hunger' (addresses can be found in the London telephone directories) to find out about work to end world hunger.

Things to discuss

What should be done to help old people who,
(a) Are lonely and feel that their lives are no use to anyone?
(b) Cannot manage their own shopping and cooking?
(c) Are ill, but not so ill that they need hospital care?

The future at work and play

What shall we do with our added wealth and leisure?

This is the great question for our time. In the past, most people had to work so hard that for them the question did not exist. Now most people have leisure and must choose how they spend it. They will probably have more leisure in the future. Computers and automated factories doing our work for us mean that we can look forward to earning and producing more than we do now, even if we have a six-hour day and a five-day week. We shall have immense time and energy for enjoying life and adding to its value. What shall we do with it? Most people get bored after a time with watching the telly. It is not very satisfactory to go on indefinitely watching other people doing things or talking about things. After a bit people are not happy unless they are doing something themselves.

The teen-agers come into the headlines

In particular, the young for the first time in history have money and leisure. In the past they had to wear the clothes and hair-dos that their

The Beatles, a pop group, on the I.T.V. programme 'Thank Your Lucky Stars', 1963.

elders chose for them, had to behave as their elders wanted, and to spend most of their spare time with their families.

Now they earn so much that they buy their own clothes and record-players; special teen-age fashions in clothes and discs are put on the market for them. Motor vehicles take them away from their own village or street for their amusements.

They do not like their own taste only in clothes, they also want their own kind of art and artists to amuse them and express their feelings, so that we had, in 1964, 'The Beatles', a group of four Liverpool boys who set up as pop singers, and with their cheerful songs took Great Britain by storm. Young people throughout the world responded to the Beatles' music. Their discs sold even in Russia, which does not approve of pop art, and when they went to America they earned the enormous sum of $1,000,000, £360,000, in one month. Since Great Britain needed dollars, they were an important national asset.

There is not only pop art like the Beatles' music. There is also an important musical movement in the new folk-songs. Many of the songs are beautiful and interesting and of a high musical standard, as well as being popular; some of them are amusing; others show deep feeling about the fortunes and misfortunes of humanity. It seems from these songs that the new generation, when it takes over, will have as much indignation over things that are wrong and as much determination to improve things, as any generation in the past.

We shall o-ver-come....   We shall o-ver-come....

We shall o-ver-come one day - - - - -

Deep in my heart   I do be-lieve

We shall o-ver-come some day.

(2) We shall end Jim Crow, etc.

(3) The truth shall make us free etc.

(4) We shall live in peace.

This is sung in America by marchers demonstrating on behalf of the Negroes. It is also sung by people on both sides of the Atlantic who take part in peace movements.

The young are lucky now, and the old unlucky. One of the jobs of the next generation will be to see that everyone can look forward to old age without fear, and to see that we spend our wealth and time in ways which make life happier and more interesting, instead of giving our energies to piling up our houses with things which the advertisements persuade us to buy.

The future is in your hands

What you choose in the way of work, art, interests and politics, will decide what is in the history books of tomorrow.

Things to do

1 Find out what interests members of your class would like to follow if they had the opportunity. Find out if the local council, or any other body, enables people to pursue these interests.

2 Collect modern folk-songs which deal with things which concern history or public affairs and discuss what they mean.

Things to discuss

1 What great changes are taking place which are not mentioned in this book? How important are they compared with automation and the new freedom of the young? What changes mentioned in this book have ceased to be important by the time you read it?

2 What changes would you like to make in society? For instance, would it be a good thing to have the vote at eighteen? Would it be a good thing to arrange for everybody between the age of seventeen and nineteen to go to a work camp and to do a year of social service at such things as forestry, decorating the houses of invalids and the old, or improving the sea defences?

Books to read

R. Banham, *Guide to Modern Architecture*, Architectural Press

R. Calder, *Men Against the Desert*, Allen and Unwin

Walter Earnshaw, *Discovering Houses*, University of London Press

G. R. Halson, *Discovering Railways*, University of London Press

A. Hancock and R. Robertson, *Ourselves*, Longmans

A. H. Hanson, *Lives of the People*, Heinemann

E. Larsen, *Transport*, Phoenix House

G. Leach, *The New Materials*, Phoenix House

M. Storm, *The Urban Growth of Britain*, Oxford University Press

G. Trease, *This Is Your Century*, Heinemann

Index

Numbers listed in italics (e.g. *15*) refer to the captions of illustrations and maps.

Acknowledgements

Airviews (M/c.) Limited : 208
Albright & Wilson Ltd : 210
Architectural Press Ltd : 130, 132, 138, 235, 236
Associated Newspapers Ltd : 61, 113, 117
Associated Press Ltd : 70, 141, 145
Beaverbrook Newspapers Ltd : 115
Berne Tageblatt : 94/95
B.O.A.C. : 208
British Gazette 1926 by permission of the Controller of Her Majesty's Stationery Office : 66
British Museum : 176, 179, 202
Central Office of Information : 99, 221, 222
Central Press Photos Ltd : 89
CoID photo : 195
Charles Chaplin *My Autobiography* The Bodley Head : 197
Crown Copyright Science Museum, London : 201
Cumbernauld Development Corporation: 235
Daily Express : 72
Daily Worker : 79
Geoffrey Drury : 213
Essex Music Ltd, Zilphia Horton, Frank Hamilton & Guy Carawan, copyright Ludlow Music Inc : 246
Farmer's Weekly : 202
Fox Photos Ltd : 242
General Post Office, Dublin : 190
General Post Office, London : 83, 102, 133
Sir Alexander Gibb & Partners : 205
Glaxo Laboratories Ltd : 214
Greater London Council : 15, 21, 65, 127, 134, 213, 243
High Commission of India : 160, 165, 168, 169
Illustrated London News : 12
Imperial War Museum : 31, 36, 39, 40, 44, 47, 48, 101, 105, 110, 111, 114, 188, 207
Keystone Press Agency Ltd : 77, 89, 113, 119, 125, 135, 144, 147, 150, 151, 152, 153, 154, 166, 205, 231, 245
Keystone View Co of New York : 197
Magnum, John Hillelson Agency, photo Ian Berry : 181
Mansell Collection : 7, 84/85
Marconi Company Ltd : 200

Marconi Marine : 199
Marples Ridgeway Ltd : 205
J. McKay : 164, 198, 215
Mount Everest Foundation : 135
Museum of Modern Art, New York : 86/87
National Maritime Museum, Greenwich (photo Science Museum, London) : 199
Odhams Press Ltd : 93
Paul Popper Ltd : 43, 162, 173, 178, 183
Press Association Ltd : 157
Punch Publications Ltd : 16, 16/17, 26/27, 56/57, 62, 97, 107, 121, 124, 129, 149, 203
Radio Times Hulton Picture Library : 8, 10, 22, 23, 24, 35, 49, 53, 59, 65, 67, 76, 82, 84, 98, 122, 123, 126, 163, 201
Ronan Picture Library : 204
South Africa House : 180, 182/183, 184, 185
St Thomas's Hospital : 223
Studio Vista Ltd, J. Laver, *Britain between the Wars* : 80
Trades Union Congress : 66, 81
United Africa Co Ltd : 173, 174, 175, 177, 178
United Nations : 161, 216, 219, 220, 225, 227, 230, 238, 239, 240, 241
United Press International : 73
United States Information Service : 209
Weekly Illustrated : 92

TEXT ACKNOWLEDGEMENTS

Chatto & Windus Ltd : 42
Siegfried Sassoon : 42

ARTISTS' CREDITS

A. W. Gatrell & Co Ltd : 33, 38, 50, 91, 103, 108, 142, 143, 158/159, 171, 172, 193, 229
Edward Poulton : 170
Penguin Education Art Department : 14, 100, 101, 102, 105, 146, 153, 154, 164, 165, 166, 167, 189, 191, 218, 232, 233, 246